An All-Star's
Cardboard Memories

An All-Star's
Cardboard Memories

Tom Zappala, Ellen Zappala, Joe Orlando
with Rico Petrocelli

FOREWORD BY DR. JIM LONBORG

Peter E. Randall Publisher
Portsmouth, New Hampshire
2018

© 2018 by Tom Zappala and Ellen Zappala

ISBN: 978-1-937721-58-9

Library of Congress Control Number: 2018938971

Produced by Peter E. Randall Publisher
Box 4726, Portsmouth, New Hampshire 03802

www.perpublisher.com

Book design: Grace Peirce

Photography credit: Chrissie Good Photography

Player card images provided by Professional Sports Authenticator (PSA)
www.psacard.com

Memorabilia provided by Brian Seigel and Joe Orlando

Additional memorabilia provided by Heritage Auctions
www.ha.com

Memorabilia also provided by Memory Lane Inc.
www.memorylaneinc.com

Additional copies available from: www.TomZappalaMedia.com

Printed in China

To Lucy, Emmie, Anna, Johnny, Tommy, Sloane,
and our future little All-Stars.

Always step up to the plate and take a swing.

Acknowledgments

OF ALL THE BOOKS THAT WE HAVE WRITTEN, this one was the most satisfying. The behind-the-scenes stories of these Hall of Famers (some of which we could not publish!) along with the great information on their baseball cards is entertaining, educational, and gives us a glimpse into the personalities of these greats. This book is the result of a great team effort.

First and foremost, special thanks to my friend and colleague, Red Sox Hall of Famer, Rico Petrocelli, for his insight and his analysis of the traits and playing styles of the Hall of Famers featured in this book. It has been a pleasure working with Rico on this project as well as co-hosting *The Great American Collectibles Show* with him. Rico is a fan as well as a great player, and that is what makes it all worthwhile.

Special thanks to our co-author and dear friend, Joe Orlando, CEO of Collectors Universe, Inc. and president of PSA (Professional Sports Authenticator). The information Joe provided on the cards that accompany the player stories is an invaluable resource. For each of the great players featured in the book, you'll find everything you need to know about their cards including some of the most valuable, rarest, and the cards to watch. We would also like to thank PSA for providing the wonderful player card images used throughout the book.

A special shout out goes to Red Sox Hall of Famer and former American League Cy Young Award winner, Dr. Jim Lonborg, for writing the foreword to this book. Jim will always be remembered as the pitcher that carried the 1967 Impossible Dream Red Sox to within one game of beating pitching great Bob Gibson and the powerful 1967 St. Louis Cardinals. Jim was one of the architects of what today is referred to as Red Sox Nation.

The beautiful photographic images that you see on the cover and throughout this publication showcase the talent of Chrissie Good, photographer for Collectors Universe. The images are brilliant and capture the very essence of what we were trying to accomplish. Thank you so much, Chrissie.

Special thanks also to Jackie Curiel, PSA content manager, for her help and support. We enjoyed the opportunity to work with her on yet another project, and it couldn't have happened without her. Jackie helps to steer the ship.

Most of the fabulous, authentic memorabilia showcased in the full-page photo images was loaned to us by renowned collector, Brian Seigel. Brian's collection is breathtaking. Thank you, Brian.

Many thanks to Heritage Auctions for providing some of the wonderful collectibles used for the cover photo.

Heartfelt thanks to Memory Lane, Inc. for also supplying some of the great memorabilia used for the photo shoots.

This is the fifth book project we have worked on with Peter E. Randall Publishers. As always, the knowledge and expertise of the staff is greatly appreciated. Special thanks to Deidre Randall for her guidance and her pursuit of excellence. Once again, the creativity of designer Grace Peirce is evident on every page, and we especially appreciate the careful editing of Zak Johnson. Because of their efforts, the finished book is one we can all be very proud of.

Finally, thanks to you, the fans and collectors. If it were not for you, none of this would have taken place. From the very bottom of our hearts we thank each and every one of you.

Contents

Foreword

TWO OF MY SONS, JOHNNY AND JORDIE, WERE
at the kitchen table one day with their baseball cards
scattered about, discussing the stats and the stories
found on the backs of these little pieces of cardboard.
Johnny, age eleven, was helping Jordie, age eight, with
some of the meanings of the numbers and the words.
Little did they know that some of the names on the
cards, like Mickey Mantle, Bob Gibson, and Sandy
Koufax were Hall of Fame players. They would ask me if
I had ever pitched against some of these great, talented
ballplayers, why I was not in the Hall of Fame, and
what was it like to be on the mound. I answered their
questions and was happy they were learning new skills,
like the mathematics of figuring out batting averages,
and for Jordie, new words that would help him with
reading in the years to come.

Personally, I had a much different experience with my
baseball cards while growing up in San Luis Obispo,
California, a quiet college town where my father taught
agriculture at Cal Poly. I would collect two or three
duplicate cards of the players from the 1940s and
1950s. I would study them all from the front to the
back. One day, I decided that it would be easier to glue
the backside of one card to the album paper next to the
front side of the same card, so I could read everything
about the card without having to turn them over. Who
knew that these cards, especially the Hall of Famers,
would become valuable commodities in the future?
When I did find out that there might be some value, I
tried everything to dislodge the cards from the paper—
from steaming to razor blades to microwave ovens! The
glue would not disappear, but the value of the cards did!

My dear friend Rico Petrocelli has brought to life,
through words, his own personal experiences of playing
with and against 56 Hall of Fame players enshrined
in Cooperstown. I first met Rico in the summer of
1964 in Seattle, Washington. We were playing for the
Seattle Rainers, a Triple A affiliate of the Boston Red
Sox. Rico had spent some time with the Red Sox at
the end of the 1963 season playing shortstop but was
returned to Seattle for the 1964 season in order to get

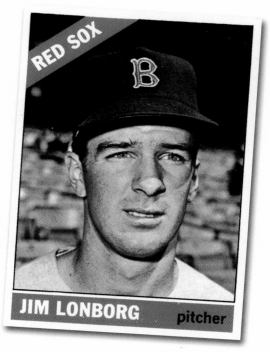

more experience that would lead him to a great 13-year
career with Boston. What a joy and honor it was to play
alongside Rico from 1965–1971, before I was traded to
Milwaukee in 1972. We knew we were in the presence
of greatness many times as we faced or played with guys
like Yaz, Mantle, Aaron, Carlton, Schmidt, Jackson,
Palmer...the list goes on. Now you can learn more about
these players from Rico's perspective as he chronicles
their interactions with his candid and thoughtful
comments.

Maybe you have old baseball cards around somewhere
that you can read to your kids or grandkids or for your
own personal enjoyment. You will be able to get a better
sense of their historical importance as Joe Orlando
describes the nuances of each of the players' baseball
cards. Hopefully, this book will bring back memories of
good times in the long-lasting history of baseball. For
me personally, these are memories that I will always
cherish. I was fortunate to play the greatest game in the
world with some of the greats of the game.

Jim Lonborg

Introduction

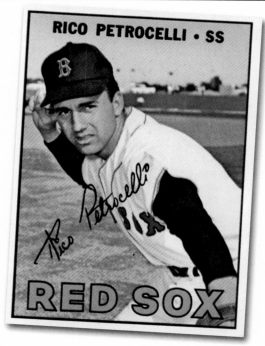

WHEN JOE ORLANDO AND I BEGAN DISCUSSING another book project, we tossed around a few ideas. After the release of our two most recent books, *The 100 Greatest Baseball Autographs* and *Legendary Lumber: The Top 100 Player Bats in Baseball History*, we both agreed that it would be good to get back to a book about baseball cards.

Once the wheels began to turn in my head, I decided to contact my friend and colleague, Red Sox Hall of Famer, Rico Petrocelli. A Boston favorite, Rico played for the Sox for his entire major league career (1965–1976). The two-time All-Star was a slick-fielding shortstop who later became a third baseman so the newly-acquired, future Hall of Fame shortstop, Luis Aparicio, could move into the shortstop position. By the way, Rico blasted 40 homers in 1969, which was the record for most home runs by an American League shortstop until Alex Rodriguez broke it in 1998.

I asked Rico if he would be interested in participating in a book project that would not only discuss the various card issues of certain Hall of Fame players, but would also give the reader a glimpse into the lives of these great ballplayers. Rico played during a time when names like Mantle, Koufax, Aaron, Mays, Bench, and Yastrzemski dotted the Major League landscape.

We compiled a list of 56 Hall of Famers who Rico played with, or competed against, during his 13-year career. Our idea was to get Rico's observations about these baseball greats. What was his teammate Yaz really like in the dugout and the clubhouse? What was it like to know and compete against Bob Gibson, Harmon Killebrew, or Johnny Bench? What made them unique when they swung a bat, fielded a ball, or fired a fastball across the plate? Although not personal friends with all of these talented Hall of Famers, Rico did develop good relationships with most of them, and his opinions and recollections are interesting, entertaining, and insightful.

Also included are four Hall of Famers who were managing or working in some capacity in baseball during that time. For example, one of the greatest pitchers of all time, Satchel Paige, is included in the book because Rico had the honor of watching him in an exhibition game between Kansas City and Boston when Satchel was in his sixties. Although Rico did not play in the game, the story is pretty neat!

As a tribute to Rico's great friendship with him, one player is included in the book who is not in the Hall of Fame. The name Tony Conigliaro still resonates with many in the world of baseball, and we are honored to share some of Rico's memories about him with you.

We hope that you enjoy Rico's take on a very special time in MLB history and the players who captured the hearts of every baseball fan in America. In addition to Rico's recollections, you will find images of the most important card issues for every player included in the book along with expert card analysis provided by Collectors Universe, Inc. CEO and PSA president, Joe Orlando, making this a very entertaining and informative read.

So, sit back, pull out a wad of bubble gum or a pack of sunflower seeds and enjoy *An All-Star's Cardboard Memories*. We hope you have as much fun reading this as we did writing it.

Tom Zappala

1

Playing Against Golden Age Greats

(to 1969)

I'm sitting in a great little Italian deli, about a half-hour north of Boston, with one of the most beloved players in the history of the Boston Red Sox. Americo "Rico" Petrocelli played both shortstop and third base for the Sox from 1965 through 1976. He was one of those players that you could not help but love. Rico's self-deprecating style and sense of humor made him a fan favorite, not to mention that he could hit and field with the best of them. This Red Sox Hall of Famer played in some of the most important and exciting games in Sox history. He also played with and against some of the greatest players that our National Pastime has ever seen. This book is not about Rico. In typical Petrocelli style, he wants us to focus on the Hall of Famers in this book and not on his career. It's Rico being Rico. That's why Boston loves him.

As we pick up our Italian subs (that's what they are called in Boston) stuffed with salami, prosciutto, Italian peppers, and fresh provolone cheese, along with a soft drink, we decide to sit at a table tucked in a corner. That way we can chat undisturbed about Rico's career and what it was like to play in a great

period of baseball history with some of the greatest of all time. Rico knew some of them better than others, but he shares his thoughts on their playing styles and, in a number of cases, personalities. With the extra virgin olive oil dripping out of the sides of the hot Italian bread, we're going to need about 20 napkins. In this first chapter, we talk about the Hall of Famers who played until 1969. Many of them were playing long before Rico's rookie year (1965), but they all played well into the 1960s. In their own way, they each helped to shape our National Pastime.

YOGI BERRA

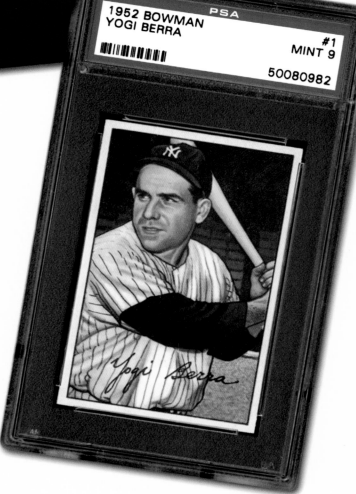

JUST ABOUT EVERYTHING HAS BEEN SAID about Yogi. It is true that he would sometimes leave players, coaches, and managers scratching their heads after a conversation. Growing up a Dodgers fan, I also loved watching the Yankees, and Yogi in particular, not only because he was such a great catcher but because he represented the Italians in New York and was very proud of it. Yogi was kind of a role model for us kids in New York. He wasn't the fastest or strongest, but he had a great approach to the game. They really broke the mold when he played for the Yanks. Yogi was a great bad-ball hitter. He would golf a pitch below the knees over the wall, or swing at a pitch up around his numbers and still make contact. He was also great defensively. He really did everything we were taught not to do, but he always had great success doing it. I never got to play against Yogi, because he was exiting baseball as a player as I was entering.

Many of us thought that Yogi was the greatest of all time at the position. I also played against Bench, so it is hard to compare the two, but both were great catchers. Our guy Fisk was no slouch either. For Yogi though, three MVPs and ten championships is not too shabby. Yogi loved to talk to hitters when they came up to bat. He was always trying to throw off their concentration and timing. Ted Williams used to complain about Yogi's chatter. One time, Yogi got Ted so aggravated that Williams told Berra "to cut the crap and play ball." Williams then popped up to second out of frustration.

I got to know Yogi in 1970 when he was coaching with the Mets during spring training. We started talking about growing up in very similar households and he asked me where in Italy my parents were from. When I told him, he said that it must be a new town in Italy because he had never heard of it. Of course, that had me scratching my head. I was not afraid to tell Yogi that he was one of my idols when I was growing up. When he broke into the big leagues, I was only about four or five years old, and his last year was in 1965, my rookie season. I regret that I never got the chance to play against him like I did Mantle.

Yogi and I re-connected in the 1980s when he was coaching with the Houston Astros. Again, we talked about our Italian heritage and especially about growing up in New

York. It seemed that a lot of our conversations revolved around food, actually sauce. We would compare sauce recipes. Between Yogi and Mantle, and the rest of the Bronx Bombers, I could not get enough baseball growing up. He paid me some very nice compliments about my career. We joked about how I grew up a Yankees fan, yet played my entire career with the Red Sox. It was nice to spend time with someone who was brought up very close to the way I was brought up. Yogi was very proud of all of the Italians who had made it to the big leagues. He would keep track of many of us. His wife Carmen and his three boys were great people. Thinking back, I was lucky to know him. He was a true Hall of Famer both on and off the field.

THE CARDS

As a member of the New York Yankees juggernaut, Yogi Berra was a leader who helped bridge the gap between the Joe DiMaggio and Mickey Mantle eras. During that time, the beloved backstop also found himself on cards that spanned over three different decades. From the late-1940s to the mid-1960s, Berra appeared in numerous mainstream and regional sets. Due to Berra's immense popularity, virtually all of the cards that bear his likeness are considered desirable.

While Berra did make early appearances in the Exhibit and Tip-Top Bread card sets, this perennial All-Star became a staple for Bowman (1948–1955). In fact, Berra was chosen as the #1 card for Bowman in 1952 and he appeared on one of the first multi-player cards for them in 1953, along with

teammates Mantle and Hank Bauer. Berra reappeared alongside Mantle on another extremely popular multi-player card in the 1957 Topps set entitled *Yankees' Power Hitters*. When Topps emerged to challenge Bowman in the early 1950s, Berra was one of the noteworthy names that could be found in both issues each year, unlike fellow stars like Mantle, Stan Musial, and Ted Williams.

During the 1950s, Berra found himself on several regional and food-issue cards. From the condition-sensitive 1950 Drake's Cookies set to the oversized Red Man Tobacco cards (1952–1955) to the seldom-seen 1959 Yoo-hoo issue, Berra's face appeared on a variety of cardboard. This trend continued into the 1960s. Beyond the traditional Topps sets, Berra made his way into more non-mainstream issues, such as perforated and/or hand-cut productions released by Jell-O and Post Cereal. Some of these Berra cards had to be removed from the boxes by the collector after purchase of the product.

As the decade progressed, Topps continued to get more creative and experimental in their offerings. Berra's last appearance came in 1965 as a catcher/coach for the New York Mets, and even though

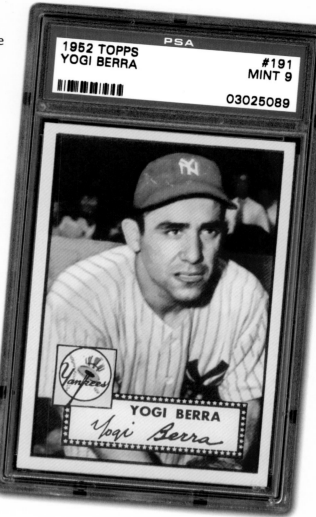

he retired as a player before several new Topps issues were released, the Hall of Famer did manage to make it into some new concepts. In the early 1960s, Topps issued a couple of stamp sets, and in 1962, the manufacturer created a set of faux currency called Topps Bucks. Berra appears in each oddball issue. The black-and-white Exhibit card sets, which have become more popular in recent times, included Berra near the beginning and towards the end of his playing career.

"Due to Berra's immense popularity, virtually all of the cards that bear his likeness are considered desirable."

The YOGI BERRA CARD

Some would argue that even though Berra's 1952 Topps is not his rookie or his most difficult card, it might be the most popular one on which the 10-time World Series champion appeared during his playing days. It has its advantages, including a slightly larger format, nice color, and the card is part of the most important post-WWII set in the hobby. That said, the nod would still have to go to Berra's mainstream debut (#6) in the 1948 Bowman set. The issue may not receive any awards for outstanding design, but its simplicity is part of the appeal. The black-and-white format showcases a young Berra who helped continue a tradition of great Yankees catchers after Bill Dickey left the game. Berra's Bowman rookie remains one of the keys to this 48-card set that contains several other Hall of Famer rookies like Musial and Warren Spahn.

ONE CARD TO WATCH

As we stated earlier, Berra collectors have a lot to choose from outside the mainstream Bowman and Topps sets, which dominated the hobby during his playing days. Before Topps unveiled their 407-card 1952 set, they dabbled in manufacturing a few small yet interesting releases. One of those releases was the 1951 Topps Major League All-Stars set (some refer to it as Current All-Stars). This very intriguing, but brutally tough, set consisted of 11 die-cut cards, each measuring 2¹⁄₁₆" by 5¼". Not only are they extremely difficult to find in high grade, they are tough to find at all. Aside from the three mega-rarities (Jim Konstanty, Robin Roberts, and Eddie Stanky) that were never released to the public, Berra is the most popular name in the set. The unique design, strong eye appeal, limited production, and its status as a true condition rarity make this Berra card one to watch and one of his most valuable as well.

DON DRYSDALE

I LIKED DON DRYSDALE. We used to play the Dodgers quite a bit during spring training up in Vero Beach, Florida, and I actually hit him pretty good back then. Don had this big sweeping fastball from his side. He was not afraid to give you a little chin music if he had to. Thank God I never got plunked by him, but it was spring training. Sometimes, however, that fastball coming in from the side would get you. He also had a nasty sinker and slider. Don had very good control, and you know, he was also a very good hitter to boot. We had a tough time at the beginning with the Dodgers during spring training when I first broke in. We were a pretty weak team in 1965 and 1966 and the Dodgers were outstanding.

I remember when Don and Sandy Koufax held out. I think it was in 1966. That really started the whole collective bargaining thing. He said that it was the only leverage that they had, he and Sandy holding out together.

Don told me that when he pitched, the outside corner of home plate was his territory. Today he would be plunking guys left and right if they were hot dogging. Back then, even if you weren't hot dogging, Drysdale was not afraid to clip you. I was kind of lucky because the two premier pitchers not afraid to throw at you, Drysdale and Bob Gibson, were in the National League. Thank goodness!

In 1967, I was thrilled to make the All-Star team for the first time, but I didn't get to face Drysdale, who was on the National League team. I faced Juan Marichal instead and popped out. Drysdale was a big part of the Dodgers success. I remember back in 1968 the Big D was on a roll. That was the year he broke records for shutouts and scoreless innings. When I was a kid, I loved the Brooklyn Dodgers. Don was only with them a couple of years before they moved to Los Angeles. He did a good job in Brooklyn, but his career really took off when they got out to the West Coast. Don and I always got along. He knew that I was a diehard Dodgers fan when I was a kid and they were my hometown team, and since I played for Boston, he would kid me about it. I'd get him back by telling him I was only thirteen years old when he broke in.

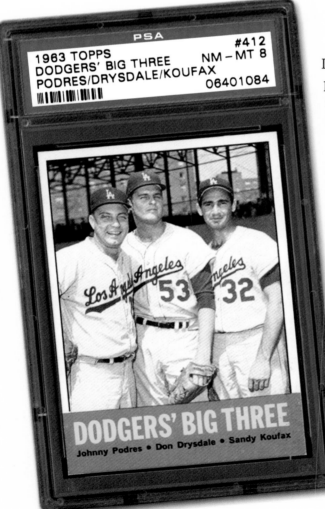

One of the most daunting factors about Drysdale was his size. He stood about 6'5" and weighed about 220 pounds. And it wasn't just his size. It was that we all knew he was not afraid to knock hitters down. I'd say he was as intimidating a pitcher as there was. As I said though, for whatever reason, I hit him pretty well in spring training. Drysdale retired, I believe, around 1969 and went into broadcasting. I would run into him periodically. It really was tragic how young he was when he died. I really liked Drysdale because he was a no-nonsense guy on the field but he was also very friendly. As the years have gone by, I look back and I realize that I was very lucky to play against Don because I could see first-hand how good he really was.

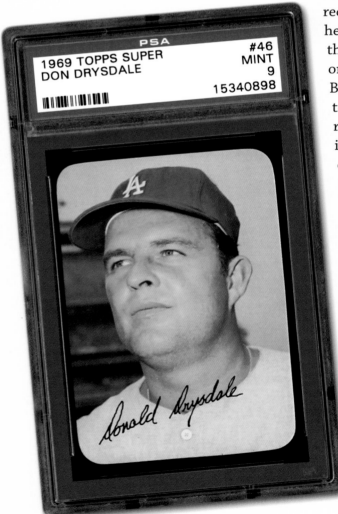

THE CARDS

Like his famed teammate, Sandy Koufax, Don Drysdale had a somewhat short yet dominant career on the mound. Thus, Drysdale's image can't be found on nearly as many mainstream card issues as some other contemporary stars during his Hall of Fame career. That said, unlike his left-handed ally, Drysdale's career extended into the late-1960s, which gave him an opportunity to make appearances in a few more issues as the decade came to a close. The latter part of the decade saw Topps continue their experimental ways, which resulted in more cards for the collector.

When Drysdale debuted with Topps in 1957, the manufacturer was coming off a run of well-received annual sets, which helped the company take over the marketplace from their only major competitor in Bowman. After 1955, Topps took command. Their 1956 release was somewhat similar in appearance to their 1955 offering, but Topps changed their approach entirely in 1957. After some degree of artwork or colorized photos dominated the format from 1952 through 1956, Topps modified the approach by using photography and a more simplistic overall design. Ironically, the design looked a little like the 1953 Bowman issue. No frills, just great poses surrounded by a basic frame.

As the years went by, Drysdale appeared in numerous basic Topps issues and a host of

terrific regional and food-related productions. Some of those sets include Bazooka, Bell Brand, Hires Root Beer, Jell-O, Morrell Meats, and Post Cereal. The Bell Brand and Morrell Meats sets were completely dedicated to the Dodgers, who packed a lot of star power on the roster, from Roy Campanella to Koufax. In fact, Drysdale was also included in Fleer's 1963 set, and he remains one of the keys along with fellow legends like Roberto Clemente, Willie Mays, and Brooks Robinson. It would be Fleer's last attempt of the decade.

Even though Drysdale was part of what many consider the most dominant one-two punch in the majors, aside from various league leader cards, he only appeared on one multi-player card with Koufax. In 1963, Drysdale, Koufax, and Johnny Podres were pictured together on a card entitled *Dodgers' Big Three*. Within the decade, Drysdale was included in some fantastic Topps test sets and other creative issues from the company. Topps produced oddball sets that included coins, decals, faux currency, peel-offs, stamps, and tattoos to name a few. Some of the more popular Topps issues that feature Drysdale include 1964 Topps Stand-Ups and 1969 Topps Supers.

"Drysdale was part of what many consider the most dominant one-two punch in the majors."

The DON DRYSDALE CARD

Drysdale has several regional and non-mainstream cards that offer a relative scarcity not found in the basic Topps sets, but the card that most collectors clamor for is his 1957 Topps #18 rookie. The simple design and great portrait of the big righty is a study in contrast. Along with Bob Gibson, there may not have been a more menacing man to step on the mound during his playing days, yet Drysdale's nearly ear-to-ear smile on his cardboard debut gives you the opposite impression. That is, of course, until you stand too close to the plate and wind up with a fastball near your melon. Like most other 1957 Topps cards, the Drysdale rookie is commonly found with print defects in the background, along with subpar centering, but the card is attainable in high grade with patience.

ONE CARD TO WATCH

As we have noted, once Topps took over the baseball-card market, they began to expand their horizons by experimenting more often. They did this to complement their standard, annual releases. By the end of the 1960s, Topps tried just about every kind of medium and design you could think of, which provided the hobby with a diverse selection of collectibles. Some of these productions were released to the public while others were left in the laboratory. In the beginning of the decade, one of those experiments took place. The cards never made it to the street, but some escaped the factory. The 1961 Topps Dice Game test set contains some of the greatest rarities the hobby has ever seen, and one of only 18 players included in the set happened to be Drysdale. It is, by far, his toughest card and one that is seldom seen. You might have a better chance meeting Sasquatch for lunch than finding this rarity. What is it worth? As much as someone is willing to pay for it.

WHITEY FORD

1953 BOWMAN COLOR
WHITEY FORD #153
PSA
MINT 9
50001127

A HELL OF A GUY and another player that, as a kid, I followed closely, Whitey Ford was not an overpowering pitcher but he had excellent command to go along with a nice sinker and very good curveball. He was a very reliable guy you knew could finish a game. I faced him a couple of times between 1966 and 1967, but the game that sticks out in my mind, and was one of the thrills of my early baseball career, was when we faced Whitey on Opening Day in Yankee Stadium in 1967. It was a hell of a game!

We had a lefty rookie, Billy Rohr, who started the game. Rohr had a no-hitter going into the ninth until Ellie Howard broke it up with a single, but before that, Yaz made one of the greatest catches that I ever saw off Tom Tresh to keep the no-hitter going. It was an over-the-head diving catch that he came up with. Because of Rohr and the play by Yaz, that game is still talked about a lot by Boston fans.

1959 YOO–HOO
WHITEY FORD
NO TAB–HAND CUT
NM–MT +
8.5
24902949

Anyway, I hit a single to left off of Whitey who I think went about eight innings that day. I was so proud of that hit off Ford. I would love to have that ball today!

Whitey didn't pitch much longer after that and I think he was done by June. I remember talking to my brother, who worked at Yankee Stadium, telling him how excited I was to be facing Whitey in that stadium. There's no doubt about it, the old Yankee Stadium was a pitcher's ballpark. As I said, Whitey wasn't overpowering. He was only about 5'10" or so with at best a 90-mile-an-hour fastball, but being a lefty, he had a knack for getting batters to hit to the largest part of the field, straight away center, which was somewhere around 463 feet.

The Yanks were breaking up at the time and getting old. Guys were being traded and were retiring, but Whitey always had a good defense behind him. You know, the Yanks were a heck of a crew back in their glory days with Whitey, Mantle, Billy Martin, Hank Bauer, and the rest, but in 1967 I think Mantle, Whitey, and Elston Howard were just about the only ones left. When Whitey pitched, his catcher, Ellie Howard, made his job a little easier. Ellie always had a wet spot somewhere on his uniform.

It was there on purpose. Let's say it was on his leg. He would rub the ball on the wet spot and then rub it into the dirt, so there was a little dark spot. That made the ball move all over the place. Ellie told me about all of this after he joined the Red Sox later on that season. It was ironic that Ellie came to Boston, because he was the guy who busted up Rohr's no-hitter.

It's interesting that I played my entire career with the Red Sox but grew up in Brooklyn loving the Dodgers and the Yankees. Whitey was right there up with my idols. What the hell? He was a 10-time All-Star and how many world championship teams did he play on, six? I'll tell you though, our whole team was in awe of Whitey and for me, personally, to play in Yankee Stadium and face Whitey? It was a real thrill to face one of the greats that I watched as a kid.

THE CARDS

While Mickey Mantle and Yogi Berra were leading the New York Yankees to World Series appearance after World Series appearance at the plate and on defense, this man was the clear leader on the mound. From a hobby perspective, he is also the most desirable Yankees pitcher of the 1950s and 1960s. Whitey Ford's career in baseball and the card collecting hobby nearly mimicked his legendary teammate, Mantle, at least in terms of time. Ford and Mantle made their mainstream debut in the same set, with Ford bowing out just a couple of years before "The Commerce Comet" hung up the cleats.

Despite having a long and successful Hall of Fame career as a pitcher, Ford did not appear in quite as many card sets as some contemporary sluggers did. Pitchers often have shorter careers and primes than position players do, which simply means there are generally fewer individual cards to choose from for the hobbyist. In addition, keep in mind that Ford did not play in 1951 and 1952, resulting in no 1952 Bowman or Topps cards for the great pitcher. If collectors could wish one Ford card into existence that never was, there is no doubt it would be a 1952 Topps card.

The good news for collectors is that Ford did appear in most of the Bowman and Topps productions after entering the league. This includes his highly-desirable 1953 Bowman card, one of his most valuable. The one major exception was the 1955 Topps set, another card that collectors can only dream about owning. Ford's image can be found in a fair number of regional and oddball issues, from Red Man Tobacco to Post Cereal to Jell-O. One of Ford's most desirable regional cards is the 1959 Yoo-hoo issue, where he appears along with his batterymate, Berra. Ford can also be found on various mediums, including a few different stamp and coin sets.

Ford is noticeably absent from several popular regional and Topps (non-basic) sets throughout the 1950s and 1960s. With his standing as the ace of the most successful team in the league and as a pitcher who put up double-digit wins almost every year until his last two seasons, you would expect to find Ford in more issues. The demand for his cards had to be there, so it is likely that his absence was the result of not working out contractual terms with the manufacturer. Ford did, however, appear in several of the ultra-tough Venezuelan Topps sets in the 1960s, which are difficult to find in any grade.

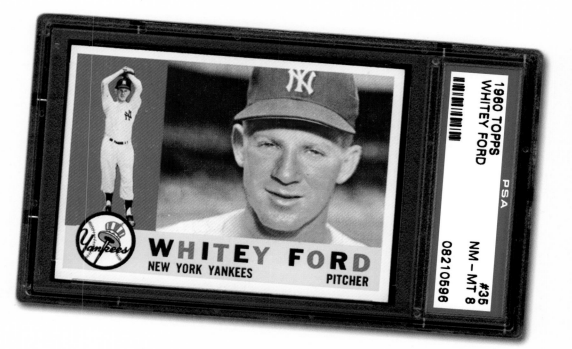

The WHITEY FORD CARD

In 1951, Bowman included three remarkable rookies in their set. Willie Mays, the aforementioned Mantle, and Ford all debuted in this classic and beautiful set. Interestingly enough, while it is hard to top names like Mantle and Mays when it comes to baseball and hobby lore, it was Ford who was selected to take the #1 slot in the set. For years, the Ford rookie was the only #1 card to feature a Hall of Fame rookie, until 2016, when Ken Griffey Jr. was inducted into baseball's hallowed halls. Griffey, of course, led off for Upper Deck's inaugural issue in 1989. The 1951 Bowman Ford offers just about everything you would want in a rookie card. The design is attractive, he played for the most popular team in baseball during their most successful run, it is part of a classic set, and it is hard to find in high grade since most first and last cards were subjected to more handling abuse than others.

ONE CARD TO WATCH

Berk Ross issued a couple of trading card sets in the early 1950s. The sets never caught on in the same manner that Bowman, Topps, or even some of the regional issues of the era have over the years, but they did produce cards with some of the biggest names in the game, like Mantle, Mays, Joe DiMaggio, and Ted Williams. In 1951, the manufacturer included a fresh-faced Ford in the set (#4–5). Along with his popular Bowman card, this Ford should be viewed as a true rookie. Granted, the card isn't quite as visually appealing as the mainstream Bowman issue due to a somewhat unfocused appearance of the image, but the value gap seems far too wide at this point. In the same grade, you can pick up the Berk Ross rookie for a fraction, and I mean a fraction, of the Bowman Ford. It will never compete with the important Bowman card, but it offers a much more affordable alternative.

NELLIE FOX

1951 BOWMAN NELSON FOX #232 — MINT 9 — 07009846

I REALLY LIKED FOX AS PLAYER. He had that big-barreled bat with no knob. It was a U1 actually, the same model bat that I used to hit 40 home runs in 1969. Fox choked up on the bat and would spray the ball to all fields. Nellie didn't hit a lot of home runs but he was a very good gap hitter. He was with the White Sox for most of his career and that was a tough ballpark to hit in. I think of him as a little "pepper pot" kind of guy—a great bunter with pretty good speed. He was a pretty quiet guy and always had that wad of chew in his mouth. You know, in that era, there were only eight teams, and they played the same teams 22 times. We knew each other's weaknesses at the plate, but Nellie had none. He was just a great singles guy that you knew would get on base.

1952 DIXIE LIDS NELSON FOX — AUTHENTIC — 26628132

Fox was an outstanding second baseman as well. When Luis Aparicio and I played on the Red Sox together, we would talk about the double play combo with him and Fox. Especially on that 1959 White Sox team, their double play combination was outstanding. They won the pennant for the first time in years in '59 and Nellie and Luis were a big part of that team. Luis liked Nellie a lot. He always said that Fox was a very smart player who really helped him when he was just starting out. The two of them became an unbelievable double play combination. Many of the little pointers that Luis Aparicio gave our second baseman, Doug Griffin, were ones he learned from Nellie Fox.

I never played against Nellie Fox. By the time I began playing, he had already been traded to Houston in the National League. Nellie was near the end of his career at that point. I did end up meeting him when he was coaching the Senators and later the Rangers. Those teams were managed by Ted Williams.

When Nellie was coaching with the Senators, we would chat a bit. He told me he liked the way I got the ball out of my hands so quickly. He also told me he really liked my stroke and that my swing was tailor-made for Fenway.

There are certain players that you try to emulate. From a defensive standpoint, I paid a lot of attention to Nellie when I was younger. I know he won several Gold Gloves and was on the All-Star team a slew of times. He was also the MVP of the American League in 1959.

Nellie died at a fairly young age from cancer. I thought he would be a shoo-in for the Hall of Fame, but it took the Veterans Committee of the Hall to vote him in. I think that wasn't until the late 1990s.

There are a couple of great statues of Luis and Nellie at the White Sox ballpark. From a defensive point, there were none better than the two of them in their heyday. After playing with Aparicio, I could clearly see how great they must have been as a double play tandem. Nellie was certainly up there with the best.

THE CARDS

Nellie Fox made his official MLB debut long before he appeared on his first mainstream baseball card in 1951, which meant he narrowly missed inclusion in some popular late-1940s sets issued by Leaf and Bowman. Once Fox entered the cardboard hobby, he became a mainstay. Fox appeared in traditional, annual sets through 1965 Topps, when the curtain closed on his collectibles career...at least from a playing days perspective. Between his card debut and his finale, Fox appeared in numerous popular regional and food-product issues of the 1950s and 1960s.

Fox was a player who signed an exclusive with Bowman when he entered the fold. As a result, he did not appear on his first Topps card until 1956,

after Bowman's run (1948–1955) ended. Unfortunately for collectors, that means Fox was never a part of the stellar Topps productions from 1952 to 1955. Every Topps set during that time is still regarded as a classic, but Fox was limited to Bowman and other regional productions of the period. Some of those regional sets include Dixie Lids, Red Heart Dog Food, and Red Man Tobacco.

While Fox did appear within a black-and-white Exhibit issue, his 1951 Bowman #232 is his official rookie card. There is no doubt that Fox is greatly overshadowed by the three powerhouse rookie cards of fellow Hall of Famers Whitey Ford, Mickey Mantle, and Willie Mays, but the association with this captivating set adds to the demand for his inaugural card. As the decade progressed, Fox found himself in other desirable issues, like the tough 1959 Bazooka baseball set, and he was pictured alongside teammate Luis Aparicio on Fox's first multi-player card entitled *Keystone Combo* (1959 Topps).

In addition to Topps, Fox continued to appear in various sets during the 1960s. He can be found in everything from Armour Coins to Jell-O to Post Cereal releases. Fox was also a part of the fun experimentation that took place at Topps during the decade. He appeared in creative faux currency and stamp issues, along with the oversized Topps Giants sets as an active player. Keep in mind that a number of the regional issues Fox was a part of had to be hand-cut by the collector in order to remove the card from a larger format, which was usually in the form of a product box.

PSA
1952 RED MAN TOBACCO   #9
NELSON FOX   NM – MT +
8.5
14628550

NELSON FOX
SECOND BASE
CHICAGO WHITE SOX
Born: St. Thomas, Pa., Dec. 25, '27
Height: 5-8   Weight: 150
Bats: Left   Throws: Right
Baby-faced Nellie, the American League's starting All-Star second baseman, appeared in 147 games for the Sox in 1951 and he batted .313. He had 189 hits, which included 32 doubles, 12 triples and 4 home runs. In addition Nellie batted in 55 tallies. Spent one full season and parts of two others with Athletics. Became regular with trade to Chicago in 1950.
(CUT ALONG THIS LINE)
1952 RED MAN ALL-STAR TEAM
AMERICAN LEAGUE SERIES–PLAYER #9

The NELLIE FOX CARD

Most of the time, the undisputed card to own of a particular player is his universally recognized rookie, but that is not always the case. Sometimes, the card to own is part of a tough or popular regional issue instead of the traditional annual set that most collectors pursue. In my opinion, that is certainly the case with Fox. His 1951 Bowman debut is hard to beat, especially since it is part of such a fantastic set, but it is bested by Fox's elusive 1954 Wilson Franks card. Those cards, which were distributed with packages of hot dogs, are visually attractive and very hard to find in high grade for obvious reasons. In addition, the extremely narrow borders leave little margin for error on centering. There are only 20 total cards in the set and the Ted Williams card is the key, a card that has fetched well into five and even six figures for a high-grade example. Fox is one of six Hall of Famers in the set.

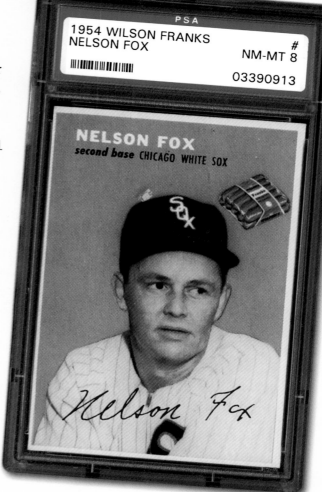

ONE CARD TO WATCH

Earlier, we mentioned the fact that Fox appeared in a variety of very popular and challenging non-mainstream sets throughout his career, especially during the 1950s. A card that is seldom offered in appealing condition is Fox's colorful and oversized (2 13⁄16" by 4 15⁄16") 1959 Bazooka card. This card, which is part of a 23-card set, was originally part of a box and had to be removed by the collector. Due to the design, which includes the way the cards were positioned on the box, it can be very hard to safely extract the card from the box without causing creasing damage. Furthermore, even though dotted lines were included in the construction of the box with the purpose of helping the collector cut the cards more accurately, many of the cards were cut well inside the lines. These cards still have value, but to achieve numerical grades, the cards must come very close to measuring fully, based on their intended design. The Fox is not only one of a handful of Hall of Famers in the set, it is also considered a short print, making it even tougher to find than most cards in the release.

SANDY KOUFAX

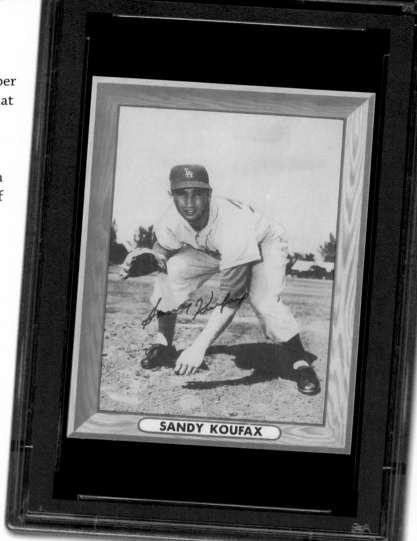

1958 BELL BRAND
SANDY KOUFAX
DODGERS
NM – MT 8
12223216

I FACED SANDY KOUFAX quite a bit during spring training at Vero Beach. He was really something. I remember how tough it was to get a hit off him. One of the things that made it difficult was that he had such a high kick, it was hard to see the ball. You would have a hard time picking up the ball, and the next thing you knew, that 95 or 97 mph fastball was on top of you. I did get a few hits off him though. I remember hitting a double to left-center field off of a breaking pitch that he threw. It had so much rotation that the ball actually whistled. His 12 to 6 rotation was amazing, and then he also had one that was three-quarters. I swear that the ball looked like it was rising sometimes when Sandy threw his fastball. It would start at your waist, and then the next thing you knew it was letter-high. You almost had to tomahawk the ball. Maybe it was an optical illusion. Who knows?

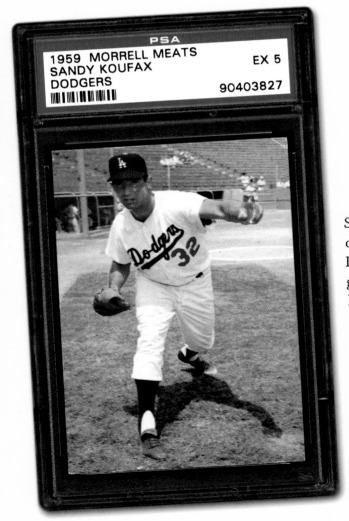

1959 MORRELL MEATS
SANDY KOUFAX
DODGERS
EX 5
90403827

Sandy was kind of a quiet guy, but I think that Drysdale brought him out a lot. They both wanted big contracts and Sandy held out with Drysdale. I'm not sure he would have done that on his own. We both grew up in Brooklyn. He's several years older than me, so we didn't play high school baseball at the same time. Sandy was an excellent hoop player and had a lot of college scholarship offers. We used to shoot the breeze at spring training about New York City basketball because he knew I made All-City as a point guard. In the early years everyone in Brooklyn was tracking this phenom. We heard the Dodgers had a young kid from Brooklyn, a left-hander, who could throw a baseball through a wall, but couldn't get it over the plate. He finally put it all together after they told him to slow down, and he was just great. Everyone in Brooklyn respected him when he wouldn't pitch in Game One of the 1965 World Series because it was on a Jewish holiday. His teammates respected him as well for his decision.

In my opinion, Koufax, Spahn, and Randy Johnson were the three greatest lefty pitchers ever, with no disrespect for Steve Carlton and Lefty Grove. Of the pitchers that I faced, Koufax is up there with Gibson and Ryan. He was very difficult to make contact with even though he was a lefty. He absolutely dominated in the 1960s. Koufax was the league strikeout leader and he won three Cy Young Awards. Besides that, he was the Series MVP in both 1963 and 1965. It's really too bad Sandy's career was cut short. Even though he won 27 games his last year pitching, Sandy retired because he got arthritis in his elbow and he was in a lot of pain. Koufax was actually one of the first pitchers to ice his elbow.

Sandy is the kind of guy who doesn't like a lot of attention. After he left the game, he married actor Richard Widmark's daughter and moved to Maine. I still see him now and then. We have played in several golf tournaments together in Florida and always have a few laughs. He's a real genuine, friendly guy. Today, I think that Sandy is working for the Dodgers in some capacity. I know he has always enjoyed working with the young pitchers in spring training. He has always been a real credit to the game.

THE CARDS

The "James Dean" of baseball had a short career, retiring at the age of 30 after the completion of the 1966 season, but his spectacular performance and immense popularity ensured the legendary lefty was part of numerous trading card sets. Koufax's image can be found in virtually all the mainstream

issues you would expect, in addition to a host of great regional releases that range in difficulty and demand. Much like contemporary superstar Mickey Mantle, virtually every Koufax card generates some measure of attention simply because of his name.

Koufax started to appear on baseball cards right as Topps took over the market and Bowman decided to exit. In fact, one of the fantasy cards that could have been but never was for Koufax includes the 1955 Bowman. Like the other two key rookies that joined Koufax in the 1955 Topps set, Roberto Clemente and Harmon Killebrew, he was exclusive to Topps when he made his mainstream debut. Koufax was a staple for Topps through 1966, and in between, the Hall of Famer appeared on many league leader cards when he put together his incredible pitching run in the 1960s.

Koufax can also be found on a few multi-player cards, alongside his teammates. In 1961, Koufax and Johnny Podres are pictured together on a card entitled *Dodger Southpaws*. In 1963, Koufax, Podres, and Don Drysdale came together for *Dodgers' Big Three*. The team was led by pitching and Koufax was at the center of it all. Koufax was also part of several of Topps' creative releases and test sets during the decade. The mound magician can be found in stamp, faux currency, coin, and tattoo sets manufactured by Topps. Perhaps the most elusive Topps Koufax is his 1967 Topps Punch-Outs card, a test issue that is rarely offered for sale and one that was designed to be used as part of a game.

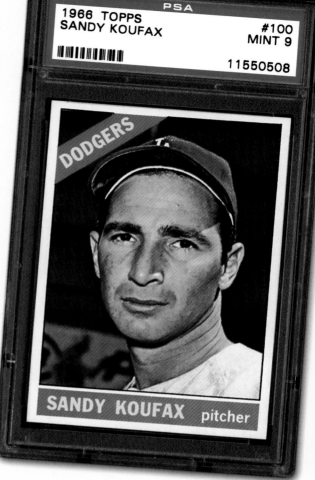

Beyond Topps' regular issue, Koufax made several appearances in the obscure Venezuelan Topps series, and he was one of several big stars to appear in the 1963 Fleer set, one that remains relatively underrated considering the set's contents and clean design. Near the beginning of his career, well before Koufax established himself as a dominant force, he was included in some great regional issues like Bell Brand (potato chips) and Morrell Meats. This started in the late-1950s but continued into the 1960s when Koufax became a perennial All-Star. In addition to the aforementioned brands, you can locate the lefty in sets issued by Bazooka, Jell-O, and Post Cereal. Koufax was also a familiar figure in a handful of black-and-white Exhibit sets, an issue that has made somewhat of a comeback with collectors in recent years.

The SANDY KOUFAX CARD

In the case of Koufax, there is no doubting the fact that his 1955 Topps #123 rookie card stands above the rest as the clear card to own of the baseball icon. While not as difficult to locate in high grade as the Clemente rookie, this card remains one of the major keys to the set, a set that has always been regarded as one of Topps' best productions. The Koufax rookie suffers from a few different condition obstacles, including subpar centering and print defects that are easily visible in the light-colored background along the face of the card. The Koufax rookie is not considered rare by any means and it exists in much greater numbers than some of the regional issues mentioned earlier, yet the overwhelming popularity of the card keeps it in a secure spot as his ultimate card.

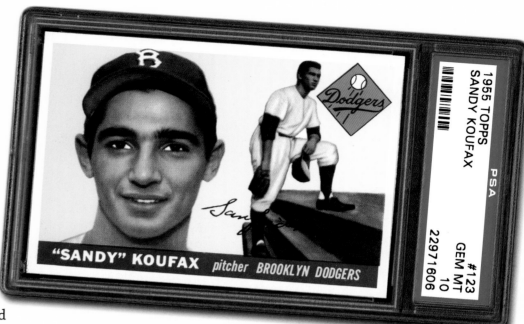

"Even if you are lucky enough to find an example, the 1967 Venezuelan Topps Koufax is brutally tough in high grade."

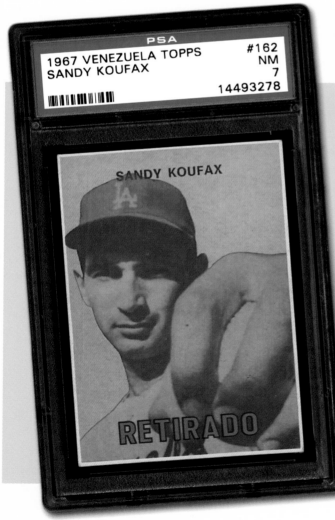

ONE CARD TO WATCH

We began with the Koufax rookie as the card to own, so we will end it with a card that appropriately wraps up his illustrious career, a card that offers the kind of scarcity that few of his other productions do. In 1967, Koufax's image can be found on a few different regular-issue Topps cards in the league leader categories, but he did not have a traditional card in the set. His 1966 Topps card was his last. That was the year he retired and some argue it was his best overall season. The next year, the 1967 Venezuelan Retirado set was released, and it was one that paid tribute to the greats of the past like Babe Ruth and Satchel Paige. Even though he had just left the game, they honored the recently-retired Koufax on card #162 of that set, a fitting tribute to one of the most dominant pitchers to ever suit up. Even if you are lucky enough to find an example, the 1967 Venezuelan Topps Koufax is brutally tough in high grade, with most known copies grading PSA VG-EX 4 or lower.

MICKEY MANTLE

WHEN IT COMES TO TALKING about Mickey Mantle, a lot goes through my mind. First and foremost, when I was a kid, he was my ultimate hero. Being from Brooklyn, I loved the Dodgers, but Mickey was my favorite player. I was only 22 years old when I played against Mantle for the first time. I was simply in awe. It was sometime in May of 1965. There I was, playing against the great Mickey Mantle in Yankee Stadium. It was a thrill that I will never forget. You know, I was only eight years old when Mickey broke in, so you can imagine how it felt to play against my idol. Wow! What a thrill. I remember when he got a home run, he hit the ball so hard and so far, it would just give you chills. By the time I got to play against Mantle his knees were pretty gone and he was near the end of his career. He still played left field at the time, but he switched to first base a couple of years later. In that first game, I got two hits off Al Downing.

As time went on, Mickey and I became pretty good friends. When he played first base, that's when we got to talk a bit. He always asked about the family and how things were going. Mickey was a very humble guy and didn't like to talk about himself too much, but we did talk baseball and how good the game had been to him. He told me to savor every minute of baseball, because it would be over before I knew it. It's pretty unbelievable, but I actually caught the last ball he hit in his career. It was off Jim Lonborg and it was a pop up. I sure wish I had kept that ball. I just casually tossed it on the mound while I was running back into the dugout. Little did I know at the time that he would be all done. I got to see Mantle hit his last home run, too. We were playing at Yankee Stadium in late September of 1968 when he drilled one off of Lonborg.

In 1967, when I made the All-Star team for the first time, it was a real kick to play on the same team as Mantle, Killebrew, and Brooks Robinson. Yaz and Conigliaro made the All-Star team that year, too. I'll never forget Mickey making his entrance into the clubhouse. We were all getting ready to go out onto the field, and in comes The Mick shaking hands

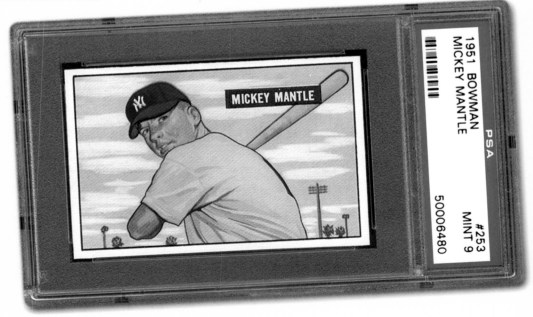

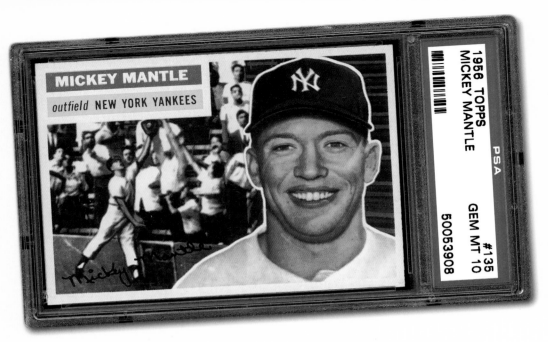

MICKEY MANTLE
outfield NEW YORK YANKEES

1956 TOPPS
MICKEY MANTLE

PSA

#135
GEM MT 10

50053908

and slapping guys on the back, joking and laughing. He went to the trainer's room, stripped down and got wrapped up like a mummy. The tape started at the ankle and went around and around all the way up to the top of his thigh. We were all watching him. Mickey was pretty much at the end of his career by then. He hung in the dugout shooting the breeze with us and I think either in the fourth or fifth inning he came up to pinch hit. Three pitches, three swings, a strikeout and he was back in the locker room, unwrapped, showered and out the door before you knew it! I guess he was an All-Star so many times it was old hat for him by then.

Everyone knows how great Mantle was with his Triple Crown, 20 All-Star appearances, three AL MVPs, and his batting title. What a talent. Mickey was as good a player as anyone.

THE CARDS

In the history of the hobby, there hasn't been a more dominant force during any era than Mickey Mantle. His ability to captivate collectors

was, and still is, something to behold. From his raw skills, to his Southern charm, to his name, Mantle seemed to have all the ingredients. This included acting as the centerpiece of the most powerful dynasty in sports history. Virtually every young boy in America wanted to be him. Babe Ruth may be the most important figure in baseball history, but no one was more universally idolized in this sport than Mantle.

Along with his unrivaled popularity came an abundance of cards to choose from during his memorable career. As a collector, you would need extreme patience and a lot of money to acquire all of them. With Mantle, where oh where do we start? His only recognized rookie card is the most logical place to do so. Along with teammate Whitey Ford and fellow superstar Willie Mays, Mantle made his cardboard debut in the 1951 Bowman set. Yes, one year later, Mantle's image would grace his first Topps card, but let's be clear: Mantle has only one true rookie, and the 1951 Bowman is it. For a couple of years (1952 and 1953), collectors were treated to both Bowman and Topps Mantle

cards, but Mantle was exclusive to Bowman in 1954 and 1955. Mantle's absence from Topps robbed collectors of two potentially classic cards.

Being the fan favorite that he was, Mantle appeared on numerous cards over the course of his career, from the basic Bowman and Topps productions to a multitude of regional issues. The slugger was also part of several great multi-player cards, as Mantle was pictured with fellow stars like Hank Aaron (1958), Yogi Berra (1953 and 1957), and Mays (1962). Once Bowman disappeared from the marketplace after 1955, Mantle reappeared in Topps' sets and he did it with a bang. Mantle's 1956 Topps card has always been a favorite of collectors, picturing the smiling icon during his best overall season, one where he won the Triple Crown.

Mantle's final Topps card came in 1969, but the Hall of Famer played long enough to make it into some of the most creative Topps sets ever made, including some test issues. Various mediums from Topps carried Mantle's likeness including stamps, tattoos, faux currency, coins, decals, pins, posters, and discs. One of the more elusive Topps test issues from the latter portion of his career would be the 1967 Topps Punch-Outs card. Bazooka, Dan-Dee, Jell-O, Post Cereal, Red Heart, Stahl-Meyer, and Yoo-hoo are just some of the brands that produced Mantle cards too, varying in difficulty and popularity. There are several black-and-white Exhibit cards that feature Mantle as well. The bottom line is that no single player appeared on more collectibles than Mantle during the era.

The MICKEY MANTLE CARD

No athlete in the history of the hobby has more individually-significant cards than Mantle, yet the answer to this question is easy. The most important Mantle card is, arguably, the most important baseball card in the entire industry. If I were to select one card to act as the poster child or the symbol of baseball card collecting, it would be the 1952 Topps Mantle #311. No, it is not Mantle's rookie card. That would be his 1951 Bowman, but the 1952 Topps card has taken on a life of its own. The card is more pop culture art than mere baseball card at this point. There is no doubt that it is the anchor of the most important postwar baseball card set ever made, but the power of its image is greater than the sum of the card's parts or attributes. If there were a Mount Rushmore of cards and it was limited to one spot, this card would get it every time.

ONE CARD TO WATCH

Unlike selecting the single-most important Mantle card, this section requires a lot more thought and it is sure to generate much more debate. There are countless Mantle cards that one could argue are ones to watch in the future. Do you prefer condition rarities like any of the Stahl-Meyer Mantles from the mid-1950s or the sheer scarcity of a nearly impossible card like the 1961 Topps Dice Game test issue? Well, I have narrowed it down to one card that neatly sums up Mantle's career, while sprinkling in a rarity twist. All of Mantle's career stats can be seen on his 1969 Topps #500 finale, but there is a variation to his already-popular last card. The 1969 Topps White Letter Mantle was produced in limited quantities, along with several other players in the set. Instead of printing the player's last name in yellow, it was done with white lettering. Was this a simple error at the factory or was it the product of something more sinister, perhaps a ploy to sell more packs? A seemingly "random" error that just happened to impact Mantle on his final Topps card? We'll never know for sure, but the variation left us with one of the great Mantle cards to collect, one that seems appropriate for the magnitude of Mantle. It was the equivalent to a walk-off home run to end a hobby career.

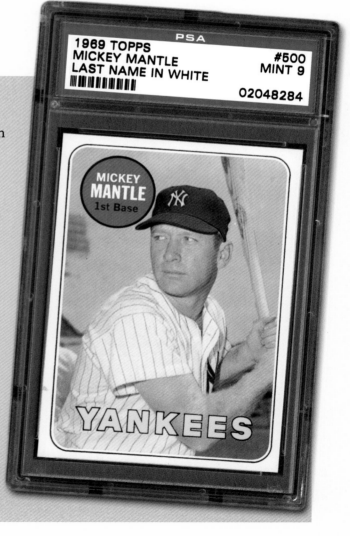

EDDIE MATHEWS

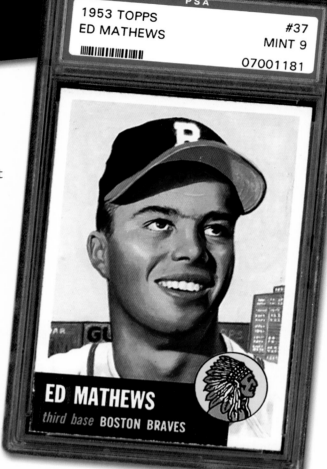

I DIDN'T KNOW EDDIE MATHEWS that well. He played for the Braves all of those years and we really never even played them in spring training to my recollection. Actually he started out with the Braves in Boston but after his first year they moved to Milwaukee. At the end of his career, he played for the Tigers and I remember him pinch hitting a couple of times against us, but at that point, he was battling some injuries and was pretty much playing out the string. Mathews did play in the World Series in 1968 though, which was not a bad way to wrap up his career.

ED MATHEWS
third base BOSTON BRAVES

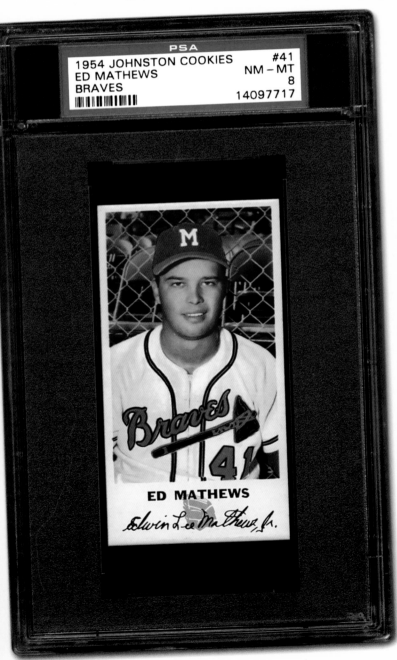

ED MATHEWS

In his heyday, Mathews was a hell of a hitter, a real home run, RBI guy. I always felt that Eddie really was overshadowed by Aaron. I believe they were teammates for most of Mathews' career. On the one hand, batting as the number three and four hitters, Mathews and Aaron put some amazing home run numbers on the board. But, on the other hand, make no mistake about it, Aaron was the superstar.

Eddie was not a spectacular third baseman like Brooks, but he turned himself into a very good fielder. With the ball coming to you at third base as fast as it does, you really don't have the time to react like you would typically in other infield positions. For a lot of years, I think that he was probably the best overall third basemen in the National League. When you can hit over 500 career homers besides playing that position very well, you are something special.

Mathews was a quiet guy but really tough. He had the reputation of being as tough as nails. Eddie got into some really great scraps with other players and he never backed down. He wouldn't take anything from anybody. I remember a pretty big fight when Frank Robinson slid into Mathews and knocked him down. Eddie went after him like a boxer and got him good. He took on Don Drysdale, too. That was after Drysdale beaned one of his teammates. Mathews was that kind of guy. If you were in a fight, you sure wanted him on your side.

I paid close attention to his career, and later on, after I switched to third base, I would study film of the greats like Mathews, Brooks, and a few others. He certainly earned his entry in the Hall of Fame. When you look at the best third basemen in the Hall of Fame, I would put Eddie in the top four or five, maybe behind Schmidt, Brett, and Brooks. His power numbers were outstanding. I know he led the league a couple of times in home runs, and he hit that 500 pinnacle. He played in three World Series and got two rings. Not a bad resume.

I know that he managed the Braves for a while in the early 1970s but was not very successful. In any event, Eddie Mathews was, in my opinion, one of the top third basemen in the game and one of the most underrated Hall of Famers. I'm really kind of sorry I didn't get to know him that well.

THE CARDS

Eddie Mathews began his career in blistering fashion, establishing himself as a premier power hitter right out of the gate. He was also part of one of the great slugging duos of all time, along with his Braves teammate Hank Aaron. Thus, Mathews cards enjoyed their fair share of demand very early on and his stellar career covered a lot of cardboard ground before he retired in 1968. Mathews' career in cards started during the early Bowman/Topps battles, but extended through the extremely experimental

Topps period of the 1960s. It was during that time when the mega-manufacturer threw caution to the wind.

Despite being exclusive to Topps during his hobby debut in 1952, Mathews would avoid exclusivity to either Bowman or Topps for the remainder of the annual brand struggle. From 1953 through 1955, when both major companies produced cards, Mathews was included in each release. His most desirable Bowman card of the trio is clearly the 1953 card, which is regarded by many to be part of one of the hobby's most appealing sets. The simple yet beautiful design continues to captivate collectors. That year, Bowman decided to integrate photos into the cards versus the artwork they incorporated into their previous designs (1950–1952).

Mathews would appear in a variety of regional sets over time. During the early portion of his career, Mathews' image was included in the visually-attractive Johnston Cookies issues (1953–1955). These sets were limited to Braves players, but the team had a few big names that helped carry the load, including Aaron (1954–1955) and Warren Spahn (1953–1955), to go along with Mathews. Another Braves-centric issue from the period was the Spic and Span series, one that Mathews appeared in several times. While Mathews was included in only one Red Man Tobacco set (1954), he did make his way into a few different Bazooka and Post Cereal sets down the road.

You can find Mathews on a mix of other mediums as well. These include a few different coins sets like Armour, Salada, and Shirriff. Even Topps produced a Mathews coin in 1964, along with faux currency, pin, stamp, and tattoo collectibles. One of Mathews' most desirable non-mainstream cards from the 1960s is his 1964 Topps Stand-Up card, a colorful issue with a unique design, one where the players were made so collectors could pop them out from their base. Mathews' last Topps card came in 1968 as a member of the World Champion Detroit Tigers. The set has always been popular. It was the beginning for future Hall of Famers Johnny Bench and Nolan Ryan, but a fitting exit to one of the best third basemen in baseball history.

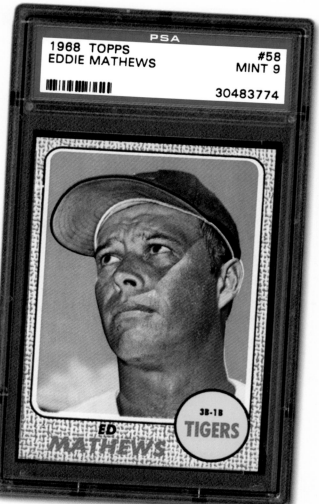

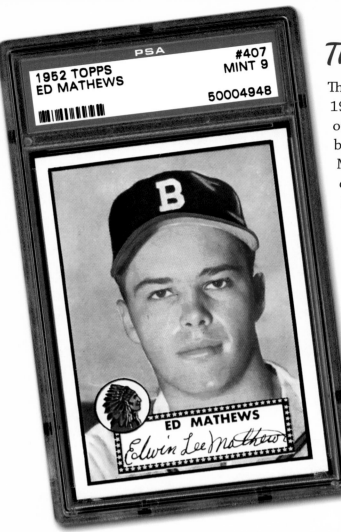

The EDDIE MATHEWS CARD

The overwhelming choice for the one Mathews card to own would be his 1952 Topps #407 rookie card, hands down. Not only is the card part of the premier postwar set ever produced and one that is anchored by the most symbolic baseball card ever made in Mickey Mantle, the Mathews is the last card in the set. Released during a time when collectors would often position the first and last cards at the top and bottom of the stack, these cards would often take additional abuse from handling since they were exposed to the elements more often than those in the middle of the stack. The elements also included rubber bands that were occasionally used to group cards together. In addition to the handling obstacles, the Mathews rookie is commonly found with subpar centering. Behind the Mantle, the Mathews is the second-most valuable card in the set, and it's by far his most valuable card ever made.

ONE CARD TO WATCH

In 1959, American Motors produced an unnumbered 20-card set to help bring attention to the new television program, *Home Run Derby*. The brainchild of renowned writer-director Lou Breslow, amongst others, and hosted by Mark Scott, this fun competition pitted many of the best sluggers in the league against each other. The participants came away with a cash prize, with the winner receiving $2,000 and a chance to return the following week. In those days, the $2,000 prize was substantial considering what the players made at the time. In fact, many players took odd jobs in the offseason to make ends meet. Mathews was one of the participants and, of course, was included in the set along with the likes of Aaron, Mantle, and Willie Mays. The black-and-white cards had blank backs and were oversized, measuring approximately 3¼" by 5¼". This collectible Mathews issue is arguably his second-most valuable card, but beware of reprints and counterfeits.

ROBIN ROBERTS

AS A BROOKLYN KID, the Dodgers were my team, but I always loved it when the Phillies came to town. Of course I rooted against the Phillies, but I did admire Robin Roberts. He had some great years. I think there was a stretch in there of about five or six years when you could count on him to win at least 20 games. Little did he know that he would play an important role in my early career without even knowing it.

God bless Robin Roberts. That's all I can say. He bailed me out. Literally. In 1965, my rookie year, I was going through what became the longest batting slump in my career. I went 0-for-32. Can you imagine? There is nothing more stressful than a slump of that magnitude. Everyone was giving me advice, my teammates, my wife, my friends. Nothing was working. When you are in a slump, it's almost like you are on an island all by yourself. The more you press, the worse it gets. The pitchers were way ahead of me. I was swinging at bad pitches.

The hitting coach and all the guys, especially Yaz, were trying to help me. I was really discouraged.

So, we went to Baltimore to play the Orioles in late April that year. Robin Roberts was their starter and faced Jim Lonborg. I knew Roberts had Hall of Fame credentials, great control, and was smart, but he was at the end of his career at the time. Even though Roberts was playing out the string, he did help the Orioles. In any event, I got two solid hits off him that day. Robin's fastball was in the upper 80s in those days, so I saw the ball well. And he threw strikes. As I recall, I hit a bloop single in the fifth and hit a line-drive double to left center in the seventh. Robin helped me end the streak! After that, I started hitting the ball a lot better. I felt like the weight of the world was off my shoulders. As a matter of fact, the Orioles beat us that day, but I was happy that I broke out of my slump.

The Orioles won the pennant the next year, but Roberts had moved on to the Astros so he missed it. Robin Roberts had some great years with the Phillies. He wasn't an overpowering pitcher but he had great command. I remember talking to my teammates before that Baltimore game about facing Roberts. It was always a challenge to face a great pitcher, even if he was at the very end of his career. You never knew what stuff they were gonna bring. That day in Baltimore, he pitched a complete game to beat us, although Lonnie gave up just a few hits. When you look at Roberts' career, the first half was spectacular. Besides all those 20-game seasons, he was an All-Star many times and he led the league in strikeouts a couple of times. The second half of his career was just okay. He lost speed on his fastball but those Phillies teams were pretty awful in those years, so without the offensive support, he didn't get as many wins. Robin was one of those guys that I really cherished facing because at one time he was as good as it gets.

THE CARDS

For a Hall of Famer, Robin Roberts had one of the strangest careers in both baseball and baseball cards. During the 1950s, Roberts put together a dominant run as a member of the Philadelphia Phillies, one where he reeled off six consecutive 20-win seasons. After leading the league in victories from 1952 through 1955, Roberts suddenly led the league in losses in 1956 and 1957. In the hobby, despite having a 19-year career, Roberts appears on a relatively limited number of cards compared to others of the period who played for a similar length of time. Whether it was due to contractual issues or a result of his roller-coaster-like numbers, collectors don't have quite as many choices as one would think.

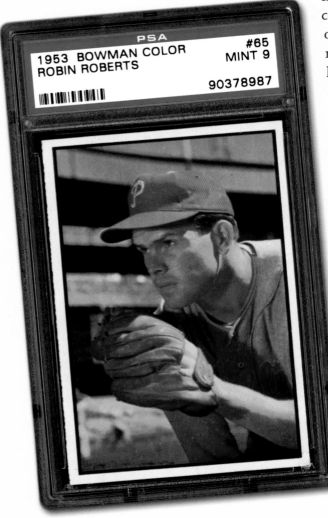

Roberts made his debut in 1949 as a part of the popular Bowman baseball set. This set features several other Hall of Famer rookie cards, like those of George Kell, Roy Campanella, Early Wynn, Richie Ashburn, Duke Snider, and Bob Lemon, along with key cards of Jackie Robinson and Satchel Paige. As you can see, this 240-card set is packed with power. After going with a black-and-white design in 1948, Bowman injected a little bit of color into their 1949 set and it paid dividends with

collectors. Roberts would appear in each of Bowman's releases from his rookie card through 1955, only surfacing once in a mainstream Topps set (1952).

Interestingly, unlike many other Hall of Famers, Roberts' rookie card does sell for the kind of premium in high grade that separates it from some of his subsequent Bowman cards. Roberts' 1951 and 1953 Bowman issues often sell in a comparable range since they are part of very popular sets, while his 1950 card has sold for slightly more than his rookie in recent years. This card is one of his toughest mainstream cards from the era to find in PSA NM-MT 8 or better. During the same decade, Roberts can be found in other issues such as Berk Ross (1951 and 1952) and the colorful Red Man Tobacco sets (1952–1954).

Beyond the basics, Roberts was included in several regional and non-mainstream issues in the following decade as he headed towards his final hobby appearance in the 1966 Topps set. Roberts can be found in Bazooka, Jell-O, and Post Cereal sets to name a few. As we noted earlier, for whatever reason, Roberts was not included in several issues where you would assume to see his image alongside contemporary players. This is especially true in the 1960s when Topps became more and more creative as the decade progressed, experimenting with all kinds of concepts.

The ROBIN ROBERTS CARD

There are some cases where selecting the single-most important card for a player is very debatable to say the least. This is not one of those cases. In 1951, Topps released a small, colorful set called Major League All-Stars (some refer to it as Current All-Stars). The set is comprised of several of the top names of the era, from Yogi Berra to Phil Rizzuto. The original set contained 11 total cards, but three of them were never released to the public: Jim Konstanty, Eddie Stanky, and Roberts. This created three of the greatest rarities in our hobby and Roberts is the only Hall of Famer in the trio. The die-cut design allowed collectors to pop the player images out from their backgrounds. The regular cards in the set are virtually impossible in high grade, but the Roberts card is nearly impossible to find—period—with fewer than six known at the time of this writing.

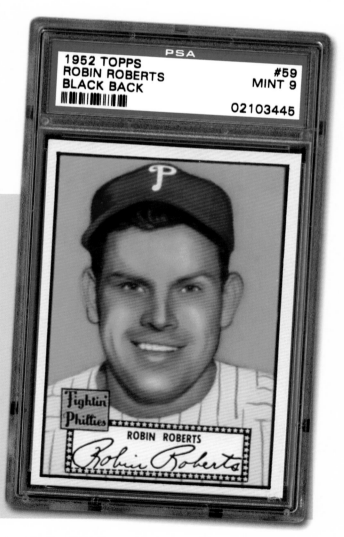

ONE CARD TO WATCH

Outside of Roberts' 1951 Topps Major League All-Stars super rarity, his most valuable card is not his 1949 Bowman rookie, but rather his 1952 Topps card. It was the first time Roberts appeared in a mainstream Topps issue and he would not reappear in one of their sets until 1956, a year after Bowman ended its competitive run in 1955. The 1952 Topps Roberts is not only part of what many consider to be the most important post-WWII set in the hobby, ensuring a high level of demand, it is also part of the low-number series. Cards 1–80 were manufactured with both red and black ink in a few different areas on the reverse, creating two distinct variations. In addition, perhaps the most challenging, inherent condition obstacle is poor centering. Finally, the card is one of Roberts' most attractive designs, offering excellent eye appeal in a year when he won a career-high 28 games.

WARREN SPAHN

WARREN SPAHN WAS A GREAT PITCHER. You can put that in capital letters. He did not have overpowering stuff, but he had a great screwball, curveball, and sinker along with excellent control. He got most of his hitters out with the screwball. It was kind of a changeup. With more than 350 wins, how can you not put him up there as one of the greatest lefties, if not the greatest lefty of all time? There is an argument for Koufax, Grove, Carlton, and Randy Johnson, but I think Spahn may be at the top. This guy made the All-Star team a zillion times, and won at least 20 games more than ten times. That one year when he and Johnny Sain dominated, it was "Spahn and Sain and pray for two days of rain." The Braves were still in Boston then and playing in the old Braves Field. They won the pennant that year, 1948. Spahn was loyal to one team, like I was. He stayed with the Braves for years after they moved to Milwaukee, pitching into his early forties.

I faced Spahn once in an old timer's game at Fenway. I was recently retired and was asked to participate. The place was packed and Spahn got a standing ovation. When I got up to the plate, Spahn was on the mound. He had to be in his early seventies. He threw one right down the middle at about 70 miles per hour and I took him deep. There I was feeling good about taking the great Warren Spahn over the fence. As I circled the bases, Ted Williams and a few of the other old timers started giving me the business for taking a seventy-year-old guy deep. Those guys called me every name in the book. I was in my late thirties. What the heck did I know? Williams and a few others were swearing at me, calling me a knucklehead. Spahn thought it was hilarious. Of course after thinking about it for a few minutes, I felt awful. After all, he was a real "old timer" and one of the greats of the game. He was very gracious and told me he would have thrown me his hook had he known.

If I'm not mistaken, I think that he was voted to the MLB All-Time Greatest Team as lefty pitcher. The guy was just amazing. He won so many games and won a bunch when he was over forty years old, too. Did you know Warren Spahn was a war hero? He was in heavy combat, not like a lot of the other baseball players in the service. Spahn was with the Army Engineers and saw action at the Battle of the Bulge. His group had to keep the bridges open and usable so the troops could move around. I think he got both the Bronze Star and the Purple Heart. Thankfully he came back in one piece and just picked up his baseball career where he left off. He was just tremendous.

When I think about some of the guys who played the game when I played, I still shake my head. I was blessed to have a successful career. I think I carried my weight for a few years with the Red Sox. One of the best things about playing in the 1960s and 1970s was being able to interact with some of the greatest players of all time.

THE CARDS

Despite missing a few years due to military service (1943–1945) near the early stages of his career, Warren Spahn had a very long and successful one, which meant the durable lefty would have the opportunity to be featured in many baseball card sets. Unfortunately for collectors, Spahn narrowly missed making it into the classic Play Ball sets (1939–1941) that captured the cardboard debuts of stars like Ted Williams and Pee Wee Reese, so collectors had to wait several years for a mainstream Spahn issue to arrive. After Spahn's playing days were over, the 300-game winner's image could be found on well over 100 different collectible cards.

While many collectors tend to focus on Spahn's first appearance in the Bowman and Leaf sets of the late-1940s, the Hall of Famer was included in a set that was released slightly earlier. The 1947 Tip-Top Bread set was a regional issue containing 163 cards, but a relatively small number of those cards pictured major stars since the game was trying to weather some

talent-deprived years during the war. However, a handful of active stars like Spahn, Yogi Berra, and Phil Rizzuto were included. This is certainly one of Spahn's tougher cards, and while it is not considered his official rookie card, it dates to the early part of his playing days.

For the remainder of his career, Spahn's image can be found in many popular sets. During the battle between Bowman and Topps, Spahn could be found in both sets in 1952 and 1953, but he was exclusive to Topps in 1954 and 1955. Spahn became a regular for Topps, in the base and some of the manufacturer's creative productions, through 1965. Some of the more interesting Topps/Spahn collectibles include coins, faux currency, pins, stamps, and tattoos, not to mention his 1955 Topps Doubleheaders card or short-printed 1964 Topps Stand-Up issue.

Beyond Bowman, Topps, Exhibit, and even Fleer in 1963, some of Spahn's most appealing cards can be found in regional issues that stretch from the 1940s through the end of the 1960s. Some of these

include Bazooka, Johnston Cookies, Post Cereal, Red Heart Dog Food, and Spic and Span. The Johnston Cookies and Spic and Span issues were completely devoted to the Braves, so Spahn remains a key alongside teammates Hank Aaron and Eddie Mathews. Unlike some contemporary stars like Willie Mays and Williams, Spahn appeared in every Red Man Tobacco set (1952–1955). These oversized, colorful cards are amongst the most visually-appealing issues ever produced.

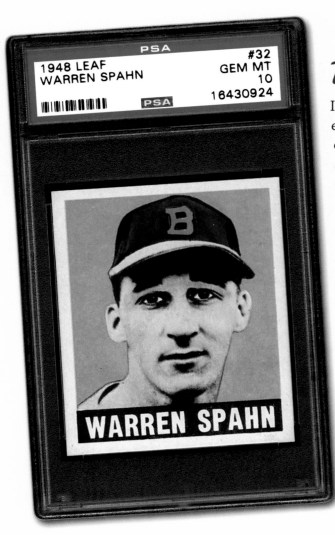

The WARREN SPAHN CARD

In the post-WWII card market, Hall of Famer rookie cards are extremely popular with collectors. Spahn, like some fellow stars of the period, didn't make his mainstream cardboard debut until several years after making his first appearance on the field. This was simply because there were no standard sets being made. The two cards that collectors deem as official Spahn rookies are his 1948 Bowman and 1948/49 Leaf cards. While both are desirable, the edge would have to go to the Leaf Spahn (#32) for the following reasons. Leaf cards, in general, are extremely tough to find in high grade due to condition obstacles such as poor centering and print defects. The Leaf Spahn has a clear edge in overall difficulty. Furthermore, the Leaf card is booming with color, giving it an edge in eye appeal versus the black-and-white Bowman card.

"The Leaf Spahn has a clear edge in overall difficulty."

ONE CARD TO WATCH

As we discussed earlier, Spahn made numerous appearances in various regional issues over the course of his career. Several of them possess great eye appeal, like his Red Man Tobacco and Red Heart Dog Food cards, while others are simply hard to find at all, like his 1947 Tip-Top Bread card. One regional set that combines an interesting concept along with a serious collector challenge is the 1950 Drake's issue. Distributed in packages of their cookies, these cards were subjected to serious handling. Each card was designed to look like a miniature television set, predating the 1955 Bowman design. These tough regional cards are surrounded by black borders, which show the slightest hint of wear, making high-grade examples very scarce. The set, while small at only 36 total cards, has better pound-for-pound star power than the previously-mentioned Tip-Top Bread issue. In addition to the Spahn (#14), fellow Hall of Famers like Berra, Roy Campanella, and Duke Snider are included as well.

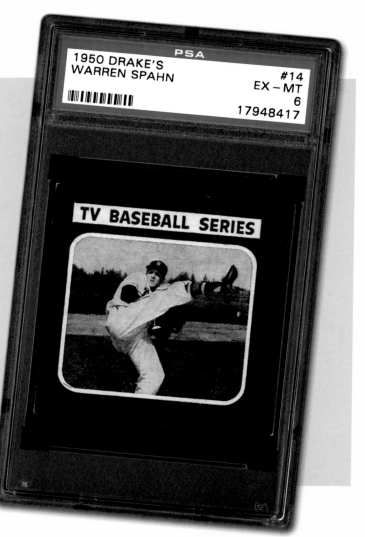

2

From Wool to Double Knits

(to 1979)

The weather in southern Florida is spectacular. It's about 80 degrees and there is not a cloud in the sky on this February day. I'm sitting on a dock with Rico and we have a couple of fishing rods going. Right now the snappers, amber jacks, and pain in the neck catfish are running. You need to be careful with the catfish because they can sting with their fins. We are using live shrimp and mullet for bait. I have a cigar going and Rico is sipping on an iced coffee. We start talking about some of the Hall of Famers that he knew who played until the end of the 1970s. It's like a who's who of the greats of that era.

PSA
1963 FLEER
BROOKS ROBINSON #4
GEM MT
10
15027991

BROOKS ROBINSON
Baltimore Orioles—3rd Base

PSA
#305
MINT 9
1973 TOPPS
WILLIE MAYS
06445748

WILLIE MAYS
NEW YORK METS
OUTFIELD

HANK AARON

I FIRST MET HANK AARON in 1965 when I was 22 years old. We were playing the Braves in an exhibition game for the Jimmy Fund, the famous clinic in Boston for kids with cancer. I made a point of walking up to him to introduce myself, because he was one of my idols when I was a kid.

The thing that struck me was that he only weighed about 175 pounds. I was expecting to meet a big hulking guy with bulging muscles, but I remember, I couldn't believe how big his hands were. They were easily twice the size of mine. I walked up to "Mr. Aaron," introduced myself, and shook his hand. He asked me to call him Hank. Wow! There I was, a nervous rookie ballplayer, meeting one of the greats of the game and he asked me to call him Hank. Since we were on a first name basis, I bravely asked if he would pose with me for a picture. He graciously said he would be happy to.

Hank was very soft-spoken and unassuming, but he carried himself like a real pro. Later on, we bumped into each other when I played on the All-Star team in 1967 and 1969, and he congratulated me on being chosen for the team both times. Even though Hank was a 25-time All-Star, NL MVP and NL batting champ, he will always be remembered for breaking Babe Ruth's record. That night, I watched the game at home because we had an off-day, and I remember jumping around like a nut after he hit the homer. I was happy because he was such a great guy and he went through a hell of a lot that season with the racial slurs and abuse from some fans. It was a damn shame.

Towards the end of his career, Hank joined the Milwaukee Brewers, who we played regularly. I remember the first time we faced them with Hank on the team. By that time, he had lost some of his bat speed and he wasn't hitting for the power he was known for. After getting a base hit, he was advanced to third. Hank asked me how I was doing, and complimented me on my play at third base. I asked him how he liked being in the American League, and he said that he was enjoying it. Hank was in his forties by then and even though he

wasn't hitting for average, he still managed to get the bat on the ball.

In 1999, when the All-Star Game was played at Fenway Park, there was an event at the Hynes Auditorium in downtown Boston that was part of the festivities. It was called FanFest. I was asked to participate and who did I bump into? Hank Aaron. He was retired and working for Major League Baseball. He warmly shook my hand and asked how I was doing. I was thrilled because this guy was still one of my great idols. I asked how he liked his job working in baseball and he told me he loved having the opportunity to still be part the game. For some reason, I had a ball in my hand, probably something to do with the FanFest event. I asked Hank to sign it and he did. Today that ball is proudly displayed in my family room. I haven't seen him in years, but I think I'm going to send Hank the picture of the two of us in 1965 and ask him to sign it. My grandkids will love it someday.

THE CARDS

Along with several other Hall of Famers of the era, Hank Aaron finds himself on some of the most iconic cards in the hobby, from mainstream issues to regional productions. In addition, since Aaron's playing career lasted a whopping 23 years, his card career spanned from the classic releases of the 1950s through the almost psychedelic designs of the 1970s. Of course, then there were all the interesting Aaron cards in between as well, which included several popular Topps test issues from the 1960s.

When Aaron first arrived on the scene, Bowman was about to exit the trading card game, leaving Topps as the only mainstream manufacturer. In fact, Aaron's only appearance in a Bowman set was in 1955, the last year of their eight-year run (1948–1955). While Bowman may have started the trend years earlier, Topps began to create more multi-player cards from 1957 onward, which have remained collector favorites over the years. Perhaps the most desirable Aaron card of this nature features the great slugger alongside New York Yankees legend Mickey Mantle in the 1958 Topps set entitled *World Series Batting Foes* as they squared off on baseball's biggest stage. It would be the only card ever made to feature the powerful pair.

As the years went by, Aaron became a part of numerous regional and food product sets to go along with his consistent presence in the basic Topps releases. This gave collectors much to choose from, beyond the standard cards that most collectors were accustomed to seeing. Bazooka Gum, Hires Root Beer, Hostess, Johnston Cookies, Kahn's Wieners, Kellogg's, and Post Cereal are just some of the brands that included Aaron in their card sets. Each set varies in terms of eye appeal, scarcity, and popularity. Fittingly, Aaron was even included in the 1959 Home Run Derby set, an extremely tough issue, which was based on the once-popular television series.

Furthermore, Aaron was active and in his prime when Topps decided to experiment, creating all kinds of new

sets and collectibles. From coins to decals to tattoos, Topps let their creative juices flow during the 1960s. In addition to some of these off-beat products, Topps developed some new concepts that didn't quite reach the finish line. These test sets never made it to the market via mass distribution. Instead, they were either part of very limited releases or were never released to the public at all, gradually escaping the factory. Aaron was included in most of these attempts such as the 1969 Topps Super set, but he did not make it into others like the 12-card 1968 Topps 3-D set. This continued into the 1970s when Aaron appeared in more Topps test issues including Candy Lids (1970 and 1972), 1973 Comics, and 1973 Pin-Ups. His final mainstream card appearance came in 1976 on card #550 in the annual Topps set.

The HANK AARON CARD

When it comes to collecting cardboard of "Hammerin' Hank," there is no disputing what card sits atop the rest. Aaron's 1954 Topps rookie card #128 is not only the key to a set filled with other stars and rookies, like those of fellow Hall of Famers Ernie Banks and Al Kaline, it remains one of the most recognizable images in the entire collecting world. As far as condition obstacles are concerned, poor centering, print defects in the orange background, and chipping along the green reverse are common. Beyond all of the accomplishments and gargantuan offensive numbers, the face of the 1954 Topps Aaron card symbolizes collecting. It may not generate quite the same reaction or illicit the same feelings that the 1952 Topps Mantle does, but it rests comfortably amongst the most important symbols the baseball card world has to offer.

"The face of the 1954 Topps Aaron card symbolizes collecting."

ONE CARD TO WATCH

In most cases, the rookie card is the pinnacle for collectors of Hall of Famers. That is certainly the case with Aaron; however, some second-year cards have begun to pick up steam in the market and deserve a closer look. While both the vertical 1954 Topps Aaron rookie and the horizontal 1955 Topps Aaron #47 are attractive cards from a design perspective, I would argue that the 1955 Topps card has the edge in eye appeal. The 1955 Topps Aaron is, arguably, his best-looking card ever produced. Each card features an identical headshot of Aaron, but the

1955 Topps card includes a batting pose versus a fielding shot on the 1954 card. The combination of bright colors and Aaron doing what he did best, coupled with the fact that the 1955 Topps card may be part of a slightly more desirable overall set, make this card one to watch.

LUIS APARICIO

LUIS APARICIO WAS THE SHORTSTOP in the American League for those years that we played. He could field, he could run, and he was a good gap hitter. Not a big guy, Luis was about 5'9" and 150 pounds. He was a very smart player and always positioned himself well against the good hitters. I was playing short for the Red Sox, but there was talk about moving me to third base because I was hitting for some power. I got a call from Eddie Kasko during the winter meetings. That was in late 1970. They tried to get Ron Santo so they could keep me at shortstop, but they were unable close the deal. Eddie told me that Luis Aparicio was available and asked if I would mind moving to third. I told Eddie that I had absolutely no problem with it because Aparicio was a perennial All-Star and Gold Glover and I felt this guy would only make us better. I had great respect for Aparicio, and as long as I would still be in the lineup, I welcomed the idea. During spring training I was fortunate to be tutored by Frank Malzone, the former great Sox third baseman.

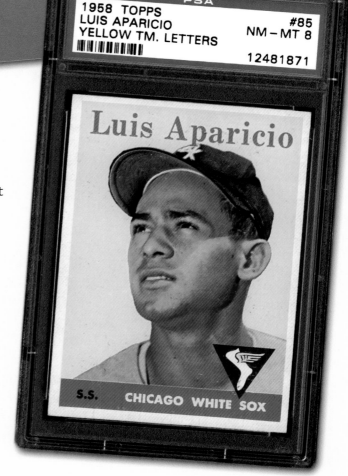

Malzie worked with me tirelessly and really made the difference in my third-base play. With Luis at short and Doug Griffin at second, we had a very good middle infield. Luis taught Doug little pointers that really made a difference in his play—how to flip the ball going to his left and how to position his feet.

Luis was a very funny guy and was very popular in the clubhouse. He would break me up in the infield, making comments about different players and coaches, all very good naturedly. He and Yaz were hilarious. They were constantly playing practical jokes on each other. Luis was always impeccably dressed and Yaz really started it when he took one of Luis' favorite ties and cut it in half. Luis got him back by cutting Yaz's pants off at the knee, and it all escalated from there. Yaz cut the toes off Luis' socks, and one day he even cut the arm off one of Luis' favorite sports coats. Yaz used to wear this really ugly "Columbo"-style trench coat. It was his favorite. One day it was missing, and of course, Yaz suspected Aparicio was behind the missing coat. Evidently, Aparicio decided to burn the coat. Finally, the manager had to intervene and tell them both to knock it off. They both had a good laugh and always remained close friends.

Luis once went 0-for-44 when he was with us which, by the way, eclipsed my 0-for-32. He was beside himself. Like me, when I was in my slump, he got advice from everyone, even the clubhouse guys. It got so bad that he even got a letter from President Nixon, telling him not to give up. He finally busted out of it. Thank God, because he was becoming pretty edgy. I think playing with Luis made me better. I worked harder because he always worked hard. He did it flawlessly. I haven't seen him in years because he went back to Venezuela. He's been very involved in baseball there and is a big sports hero in that country. He deserves it. What a great guy!

THE CARDS

Shortly after Bowman made their exit from the card manufacturing business, Luis Aparicio made his hobby debut. Playing in three different decades, Aparicio's long

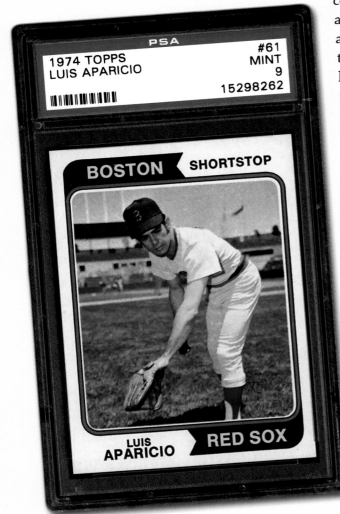

career enabled the Hall of Fame shortstop to gain entry into various trading card sets, extending from the classic Topps designs of the 1950s to some psychedelic creations of the 1970s. There is no doubt that Aparicio's playing days and era were dominated by Topps, but a nice selection of cards awaits the collector, with well over 100 cards bearing his likeness.

Early on in Aparicio's career, he appeared in one of the tougher oddball sets of the 1950s. The 1956 Yellow Basepath PM15 Pins set contains 32 total subjects and a host of Hall of Famers such as Hank Aaron, Stan Musial, and the key to the set—Mickey Mantle. Aparicio's pin was released the same year as his Topps rookie debut and it remains one of his most valuable collectibles. Aparicio became a mainstay with Topps for almost 20 years. In addition to his true rookie, another of his most desirable issues was released early on. In 1958, Topps created both white and yellow letter variations in series one, cards 1–110. The yellow-lettered cards are, by far, the scarcer of the two varieties and worth significantly more than the white-lettered cards.

As the decade came to a close, Aparicio found himself in the middle of one of the strangest baseball card sets of the period. In 1960, Leaf came back into the hobby with a 144-card baseball set. Instead of gum, the cards were packed with marbles of all things. Beyond the perplexing marble

pairing, the simple black-and-white set had very few stars despite its decent size. Aparicio was one of the few stars included and it happened to be card #1. Furthermore, a mere eight cards in the set can be found with "Large Portrait" variations. These cards are believed to have been part of a test printing and exist in very small numbers.

Over the years, Aparicio appeared in a diverse selection of issues including Bazooka, Exhibit, Jell-O, Kellogg's, Kelly's Potato Chips, Milk Duds, Post Cereal, and Transogram to name a few. The slick-fielding shortstop also appeared in a wide variety of Topps productions, beyond the regular issue. This included decals, Deckle Edge, stamps, and transfers, but it also included some harder-to-find Topps productions such as 1967 Punch-Outs, 1969 Supers, 1970 Candy Lids, and several Venezuelan cards. Aparicio's final appearance on a mainstream card came in 1974 as part of the annual Topps set, which ended his long career in cardboard.

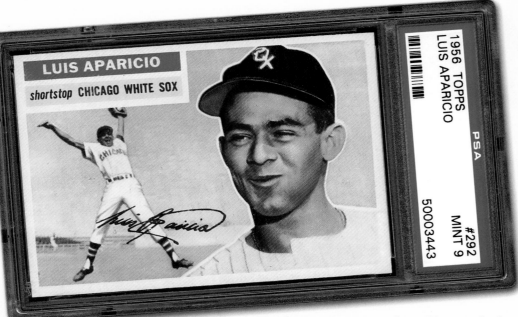

The LUIS APARICIO CARD

In 1956, the baseball card world belonged to Topps after a hellacious battle with Bowman in the preceding 1952–1955 time frame. After issuing one terrific set after another during the head-to-head clash, Topps didn't disappoint without the competition. The design was, once again, attractive and the set had its usual selection of stars, including the reintroduction of Mantle after a two-year hiatus. Of course, the Mantle is the key to the set and it doesn't hurt that the card came out during his lone Triple Crown year either. That said, the only Hall of Fame player rookie card in the entire set is that of Aparicio (#292). The card isn't considered overly difficult to find since Topps apparently ramped up production in 1956, nor is it extremely hard to locate in high grade, but its association with such a popular set and its claim as Aparicio's unquestioned rookie makes it an obvious choice.

ONE CARD TO WATCH

When it came to selecting the card to watch from Aparicio's abundant selection of cards, the choice was difficult. Would it be the ultra-rare 1960 Leaf Large Portrait or the 1967 Topps Punch-Out? How about something even more offbeat like his 1956 PM15 Pin or the 1970 Topps Candy Lid? Each card is challenging to find in any grade and worthy of consideration, but I decided to go with Aparicio's 1971 Topps Greatest Moments card (#51). This oversized 2½" by 4¾" horizontal issue contains 55 cards, and the core of the set is made up of great players who did great things. Johnny Bench, Reggie Jackson, Willie Mays, and more are all here in a set designed with vulnerable black borders. If the pesky borders weren't enough to contend with, commonly-found print defects and poor centering add to the collector's headache. The set is very intriguing, the player selection is fantastic, and the challenge is real.

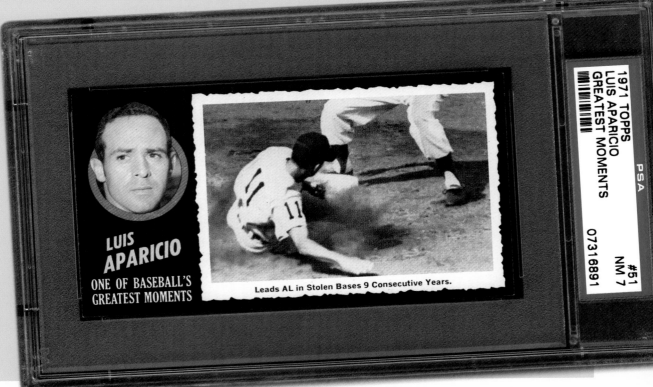

ERNIE BANKS

A GREAT ALL-AROUND HITTER, Ernie Banks could hit for power and average, and he was a very good shortstop. Of course, he moved to first base later on. Ernie and I played against each other often during spring training in Arizona. He was one of the nicest guys that I met in my entire time in the big leagues. Ernie was a very sincere guy. When I played against him, he was in his mid-to-late thirties but could still hit for power. He had this little wiggle of his thumb before he would hit, great wrist action, and a very quick bat. Some of those Cubs teams were not very good, but he really carried them as their MVP.

Ernie and I would chat outside the batting cage before spring training games, talking about the shortstop position. By that time, he was no longer playing shortstop, but told me that he always loved the position and missed it. Ernie was always very friendly and never had a bad thing to say about anyone.

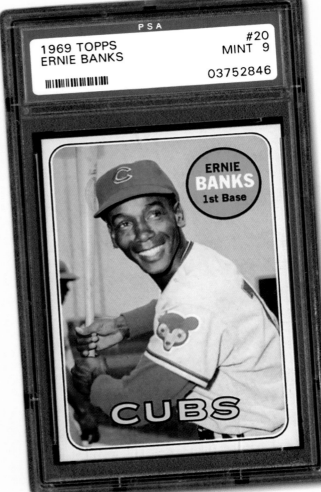

In my opinion, he was kind of overshadowed in the National League by guys like Aaron and Mays because the teams he played on were weak. He did play with some great talent like Santo and Billy Williams, but overall some of those Cubs teams were pretty weak until Durocher came on board as manager, and then they got some traction in the late-1960s and early-1970s. I think Ernie and Durocher butted heads quite a bit, but something worked because the Cubs climbed out of the cellar and had several years when they finished in second or third place in the league.

I hit 40 home runs in 1969, breaking the American League single-season record for a shortstop. I held that record until A-Rod came along in 1998. Ernie hit 47 homers one year in the National League. That was in the late 1950s, way before I started playing, and you know, he still holds that record. He was so consistent with great power numbers, too. It was pretty big news when he got 500 home runs. That was near the end of his career; 1970, I think. He was only the ninth or tenth player to hit 500, so it was pretty rare in those days. Ernie was also pretty darn good as a first baseman, too.

The thing I liked best about Ernie was how humble he was. When we chatted, it was never about him but about everyone else. He loved the way Yaz played the game, and he was a big Tony Conigliaro fan. The Cubs and the Red Sox always had a sort of kinship because both teams went for so long without winning a World Series. Anyway, here was a guy that was an All-Star for years, the National League MVP a couple of times, and a Gold Glover, and he never bragged about himself. Ernie was also a man of great faith and a very optimistic guy. He was a great ambassador to the game. The fans loved him in Chicago. They even put a statue of him at Wrigley Field. Even though he never got a World Series ring, Ernie Banks is a very deserving Hall of Famer. He was as good as they came and just a wonderful guy.

THE CARDS

Ernie Banks had a career in cardboard that any player would envy. Playing for nearly 20 years, Banks entered the hobby at a time when baseball cards were really starting to come into their own with kids, and by the time he retired, the charismatic slugger had appeared

on dozens of collectible issues over three decades. Banks made his official card debut in 1954, and he was exclusive to Topps. The very next year, Banks would appear in both the Topps and Bowman sets, with the latter manufacturer making its farewell after a nice run.

For the remainder of the 1950s, Banks would become a staple with Topps, but he also made his way into several other regional and non-mainstream issues. This included everything from Armour Coins to Bazooka to Home Run Derby, a set that promoted an upcoming television series where top sluggers in each league would face off in a one-on-one battle for prize money. One of the more interesting, and arguably undervalued, sets from the 1950s is the 66-card 1955 Topps Doubleheaders set. Banks is clearly one of the keys, but unfortunately for collectors, the dual-player card design has Banks positioned on the reverse of the perforated issue with Howie Pollet on the front.

The next decade would produce the majority of Banks' cards from his playing days. Of course, Banks appeared in every major Topps set, along with several of their creative, off beat attempts. This includes, but is not limited to, Topps products such as coins, faux currency, rub-offs, stamps, stickers, tattoos, and some elusive Venezuelan issues. In 1963, Banks would appear on his most popular multi-player card in the regular Topps set alongside fellow home run hero Hank Aaron on a card entitled *Power Plus*. Perhaps the most desirable Topps production featuring Banks, but not of the mainstream category, would be his 1964 Topps Stand-Up card. This colorful set is packed with stars and plenty of eye appeal.

Banks' career stretched into the 1970s, a time when the Chicago favorite entered the exclusive 500 Home Run Club. His last solo appearance in a mainstream set came in the black-bordered 1971 Topps issue, but it isn't his most interesting card from his final bow. Like the regular 1971 Topps set, the oversized 2½" by 4¾" Greatest Moments test issue was also surrounded by black borders, extremely condition sensitive, and significantly tougher to find than their regular-issue counterparts. The Banks card, like many others in the set, is tough to find well-centered.

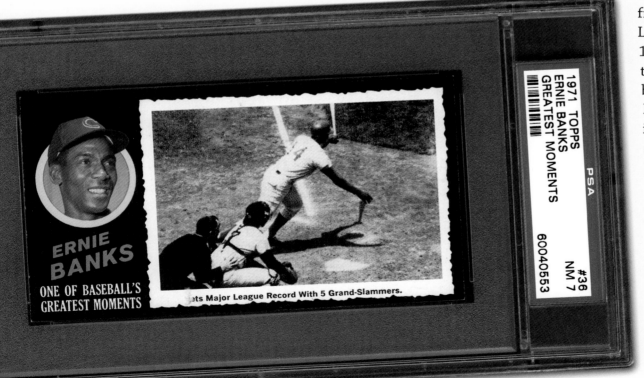

ERNIE BANKS

ONE OF BASEBALL'S GREATEST MOMENTS

...ts Major League Record With 5 Grand-Slammers.

1971 TOPPS
ERNIE BANKS
GREATEST MOMENTS

PSA

#36
NM 7

80040553

The ERNIE BANKS CARD

There is no doubt about which Banks card rests atop all others on his master checklist. The 1954 Topps issue, one of the most popular baseball card sets ever made, is home to three ultra-important rookie cards of Hall of Famers. Along with Banks (#94), Hank Aaron and Al Kaline made their hobby debuts, while Ted Williams acted as a bookend to the set appearing on cards #1 and #250. One of the great aspects of his rookie card is how young Banks looks in his headshot. In fact, Banks is almost unrecognizable, but that young kid would soon win back-to-back NL MVP Awards. The card itself can be challenging to find well-centered and absent pesky print defects in the white background. It is the ultimate Banks card.

"One of the great aspects of his rookie card is how young Banks looks in the headshot."

ONE CARD TO WATCH

Beauty is in the eye of the beholder—at least that's how the old saying goes. While there is no question that the most important and desirable Banks card is his 1954 Topps rookie, a compelling argument can be made for his second-year Topps card being the best-looking issue of his career. The rich, red background and yellow highlights combine for a card that is, quite frankly, more eye catching than its predecessor. Like his 1954 Topps rookie, the 1955 Topps Banks is part of an incredibly-popular set. This time, other rookies steal the show in Roberto Clemente, Harmon Killebrew, and Sandy Koufax. That said, the three major rookies that anchored the previous Topps set are all back in 1955. In contrast to his rookie, Banks provides an intense glare in the headshot used on his second Topps card instead of the innocent smile captured on the slugger's first card.

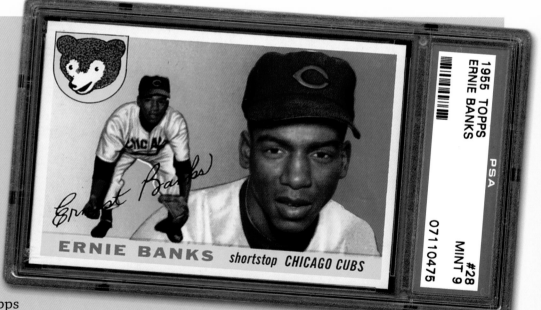

LOU BROCK

WHAT A HECK OF A BALLPLAYER Lou Brock was. He started out kind of slow with the Cubs, but by the time I was playing he was tearing it up with the Cardinals. We played them a lot in spring training and I'll tell you, he was one of the best that I ever played against. He could run, hit for average, and he was very good defensively.

Not to beat a dead horse, but as most fans know, Lou absolutely killed us in the 1967 World Series. He had our infield on edge because he stole so many bases during that Series. Brock had seven stolen bases and had his way with us offensively. I think he batted over .400. It was a real battle. We forced the seventh game, but mostly thanks to Brock, the Cardinals prevailed and our Impossible Dream season was over. Well, it sure was exciting while we were in the hunt for the pennant, and I'll never forget those World Series games. I remember one of those steals. Brock made the break and he was safe by about a foot and a half, but I was so frustrated that I started arguing with the ump, just to argue. The umpire thought I was nuts.

I told the ump that I had the tag on Brock easily. The ump just laughed. "Nice try, Rico," he said.

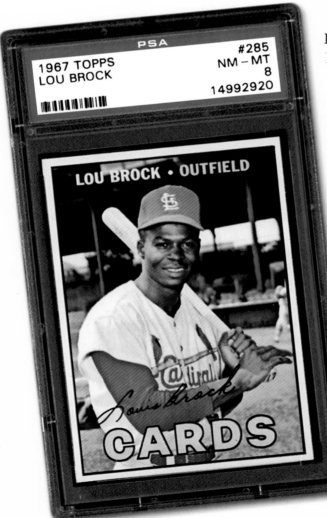

Lou was the catalyst for that team. Besides Brock, that Cards team of Gibson, Cepeda, Maris, and Curt Flood, just to name a few, were amazing, but we made them work for their rings. Brock was a quiet guy, and real easy to talk to. Nothing, by the way, against our great catcher Ellie Howard, but Lou Brock was simply so great that any catcher would have had a tough time against him. I remember talking to him one of the times he was on second and asking what his goal was as far as base stealing went. He said that it was totally up to how his body could hold up, and someday he hoped to be up there with the best. I used to follow his numbers after we had that conversation. He kept taking advantage of every opportunity and one year he had 118 stolen bases. I think he was in his mid-thirties at the time. Anyway, ten years after we played in that Series, Brock actually broke Ty Cobb's record for steals. He wasn't just up there with the best. He was the best. I was genuinely happy for him. I can't remember how many times he led the league in steals, but it was a lot. Just about every year in his prime.

He was also a hitting machine with his 3,000 plus hits. Lou retired after he hit that milestone. He was probably about forty years old at the time and I can't even imagine how he felt after all those years of aggressive play. Lou Brock was a superstar in the true sense of the word. Besides being a really good guy, he was an All-Star, Hall of Famer, and one of the all-time great basestealers. As an all-around player, Brock is right up there with the best. Of all the superstars I played with and against, he was one of the greatest five-tool players. He could do it all. I know Lou has had some medical issues recently and I wish him nothing but the best.

THE CARDS

From a hobby perspective, Lou Brock seems underappreciated considering the total package that the Hall of Famer was. Brock is a member of the exclusive 3,000 Hit Club, one of the most noteworthy achievements a hitter can reach and one that collectors respond to. Brock was a World Series champion (1964 and 1967) and played for two very popular franchises, the Chicago Cubs and the St. Louis Cardinals. Oh, by the way, when he retired from the game, no one had more career stolen bases. Despite all that Brock accomplished, most of his cards remain relatively affordable compared to those of contemporary stars.

Brock's career in cardboard began in 1962 as part of the interesting brown-bordered Topps set. Like the 1955 Bowman set, this Topps issue chose to abandon their traditional white borders for one that resembled wood grain, creating a tougher challenge for collectors seeking high-grade examples. Topps went back to the colored-border concept, at least in part, in 1963. The card design was split between a white border in the upper portion and a colored border along the bottom. Even though Brock was traded from Chicago to St. Louis in 1964 for the stretch run, the card features Brock as a Cub, making it the last Topps card to do so.

For the remainder of the decade, Brock was included in various Topps-related issues, from the scarce Venezuelan series to the 1967 Punch-Outs set, which was designed as a stand-alone game instead of a traditional card. From the 1960s through the end his career, Brock found himself in a variety of regional productions as well. He appeared in a number of non-Topps sets, which included Bazooka, Hostess, Kellogg's, Milk Duds, and Transogram to name a few. During the 1970s, Topps continued to produce complementary sets to their base issues. Brock was included in test issues like 1972 Topps Candy Lids, which ranks right up there with the 1967 Topps Punch-Outs in terms of scarcity, along with other sets such as 1974 Topps Deckle Edge and 1975 Topps Minis.

As his career came to a close, Brock was honored on several special cards as his offensive numbers started to pile up and impact the record books. In the 1979 Topps set, the manufacturer included a series of cards entitled *All-Time Record Holders*. The Brock card is extra special in that he is pictured twice as the leader in both the single-season and career stolen base categories. As a fitting finale, Brock is pictured with Carl Yastrzemski on card #1 in the 1980 Topps set. While Brock's last regular card was issued in the 1979 Topps set, this 1980 issue honors both Hall of Famers for reaching 3,000 hits during the 1979 season. In a career filled with statistical accomplishments, the 1980 Topps #1 card was a nice way to pay tribute to the St. Louis legend.

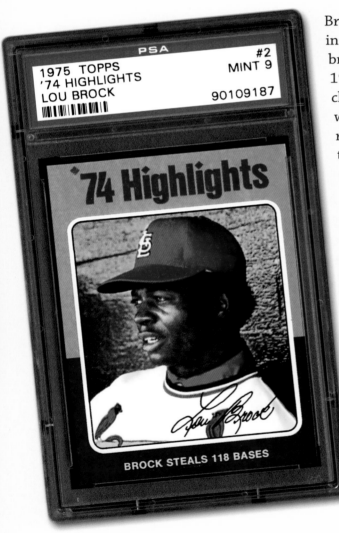

PSA   #2
1975 TOPPS   MINT 9
'74 HIGHLIGHTS
LOU BROCK   90109187

'74 Highlights

BROCK STEALS 118 BASES

"When he retired, no one had more career stolen bases."

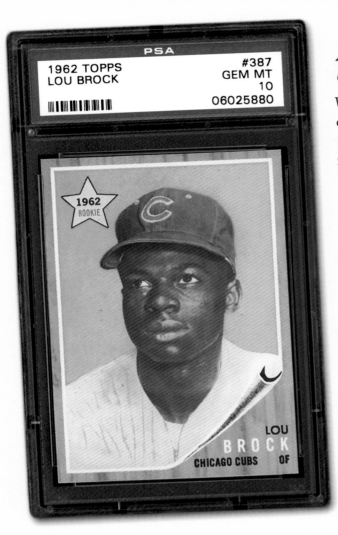

The LOU BROCK CARD

When it comes to Brock cards, there is little doubt about which one garners the most attention. Brock's 1962 Topps rookie card (#387) has always been the one to own. Brock entered the hobby right as Topps modified their design from previous releases. Topps, always known for using bright colors in their creations, decided to frame each image with brown borders. The borders look like wood grain and they vary in appearance, from a light tan color to a rich, dark patina. As a result, the cards can be difficult to find without visible wear or chipping along the edges, making it one of the toughest Topps sets of the decade to assemble in high grade. Like most other period sets, the cards can be challenging to find without problematic centering or print defects. The Brock rookie is one of three key rookies in the set, along with the debut card of fellow Hall of Famers Gaylord Perry and Joe Torre.

ONE CARD TO WATCH

For several years after Brock entered the hobby on his 1962 rookie card, the speedster was featured in each annual Topps release. In 1969, just like every year preceding it, Brock's image can be found. This time on card #85. So, what makes this Brock card so special? Is it a rare variation? No. Was it a particularly great year for Brock? Not really. It's simply a product of where Brock found himself on the sheet. The Brock card can be challenging to find well centered. Why? Brock's card was located in the corner of the sheet. When it was cut, it was often done off the mark, creating a condition rarity in one of the most popular sets of the decade. While the card isn't as valuable as Mickey Mantle's final card or the Reggie Jackson rookie, it is one of the set's most valuable cards in PSA NM-MT 8 or better.

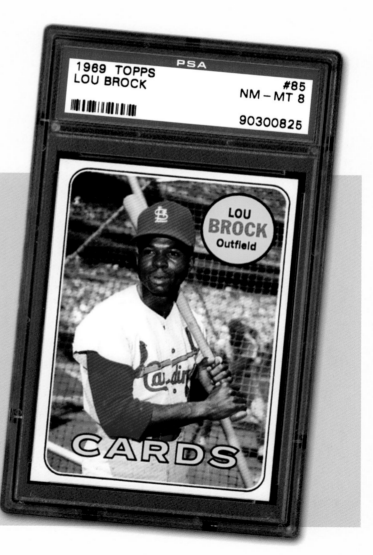

JIM BUNNING

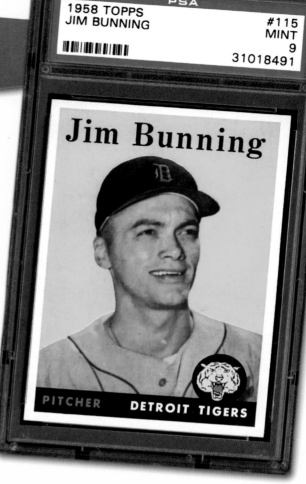

Jim Bunning
PITCHER DETROIT TIGERS

JIM BUNNING WAS ONE OF THE FEW players that I did not know very well. When he pitched for Detroit, I was just a kid, and when he was traded to the Phillies in the National League, I was just coming up through the ranks. We never played the Phillies during spring training, but being a fan as well as a player, I followed all of the great ones, and Jim Bunning had a great run as a pitcher, although he played on some weak teams over those years.

He is involved in Red Sox history though. Bunning threw a no-hitter against the Sox back in 1958. It made a real splash, however, when he tossed a perfect game soon after he moved to the National League. I remember, it was in 1964 against the Mets at Shea Stadium. You know, I have always paid close attention to the New York teams. The Mets had only been playing for a couple of years and they had just moved into Shea Stadium at the beginning of the season.

JIM BUNNING
PITCHER—DETROIT TIGERS

As the story goes, Bunning was pretty relaxed all through that perfect game. He was joking and kidding with his teammates but they wouldn't talk to him because they didn't want to jinx him. Anyway, that game made such a splash because it had been years since anyone threw a perfect game in the National League. I mean years—like the 1880s.

The guy was a perennial All-Star, so he had to be doing something right. Bunning was a sidearm strikeout pitcher who was near the top of the strikeout list for years. He really did not have an "out" pitch, but threw a very good curveball, slider, and fastball. Jim was one of those guys who was not overpowering but had great command of all his pitches. And he was such a workhorse. He pitched more innings than anyone in the league for a couple of years. Aside from his no-hitter and his perfect game, I guess he was known for being dependable and consistent. He only got 20 wins once, but you could count on him for a solid 15 to 19 wins for most of his career. Just think what those numbers would be if he had played on better teams.

One thing I am thankful for is that Bunning got involved in the Players Association. Because of Bunning and a few others, we were able to get better benefits and higher salaries. Remember, most of us had to work jobs in the offseason to make a few additional bucks. He was a tough negotiator and really laid the groundwork for all players to earn a good salary at baseball. That way we could concentrate on improving our skills in the offseason instead of trying to earn some extra cash to pay the bills. After Bunning was done with baseball, I know that he got involved with politics and became a senator. I really did not pay much attention to his political career. If you take his 17-year baseball career, and his time in politics, not to mention that he is in the Hall of Fame, Jim Bunning did pretty well for himself.

THE CARDS

Jim Bunning made his card debut shortly after Topps took control of the market. After issuing sets where three key rookies were born in each release (1954 and 1955), the class of newbies was far less powerful in 1956. With names like Hank Aaron and Sandy Koufax leading the way in the prior two sets, it became a hard act to follow. After Luis Aparicio had the set to himself in 1956, at least from a Hall of Famer rookie perspective, five new faces who eventually became members of the hallowed halls entered the fold in 1957, which included Bunning.

Bunning would become a staple with Topps for the remainder of his career, one that spanned three decades of card production. Beyond the traditional annual releases, Bunning made appearances in many creative Topps issues over the years. This included various sets and collectibles like coins, faux currency, peel-offs, and stamps. Bunning was also included in some of the elusive Venezuelan Topps issues and the related Canadian O-Pee-Chee sets during a multi-year stretch. In 1963, much like the *Dodgers' Big Three* card that showcased pitching stars Johnny Podres, Don Drysdale, and Koufax, Bunning was part of a multi-player card entitled *Tiger Twirlers* alongside Frank Lary and Don Mossi. The star pitcher also

appeared in sets like 1964 Topps Giants, an oversized issue, and 1965 Topps Embossed.

In addition to Topps, Bunning's image can be found in many other sets during the decade. In 1960, Leaf decided to enter the market once again. This time, the 144-card set is absent many of the era's stars, but Bunning is included. In fact, not only is Bunning one of the few Hall of Famers featured, he is the last card in the set (#144). This means, in many cases, his card was exposed to the elements more often than those housed in the middle of the set. This includes potential damage from rubber bands since some collectors organized their collections with their use. Other brands to feature Bunning include Bazooka, Jell-O, Post Cereal, and Wheaties.

The decade also produced a few different coin sets that include Bunning. In 1964, Topps tried their hand at a collectible coin set and they did it again in 1971, but others joined in the fun like CITGO, Old London, Salada, and Shirriff. By the 1970s, Bunning's career was coming to an end, but he did manage to make it into a couple of sets near the beginning of the decade. One of Bunning's

most interesting cards is his 1971 Topps Greatest Moments card. Oversized and featuring the same black borders as Topps' regular release did, this card is challenging to find in PSA NM-MT 8 or better condition. Bunning's final regular card can be found in the 1971 Topps set. This black-bordered, 752-card issue is the toughest mainstream Topps set of the decade to assemble in high grade because of inconsistent centering, print defects, and ultra-sensitive edges.

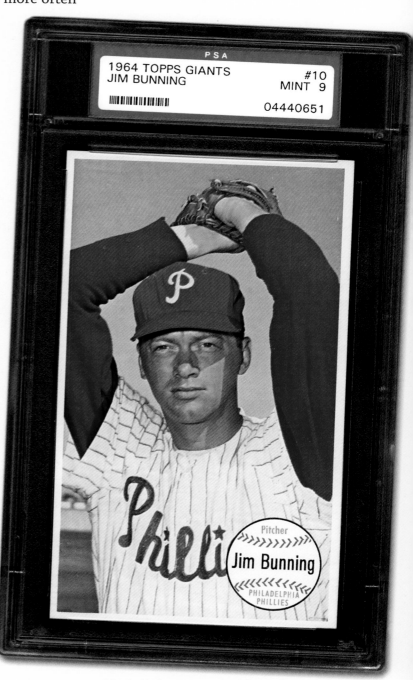

The JIM BUNNING CARD

In 1957, Topps abandoned their use of artwork and instead used real images of each subject as part of their design. The result gave collectors a set that became one of the more popular Topps releases of the decade. The simple, clean look was similar to the 1953 Bowman set from a few years earlier. Inside the 1957 Topps issue are a handful of key Hall of Fame rookie cards. This includes Don Drysdale, Bill Mazeroski, Frank Robinson, Brooks Robinson, and of course, Bunning at card #338. While Bunning isn't quite as popular with collectors as the other four, the demand for postwar Hall of Fame rookies, coupled with the popularity of the set itself, ensures that the 1957 Topps Bunning card is a necessary component of many personal checklists. The card is not considered a condition rarity, but it is commonly found with print defects in the background along with marginal centering.

"The 1957 Topps Bunning card is a necessary component of many personal checklists."

ONE CARD TO WATCH

Post Cereal was one of many companies that produced baseball cards and collectibles during a time that Topps dominated the mainstream market. Not only are some of these sets appealing, they can also be very tough to assemble in high grade. Part of that is due to the fact that the cards had to be removed from the packaging by hand. A good portion of collectors cut the cards from the boxes poorly, resulting in individual cards that are damaged in some way or simply too small to issue a numerical grade. Furthermore, some cards were manufactured in far fewer quantities than others. Bunning was included in the 1963 Post Cereal issue. This card (#53) remains one of the tougher cards to find and a key in the 200-card set, one that contains legends like Roberto Clemente, Sandy Koufax, and Mickey Mantle.

ORLANDO CEPEDA

CHA CHA... I SAW ORLANDO CEPEDA for the first time in Arizona during spring training. He was with Mays and the rest of those guys. The Giants had a great hitting lineup at the time. Man, could Cepeda hit, but he couldn't run. Not even before he tore his knee up pretty badly. Orlando was a righty hitter and could hit the ball to the opposite field as well as anyone. He was an All-Star almost every year with the Giants, but he was really overshadowed by Mays and McCovey.

Cepeda was traded to the Cardinals in 1966 and we played them in the World Series the next year. Even though Orlando was the MVP of the National League and an All-Star in 1967, he really didn't do that much damage to us in the Series. As I recall, he really struggled. Roger Maris, Lou Brock, and Julian Javier, now those were the guys who killed us. Defensively, Orlando was an adequate first baseman, but offensively, he was a real powerhouse. He was a power hitter and led the National League in home runs early in his career.

Orlando was an RBI guy, too, and hit for average. I think he ended up with a career average just under .300.

In 1973, near the end of his career, Cepeda became our teammate. He was probably in his mid-thirties at the time. He had bad wheels, but we all had great respect for him because of his past accomplishments. He was a terrific hitter and he loved baseball. Orlando was actually the first designated hitter in Red Sox history. One thing that really stands out is that he swung about a 42-ounce bat. It was a real log but the handle was really thin. I'm not sure if he shaved it or not. I hit behind him for part of that season. All the guys tried to pitch him inside, but if he got a hold of one, he would just nail it.

Orlando was an outgoing guy. He liked to play Latin music in the clubhouse and loved talking about Puerto Rico. He had a blender in the clubhouse and concocted an energy drink of papaya, pineapple, and some other exotic fruits. I decided to try drinking it, too, but I only lasted a couple of days with it. I told Orlando it didn't energize me, it just made me feel like taking a nap! He was a good guy, and pretty funny. We'd go out to dinner on the road and have a few laughs, especially about splitting the check. He was also a big help to other Latino players.

Orlando only played for us that one year, and it was a great year for him. He smacked 20 home runs, and he was voted Designated Hitter of the year. I can remember how difficult it was for him to round the bases because of his gimpy knees. He finally retired the next year, in 1974. After that, I know that he had some personal and legal problems, but he bounced back pretty well. He began working in baseball again and turned into a great ambassador for the game. I haven't seen him in years, but I'm glad that he got back on the right path and eventually got into the Hall of Fame.

THE CARDS

When Orlando Cepeda's career began, Topps had established itself as the dominant player in the market and his baseball card debut came inside a set that combined different aspects of their prior releases. The attention-grabbing design that defined so many of their earlier productions was back in a big way in 1958, the year of Cepeda's undisputed rookie card. When located in high grade, the card can possess immense eye appeal. After a long and successful career, Cepeda's image can be found in three different decades of cardboard memories, which means there is plenty to choose from for the collector.

Of course, Cepeda remained a staple with Topps throughout his career, but he also made repeat appearances in other issues as well. This included the related Venezuelan Topps sets and Canadian O-Pee-Chee issues, both of which can be hard to find in any condition, not to mention independent brands like Bazooka, Exhibit, Jell-O, and Post Cereal. Since Cepeda was an instant success at the major-league level, winning the National League Rookie of the Year in 1958, it helped him gain entry in a variety of collector issues. Two brands that produced competitive sets to Topps in the 1960s were Fleer and Leaf. The 144-card 1960 Leaf set lacks the kind of star power possessed by the 66-card 1963 Fleer set, but both included Cepeda.

Cepeda found himself in the midst of, arguably, Topps' most creative decade. His image can be seen on a plethora of interesting Topps products, including mediums like coins, faux currency, peel-offs, stamps, stickers, tattoos, and transfers. Two of the more intriguing, non-mainstream Topps sets to include Cepeda are the 1964 Stand-Up set and the 1967 Punch-Outs issue. The 77-card colorful Stand-Up is packed with stars and offers a unique design, while the Punch-Outs test issue is one of Cepeda's more elusive cards overall. Surprisingly, Cepeda never shared a multi-player card with slugging teammate Willie McCovey, outside of the *League Leader* variety, but he did share the limelight with Willie Mays in the 1964 Topps set on a card entitled *Giant Gunners*.

Once Cepeda's playing days were coming to an end and his career was in the home stretch, the slugger appeared on more non-mainstream collectibles than traditional Topps cards. This includes everything from the tough 1971 Topps Greatest Moments set to the 1972 Puerto Rican League Stickers issue, which has special meaning since these stickers were produced in Cepeda's home country. Other brands such as Bazooka, Kellogg's, and Milk Duds featured Cepeda in their sets during his last few active seasons as a player. Cepeda's last regular Topps card (#83) can be found in the 1974 set, one that is anchored in part by the rookie card of fellow Hall of Famer Dave Winfield.

The ORLANDO CEPEDA CARD

After changing their design somewhat dramatically in 1957 in terms of size and appearance, Topps decided to blend the new size standard with the kind of look collectors were used to seeing a few years earlier. The simplicity of the 1957 Topps set was replaced with eye-popping colors that really grab your attention. Their appearance in 1958 was similar to Topps' 1954 or 1955 productions, minus the artwork. Despite being numbered to 495, there are only 494 cards in the set, as no #145 was issued. The set begins with Ted Williams at card #1 and ends with a Herb Score All-Star card at #495, with plenty of star power in between. Interestingly, the only Hall of Fame rookie card to be found is that of Cepeda (#343). The card can be challenging to find in high grade due to print and paper quality issues throughout the set. White print specks are often visible in the bright-colored background. The *San Francisco Call-Bulletin* issued a Cepeda card in 1958 as well, but the Topps debut is considered his only official rookie card.

ONE CARD TO WATCH

Just one year after entering the hobby on his Topps rookie card, Cepeda was chosen to be a part of the relatively exclusive 1959 Bazooka issue. This set contains a mere 23 cards (one per box) and several of the players featured were major stars at the time, from Hank Aaron to Mickey Mantle. They are both oversized at 2¹³⁄₁₆" by 4¹⁵⁄₁₆" and colorful, making for one of the most attractive issues of the decade. More importantly, they are brutally tough to find in top condition since each card had to be removed from the bottom of the box. Dotted lines were included in the design to provide guidance on how to cut them, but very little room for error was given. This meant that many of the cards were cut inside the lines or damaged from unsteady hands during the removal attempt. This is one of Cepeda's best-looking and most difficult cards, one that is part of a very popular set.

ROBERTO CLEMENTE

AS A KID, ROBERTO CLEMENTE was one of my favorites, one of my idols. For me, he was right up there with Mantle. When I got up to the big leagues, it was a great thrill to play against him a lot because we played the Pirates many times during spring training. I loved watching him because his batting style was so unorthodox. He would lift his leg, twirl his bat, and make great contact. Sometimes he would step into the bucket, hit a ball on the outside corner, and drive it down the right field line. He was a master at that. Roberto had a great arm in right field and the way he ran was just incredible. Everything about him was unique. He was very gifted both offensively and defensively, and he was one of the most athletic players in the game at the time. Clemente was such an aggressive yet fluid runner. I think of him as a thoroughbred.

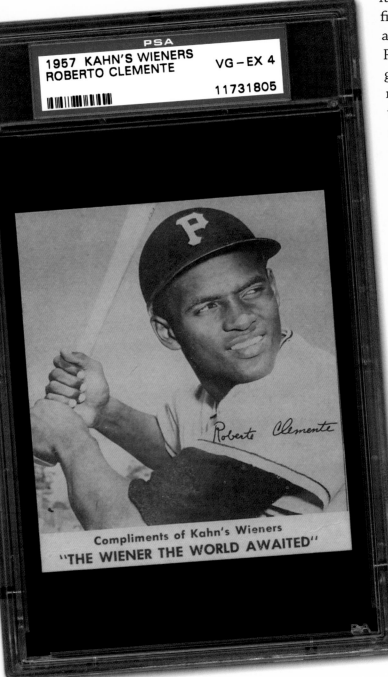

Compliments of Kahn's Wieners
"THE WIENER THE WORLD AWAITED"

One thing that really sticks out in my mind about Clemente was his approach to hitting during spring training. Roberto would actually get aggravated if he got a hit in a pre-season game. I could never figure out why, so I asked him about it one day. He was a pretty superstitious guy and he had this idea that the number of hits he would get in a year was predetermined. He explained that he didn't want to waste a hit on spring training. He wanted every hit to count, in a real game.

In 1967, Major League Baseball put together a team of All-Stars to go to Puerto Rico as ambassadors and to appear in an instructional film. Aaron, Yaz, Clemente, Mazeroski, and Brooks Robinson were named to the team and I was thrilled to be invited as the shortstop. We put on a series of clinics for prospective Major Leaguers. I talked about shortstop play and the other guys did their thing. Clemente acted as our host. We were there for a week and had a great time.

Roberto was always very friendly and cordial to me, but there were two sides to him. There was the Clemente who would complain to umps and scorers and get on them pretty good. Then there was the helpful, soft-spoken Clemente, a real gentleman, who would give advice to other players.

There's no doubt that Clemente was a leader in the clubhouse. There were a lot of Latin players on the Pirates teams, and Clemente took them under his wing. He was instrumental in helping them become better players, both in hitting and fielding.

Because we played the Pirates many times and because he was one of my boyhood idols, I paid close attention to Roberto Clemente's career. The guy won a slew of Gold Gloves and quite a few batting titles. On top of that, he was a perennial All-Star, MVP of the National League, and the hero of the 1971 World Series. I was genuinely shocked when I found out about his death. I just couldn't believe it. I'm glad that they didn't wait to vote him into the Hall of Fame. It was such an honor to play against him and develop a friendship with him. Looking back, I was blessed to know him.

THE CARDS

When Roberto Clemente entered the hobby on his first card, Topps was one year away from total domination, since Bowman made its last stand in 1955. Even before it was over, Topps really made their point during Bowman's final year, capturing the three most important rookies of the season in Clemente, Sandy Koufax, and Harmon Killebrew. The 1955 Bowman set, while still interesting since they locked in Mickey Mantle to an exclusive deal, was left with

no major rookie cards outside of umpires. For the remainder of his career, the popular outfielder's image can be found on just about as many cards and collectibles manufactured during the era as Mantle.

Beyond Topps, Clemente started appearing in other issues in the 1950s. This included Kahn's Wieners, a regional issue that included the Pirates star in several sets through the mid-1960s. In 1958, Clemente was included in the regular Topps set, but a more desirable variation of the regular card exists. This variation features yellow lettering on the team name versus white, the more common color used in the design. The tougher, yellow letter variation cards sell for a noticeable premium. In 1959, Clemente would appear on his first multi-player card from Topps entitled *Corsair Outfield Trio* alongside teammates Bob Skinner and Bill Virdon.

The 1960s were a time when Clemente put up his best individual seasons and he also stamped himself as a hobby favorite. Clemente appeared in numerous issues of all types. The regional and non-mainstream sets loved Clemente, year after year, as he can be found in issues such as Atlantic Oil, Bazooka, East Hills Pirates, Exhibit, Jell-O, Post Cereal, Nabisco, Salada, Shirriff, Sugardale, and Wheaties to name a few. It was also perfect timing with Topps, as they remained creative throughout the decade, producing coins, faux currency, peel-offs, pin-ups, stamps, stickers, and transfers with Clemente's image. Two of the more popular unconventional Topps Clemente cards are his colorful 1964

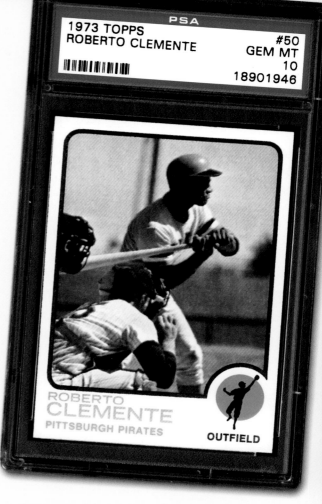

Topps Stand-Up and striking 1969 Super card. He was also chosen for the first major attempt by Fleer to compete with Topps in 1963.

As Clemente's career in cardboard entered the 1970s, many of his most popular issues were behind him, but there were still some excellent cards created for collectors. Two of the more attractive Clemente issues are his condition-sensitive 1971 Topps card and the scarce 1972 Topps Cloth Sticker test card. The decade also produced other Clemente cards from brands like Bazooka, Kellogg's, Milk Duds, O-Pee-Chee, and Transogram. Clemente's final mainstream card (#50) came in 1973 as part of the regular Topps set. It has never been considered extremely desirable due to the lackluster design that Topps employed that year, but it provided closure to a career and life cut too short.

The ROBERTO CLEMENTE CARD

Without a shadow of a doubt, the Clemente card that garners the lion's share of collector attention is his 1955 Topps rookie card (#164). Along with debut singles of Koufax and Killebrew, the Clemente rookie anchors a set that many believe to be one of Topps' best overall productions. While the Koufax and Clemente cards offer tremendous visual appeal and are extraordinarily popular, one of the advantages the Clemente rookie has over the Koufax is its difficulty to find in high grade. The card is clearly more elusive in PSA NM-MT 8 or better than the Koufax, and the price for cards of that quality are reflected in the marketplace. There are Clemente cards that possess superior scarcity, but no other card can compete with his official rookie when it comes to demand.

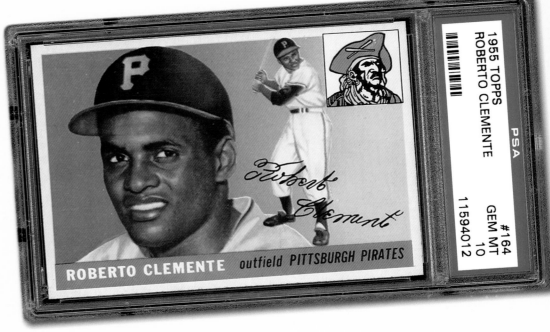

"The Clemente rookie anchors a set that many believe to be one of Topps' best overall productions."

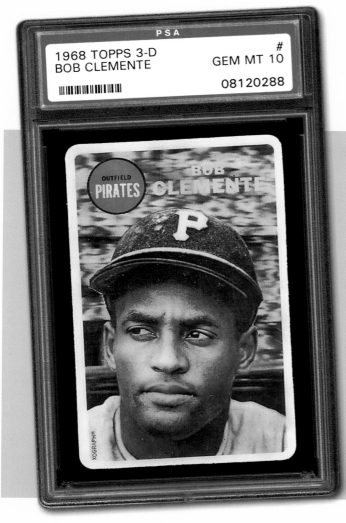

ONE CARD TO WATCH

In every collectibles field, rarity becomes a greater and greater factor in valuation over time. The idea is that collectors love to own items that very few or no other collectors own. Pride of ownership should never be underestimated. When it comes to Clemente, there are a host of cards to choose from during his playing days, and some of them offer the exact kind of elusiveness that collectors clamor for. One Clemente card, however, offers a combination of scarcity and intrigue that is hard to beat. In 1968, Topps released another in a long line of test issues. Topps called this 12-card set 3-Ds, and these were no ordinary-looking cards. The images of the players were set against blurred backgrounds on the plastic fronts, creating a revolutionary 3-D effect. There is nothing like it from that decade or before, and with Clemente as the clear key in the set, it remains a card to watch in the future.

BOB GIBSON

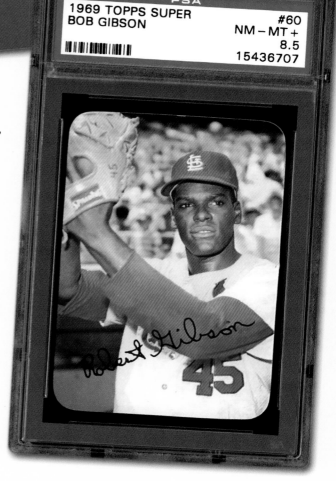

I'VE ALWAYS SAID THAT BOB GIBSON, along with Nolan Ryan, were the two toughest pitchers that I ever faced. They both threw nasty heat. Gibson always kept you off-balance because he was certainly not afraid to serve up a little chin music. Like other fireballers, he would use the top of the strike zone to make your life miserable. Gibson had great stuff. He threw in the middle-to-upper 90s. He had an excellent slider and a changeup that he threw occasionally, but he liked to throw the fastball and it was very tough to hit. Tim McCarver told me that every once in a while when he would walk out to the mound for a conference with Gibson, Bob would look at him like he had two heads. He would say to McCarver, "How can you possibly tell me anything about pitching?

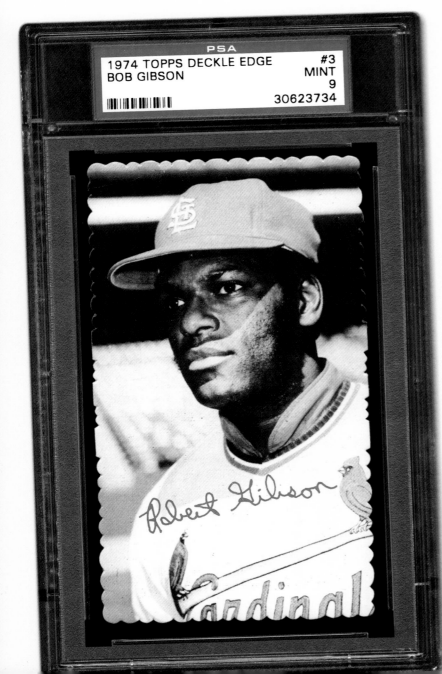

Get back behind the plate." McCarver would just smile and walk back. They were such a great tandem and great friends. I believe Tim caught more than 200 games for Gibson.

I faced Gibson several times in spring training, so going into the 1967 World Series against the Cards, I kind of knew what to expect from him. I knew he threw hard, and that he was a great pitcher. I knew he hated giving up hits, and he pitched mean. He would knock guys down. For the record, I was never brushed back when I came up to the plate. Gibson was one of those players who never wanted to get friendly with the opposition. No small talk, nothing. We were the enemy. If you got a hit off him, he would pitch very aggressively your next time up. He was not afraid to throw at anyone. Also, for a pitcher, he was outstanding defensively and he was a pretty good hitter. Gibson went out there to beat you. He was such a great competitor, and he worked fast, too. He kicked our ass in the 1967 Series. In Game One, I struck out three times against him. He was unbelievable. I did manage to get a double deep down the left field line off him in Game Seven. I remember

Boomer (George Scott) hit a triple in that game. As I recall, Gibson gave up only three hits that day.

Gibson was the '67 Series MVP and deservedly so. He gave up, I think, only three earned runs over the three games in which he pitched. He absolutely owned us in that Series. Actually, our guy Jim Lonborg pitched very well himself. I still think that if Lonborg was rested longer for Game Seven, we could have won the Series. That St. Louis team was unbelievable though, with Gibson, Maris, Brock, Flood, Cepeda, McCarver, and the rest of those guys. Bob was really at the top of his game at that time. The next year he was the MVP of the National League and he won the Cy Young Award for the first time. He got another Cy Young a couple of years later. And of course, he was always on the All-Star team. Even when he was playing, Gibson was considered to be one of the great all-time pitchers. He made it to the Hall of Fame on the first ballot. That tells you something right there.

THE CARDS

Bob Gibson's career in cardboard covered three decades, which produced dozens upon dozens of great Gibson cards and more to collect. The Hall of Fame pitcher entered the league at a wonderful time. Gibson experienced his prime years as a player when Topps was experimenting with new concepts and various regional sets were being created by a host of brands. A lot of baseball experts argue that Gibson was in a league of his own during those prime years, so it is fitting that the flame-throwing right-hander remains the only Hall

of Fame player to have a rookie card in the 1959 Topps set. From that perspective, all eyes are on Gibson. It was the first, last, and only card from the decade to feature Gibson.

After a slow start as a pitcher, Gibson really came into his own during the 1960s and that's when the bulk of his cards were made. Of course, Gibson was included in all the mainstream Topps sets, but this was a decade of creativity for the manufacturer. Thus, Gibson's image appeared on various Topps mediums like coins, decals, rub-offs, stamps, and transfers. Topps also produced interesting card sets with the intention of complementing their traditional ones. These sets include more commonly-found releases like 1964 Topps Giants and 1965 Topps Embossed, as well as more elusive issues like their Venezuelan or test sets like 1969 Topps Super.

One interesting note is that Gibson, unlike many stars of the day, was never featured on a Topps multi-player card other than cards of the *League Leader* variety. In 1968, a year that has special meaning for Gibson collectors due to his remarkable performance, a Milton Bradley board game was made using baseball cards that are virtually identical to the regular Topps issue from the same year. The subtle difference is in the color used on the reverse, which is a brighter yellow on the game cards, or the occasional presence of a white line along the border of the game card fronts. Gibson was one of the stars of the day to appear in Fleer's big attempt to compete with Topps in

1963. Gibson was also included in many other issues outside of Topps. These sets include Bazooka, Jell-O, Nabisco, and Post Cereal.

Gibson's career extended well into the 1970s, which gave him a chance to be included in several interesting mainstream and non-mainstream sets. Some of the more interesting Topps issues of the decade include 1971 Greatest Moments, 1972 Candy Lids, 1974 Deckle Edge, and 1975 Mini, which was simply a smaller version of the regular 1975 set, a set that contained Gibson's last regular card from his playing days (#150). Gibson also became a regular with Kellogg's and O-Pee-Chee, while making appearances in other issues like Bazooka, for the final time, and Hostess near the end of his memorable run as a dominant mound presence.

The BOB GIBSON CARD

Like many other Hall of Famers of the era, the Gibson card that many collectors clamor for is his rookie. In 1959, Topps issued another colorful set that was full of stars, multi-player cards, and included an All-Star run in the high-number series. While the set has a lot to offer overall, the only Hall of Fame player rookie card is that of Gibson (#514), making it a clear key for collectors. It is also one of the more eye-catching cards in the set, featuring a bubble-gum-colored background and a perfectly placed facsimile signature beneath Gibson's smiling image. That's right. Gibson is smiling. Much like the irony found on the 1957 Topps Don Drysdale rookie card, one of the most intense competitors in baseball history has a joyful look on his face. Behind the intimidating glare was a real person. The Gibson rookie is not terribly difficult in high grade, but finding a well-centered copy that is absent print defects in the light-colored background may be somewhat challenging.

"The 1962 Topps card is one of the toughest Gibson cards to find in PSA NM–MT 8 or better condition."

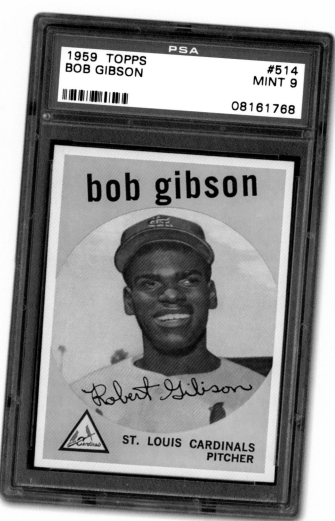

ONE CARD TO WATCH

Gibson appeared in a number of interesting regional sets over the course of his career, but one of the cards really worth watching is another mainstream Topps issue. In 1962, Topps abandoned their traditional, colorful format and decided to frame each card with a faux wood grain border. In terms of design, the set really stands out from all the other Topps releases during the 1960s. The design was not only unique, it created an increased challenge for collectors seeking high-grade examples since wear along the edges and corners is often clearly visible. The 1962 Topps card is one of the toughest Gibson cards to find in PSA NM–MT 8 or better condition, and it was also a short print, which enhances the difficulty. The combination of the set's popularity and the condition-sensitivity of the card design make this Gibson one to watch in the future.

CATFISH HUNTER

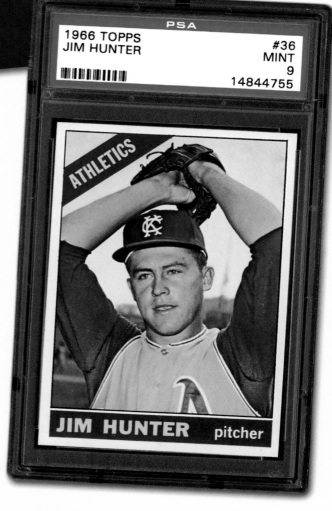

HE WAS NOT OVERPOWERING, but Catfish Hunter was a very good pitcher. Catfish had great command and was one of those guys who would give you a comfortable 0-for-4. He would work you high and outside and just catch the corners with his fastball. You'd go after it because it just looked so good, and it would pop up. When his control was on, he was a great painter. He also worked fast. When he was off, though, he made a lot of mistakes out over the plate, and was hittable.

One of the things about Catfish that separated him from most, was that he was a big game pitcher. He was clutch all the way, especially in the World Series. Hunter was the Athletics go-to guy during those really good years. Over the course of our careers, I had some success against him. I faced Hunter quite a bit and he always tried to keep me off balance, but I hung in there.

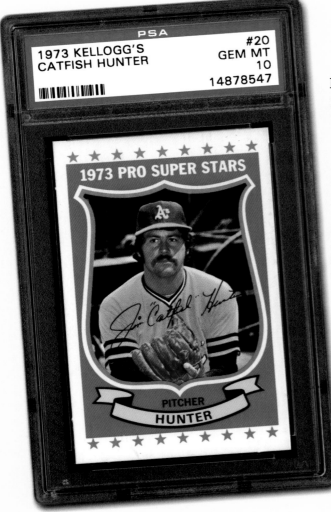

I feel like I had more success facing Catfish when he was a 20-game winner than when he was a sub .500 pitcher at the beginning of his career. He was known for being particularly tough in the late innings, especially with men on base.

When Catfish was with Oakland, the players absolutely hated Charlie Finley, the owner. Finley really liked Catfish. He personally traveled to North Carolina to sign him back in 1965 when the Athletics were still in Kansas City, and Finley was the one who gave Jim the name Catfish. We both came up in 1965. He was with the Athletics through the 1974 season, so most of the time I faced him as part of the Athletics team. As I recall, he absolutely killed it in his last season with them. That year he won 25 games and won the Cy Young Award. As I understand it, Finley paid Catfish well over the years, but when he came up for free agency, Finley lied to him. He told Catfish he would give him a huge contract, but he never came through with it by the deadline. Finley reneged on his word. The Yankees offered Catfish a ton of money and he joined them. I think he was probably the highest paid player in the game when he signed. The guy was a real gamer though, playing on three championship teams with Oakland and two with New York.

The year that he won the Cy, I could not touch him. His control was lights out. Even though we were not close friends, we would chat occasionally. He was a real nice guy, very cordial. Jim was one of those guys who seemed to live very simply. He loved to hunt and fish. I am not a hunter but I love to fish, so we would talk about that once in a while. It's really tragic that he died in his fifties from Lou Gehrig's disease. I think Catfish was a worthy candidate for the Hall of Fame. To be honest, I always use Hunter's numbers when I'm lobbying for my dear friend and teammate Luis Tiant to get into the Hall. Luis's numbers are very similar to Hunter's. Both of them were very competitive, clutch pitchers, and I hope that Luis can follow Catfish into the Hall.

THE CARDS

Catfish Hunter began his career when Topps, the dominant manufacturer of cards at the time, was right in the middle of their most creative run of innovative sets. Since Hunter was still a young player trying to establish himself, he missed the cut in some of Topps' most desirable productions in the 1965–1970 period, but the Hall of Fame pitcher was able to make appearances in some of their classic issues. Of course, it all began for Hunter in the 1965 Topps set when he made his debut on a four-player rookie card. The set has a very attractive design and remains popular with collectors.

For the remainder of the decade, Hunter did appear in all the regular Topps sets along with some that were outside the norm. Hunter can be found in everything from Topps Plaks to stamps to stickers. This is in addition to the related Canadian O-Pee-Chee and Venezuelan issues. During the last half of the decade, Hunter also appeared in some regional issues like Bazooka and Jack in the Box. Once Hunter's career turned the corner and extended into the 1970s, the A's pitcher found himself in dozens of interesting collectible sets beyond the standard Topps sets.

In the 1970s, some of the more interesting Topps productions that featured Hunter include the tough 1974 Deckle Edge set, one of his most valuable cards, not to mention 1971 Coins, 1973 Candy Lids, and 1977 Cloth Stickers issues. Hunter was also a part of many non-Topps sets as a member of both the Oakland A's powerhouse in the first half of the decade and the New York Yankees near the end of it. Hunter seemed to be in the postseason every year. You can find the pitcher in sets made by Bazooka, Burger King, Hostess, Kellogg's, Milk Duds, Sportscaster, and SSPC.

As Hunter's career came to a close, Topps was still king, but they were outnumbered by a gang of non-

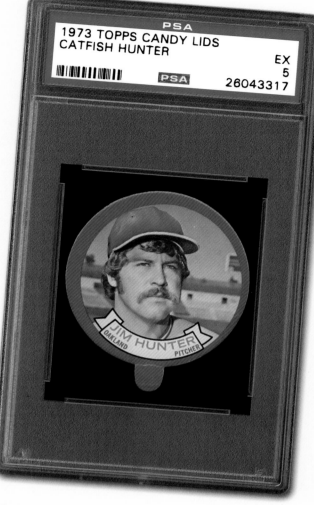

mainstream products. One of the concepts that seemed to catch on with collectors in the mid-1970s was the medium of discs. This included discs issued by Buckmans, Carousel, Chilly Willee, Crane Potato Chips, Dairy Isle, Detroit Caesars, Holiday Inn, Islay's, MSA Sports, Orbaker's, Safelon, Towne Club, Wendy's, Wiffle, and Zip Z. Apparently, collectors really liked them. In the era of disco, it seems fitting that so many discs were created. Most of them are not hard to find today, nor will they break the bank. Hunter's final Topps appearance came in 1979 on card #670 in a set dominated by the Ozzie Smith rookie card.

"Hunter seemed to be in the postseason every year."

The CATFISH HUNTER CARD

Many collectors tend to focus on rookie cards of Hall of Famers. While this is true in every sport, it is especially true with postwar baseball card collectors. In the 1960s, Topps started producing multi-player rookie cards. Hunter is one of several Hall of Famers to be pictured on multi-player rookies during the decade. The other players pictured on the card don't often turn out be Hall of Famers or even stars in their own right. The Hunter rookie was no different. The 1965 Topps set, however, contains four separate Hall of Famer rookie cards, including those of Joe Morgan, Steve Carlton, and Tony Perez in addition to the Hunter (#526). The Hunter rookie, which is considered a short print, features teammates Rene Lachemann, Johnny Odom, and Skip Lockwood as well. The card can be challenging to find well centered and absent print defects in the background.

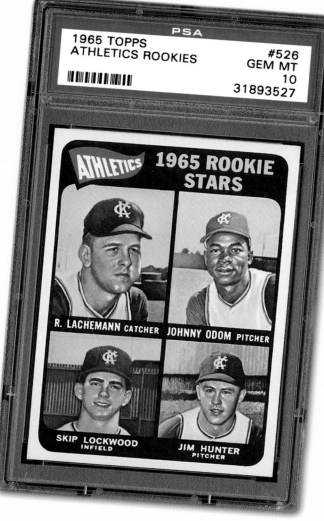

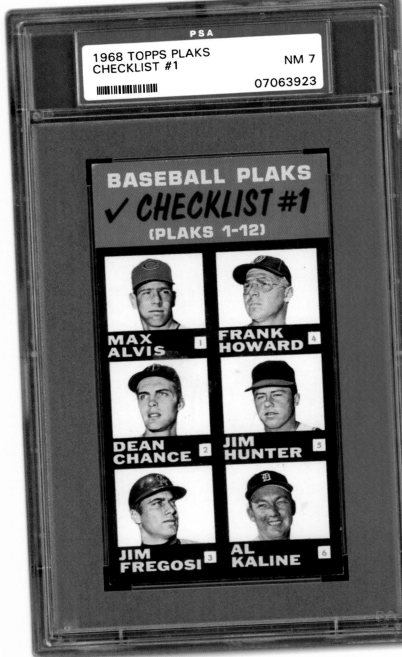

ONE CARD TO WATCH

In 1968, Topps continued to produce test issues as their decade of experimentation continued. One of their most elusive productions was the 24-piece Plaks set. The Plaks were miniature plastic busts of different stars. The likes of Roberto Clemente and Mickey Mantle can be found here. Hunter was amongst the limited group of players included. In addition to the unassembled bust, a colorful checklist card was inserted into each pack. There were two different checklists, one for Plaks 1–12 and the other for Plaks 13–24. Each checklist showcased six color player photos on each side and Hunter appears on the face of checklist #1. These oversized cards measure 2⅛" by 4" and feature colored borders, a mix of red and black, which make these rarities condition sensitive. Pound-for-pound, this is the most valuable card to feature Hunter during his playing days.

AL KALINE

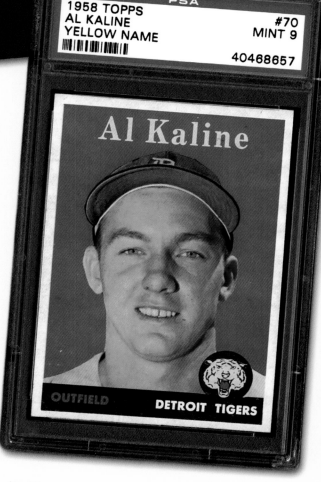

A CLASSY GUY AND A REAL GENTLEMAN, Al Kaline was just a perfect ballplayer. When I say that, I mean he made it look so easy. He was an outstanding outfielder. He hit for some power, and he hit for decent average. Everyone respected him. We played Detroit a lot and they had some very good-hitting teams. With guys like Bill Freehan, Willie Horton, Mickey Stanley, Kaline, Jim Northrup, and Dick McAuliffe, they were darn good. Their pitching was very good, too, with Denny McLain, Mickey Lolich, and Earl Wilson.

Kaline was such a tough hitter that we tried to figure out what his approach was. It seemed to us that Kaline was a zone hitter. He'd look outside and looked inside sometimes, and when he was ahead in the count 2–0, 3–1, he waited for his pitch, and a lot of times he hit home runs. There was one game in particular. I just couldn't believe it. Kaline had a pitch, low and away. We had pitched him two fastballs inside, one ball and one strike. Then he gets this breaking ball, low and away, a real pitcher's pitch. Kaline reaches for it like he knows it's coming, lines the ball to right-center field, and it was a double. He had to be zoning to do that. He had an uncanny knack for anticipating the zone. Anyway, he was a terrific hitter and a tough out. Kaline also had an outstanding arm, an accurate arm.

In my era, early on, you couldn't talk to players from the other team before the games or you'd get fined. They were afraid of the gambling stuff.

Umpires were in the stands before the game, and when you went across to batting practice you could look and say hello but that was it.

Al and I would chat when he was on base. That was considered okay to do. You know, small talk. How is the family? How is the season going? Stuff like that.

In 1967, the Tigers were in the hunt right until the end. After we beat the Twins, we were in our locker room in Boston waiting and listening to their game. They were playing the Angels in the second game of a doubleheader. Detroit lost and we clinched it, and all hell broke loose in our locker room. That was one of the greatest moments of my professional life. That year, Kaline was out in the middle of the season with a broken

KALINE

hand. Who knows what would have happened if he hadn't been injured. The next year, in 1968, the Tigers had a hell of a team. They came back to win it all. Kaline was injured again that year and only played about half the season, but he played well in the Series.

Kaline started way before me and retired just a year or two before I did. He played for Detroit at least 20 years. Besides winning a bunch of Gold Gloves, he was an All-Star just about every year, he got 3,000 hits, and he got into the Hall of Fame on the first ballot. Kaline is one of the guys who made a real impression on me.

THE CARDS

Al Kaline had a long career that was filled with accolades. As a result, the Detroit Tigers icon can be found in a variety of collectible issues over 20-plus years. This includes some of the greatest rarities manufactured during the era. Kaline's start in the hobby came inside a fantastic set, as the teenager began his

career in cardboard in the beautiful 1954 Topps set. It was his lone rookie card during the Topps/ Bowman overlap. Kaline did make an appearance in Bowman's last annual set of their 1948–1955 run. This 1955 Bowman card is one of Kaline's most overlooked issues. It is one of the better-looking cards in this intriguing set.

As the decade progressed, Kaline became a staple with Topps and made appearances in some other great sets too. Kaline not only appeared in the regular 1955 Topps set, he was also selected to be a part of their Doubleheaders issue. This set paired two players in a large, perforated format. Two players share the same set of legs, so the cards could be folded in such a way that the player could be positioned against a colorful stadium background. Kaline shared the card with Corky Valentine, but the beauty of the Kaline card is that he is positioned on the front when the card is in the unfolded position. It is one of the toughest cards in the set to locate in high grade.

In 1958, Kaline would be part of the annual Topps set as always, but his #70 card can be found with either white or yellow letters on the front, the yellow being the tougher of the two variations. This would also be the first set that featured Kaline on a multi-player card; he appeared alongside teammate Harvey Kuenn. Kaline would appear on a few different multi-player cards over the years, with his most popular card coming in the 1964 Topps set. There he was pictured with Norm Cash, Roger Maris, and Mickey Mantle on a card entitled *A.L. Bombers*. It was during the 1960s that the sheer volume of Kaline collectibles really increased.

Kaline's image was seemingly everywhere. He appeared in issues like Armour Coins, Bazooka, Exhibit, Jell-O, Nu-Card Scoops, Post Cereal, and Wheaties to name a few. Topps produced everything from coins to faux currency to stamps during the decade, in addition to several creative sets like the colorful 1964 Stand-Ups. They also produced some test issues that are now very difficult to find, like the nearly impossible 1961 Dice Game rarity or Kaline's condition-sensitive 1968 Plaks Checklist card (#1). Both are amongst Kaline's most valuable cards. In 1971, Topps created another set with condition obstacles called Greatest Moments. The solid black borders can be unforgiving. Kaline's final appearance came in the 1975 Topps set on card #4, one that honors the Hall of Famer for joining the exclusive 3,000 Hit Club.

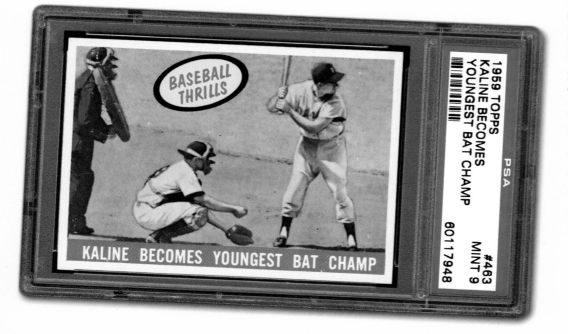

The AL KALINE CARD

The 1954 Topps set has always been one of the most revered baseball card issues of all time. With its booming colors and immense star selection, it's easy to see why. Between the Ted Williams bookends, cards #1 and #250, are three key Hall of Famer rookie cards. Hank Aaron, Ernie Banks, and Kaline made their debuts here and were exclusive to Topps that year. They not only became stars, but all three were able to play in three different decades due to their tremendous longevity. The Kaline rookie in particular is a very eye-catching card, as his portrait and the yellow Tigers logo really pop against the background. That background can vary a little in color, from a rich cherry-red to one that exhibits a hint of orange, and it can be susceptible to print defects. Regardless, there is no doubt that the classic 1954 Topps rookie is the Kaline card to own.

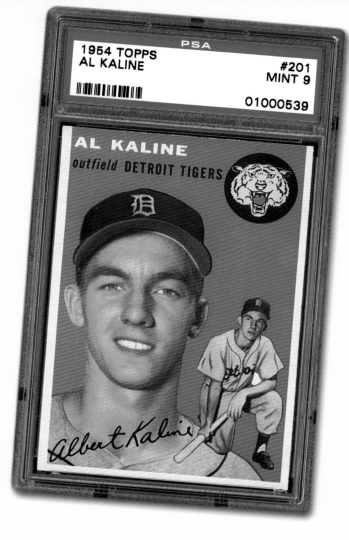

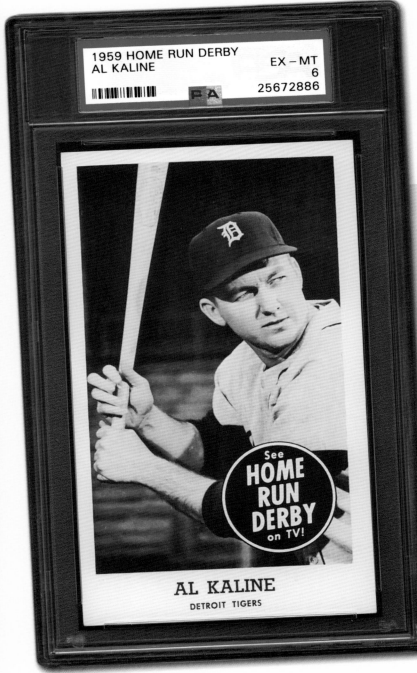

ONE CARD TO WATCH

In 1959, American Motors produced an unnumbered 20-card set to help bring attention to the new television program *Home Run Derby*. The brainchild of renowned writer-director Lou Breslow, amongst others, and hosted by Mark Scott, this fun competition pitted many of the best sluggers in the league against each other. The participants came away with a cash prize, with the winner receiving $2,000 and a chance to return the following week. In those days, $2,000 was a lot considering what the players made at the time. In fact, many players took odd jobs in the offseason to make ends meet. Kaline was one of the participants, and of course, he was included in the set along with the likes of Aaron, Mantle, and Willie Mays. The black-and-white cards had blank backs and were oversized, measuring approximately 3¼" by 5¼". This collectible Kaline issue is one of his most difficult and valuable cards, but beware of reprints and counterfeits.

HARMON KILLEBREW

EVERYBODY LOVED HARMON KILLEBREW. He was such an easy-going guy. His teammates loved him, the fans loved him, and the competition liked and respected him. When he played first and I would get on base, we would shoot the breeze about anything, depending on what was going on. The game, the family, the world, whatever. Harmon was such a great power hitter. He really killed us. The Twins had some really good teams, but even though they had other superstars, Killebrew was their power guy. He could hit the ball far and high. He had a little uppercut swing, and he was an incredible RBI guy. He had a good eye and he was a great low-ball hitter because of that uppercut swing. Killebrew was a tough out. He was a decent fielder, too.

Killebrew had some great home run years. He started in Washington and hit some home runs there, so it wasn't just the ballpark. Minnesota was more hitter-friendly though. He hit home runs to center field, left field, and right-center when the Twins were home. I remember a game when Killebrew hit one right over the light tower at Fenway. He was tailor-made for Fenway. I bet he would have had over 600 home runs if he played for the Red Sox. That 1967 Twins team was outstanding with Carew, who was a kid; Versalles, Tovar, Oliva, Allison, and Killebrew. With Jim Kaat and Dean Chance, they also had a good pitching staff.

I'll never forget the last day of the 1967 season as long as I live. It all came down to one game. I got a hit in that game, and Killebrew got a couple. He misplayed a ball for an error, though, and I think it cost them a run. In the bottom of the ninth, Rich Rollins hit that little pop up to me on the infield grass and I remember the feeling. I was more focused on catching that little pop up than any other ball ever hit to me. Once I caught the ball, all hell broke loose. We could not believe it. Dalton Jones, who was playing third for us, jumped into my arms and we both jumped into the mob scene on the mound. Hundreds of fans ran onto the field and they started carrying Jim Lonborg away. Security had to save him.

Killebrew had a great season in 1967 and probably would have been the MVP except Yaz had such an unbelievable season, winning the Triple Crown. They both hit 44 home runs that year. After that season, Killebrew had some more big home run and RBI years and he was MVP in 1969. He moved to third base and really the best thing that happened for him was the designated hitter position. He was able to play a little longer as DH. Killebrew and I played against each other many times, and we established a great relationship over the years. Later on, we would bump into each other at baseball events and chat about those great years in the '60s and '70s. Like lots of other players, he died from cancer. Harmon was just a great, easy-going guy. His place in the Hall of Fame is well deserved.

THE CARDS

As a player, Harmon Killebrew started somewhat slowly, but once the slugger found his groove in 1959, there was no doubting his Hall of Fame potential. Killebrew made his cardboard debut during a great era of baseball card production and within an exceptional set, the 1955 Topps. It would be his only mainstream rookie card, as Killebrew was exclusive to Topps during the final year in Bowman's run (1948–1955). Interestingly enough, despite his limited experience, Killebrew was also included in Topps' 1955 Doubleheaders set. He shared the perforated card with Johnny Podres of the Brooklyn Dodgers and can be seen in full view on the front when the card remains unfolded.

As the decade continued, it is important to note that no 1957 Topps Killebrew card was ever made. It would be the only time he was not part of their regular set during his entire playing career. This was most likely as result of his limited playing time at the major-league level. The following two years Killebrew can be found on cards with fantastic eye appeal. The 1958 and 1959 Topps Killebrew cards are very colorful, with the latter found in the high-number series for the issue. Collectors love the bold red background of Killebrew's 1959 Topps card, but finding one well centered and without distracting print defects can be challenging.

As a player, Killebrew's defining decade was clearly the 1960s and the collectibles bearing his image followed. Killebrew can be found in coin, decal, faux currency, peel-off, rub-off, stamp, sticker, tattoo, and transfer sets manufactured by major brands like Topps and others. There were plenty of popular regional sets that included Killebrew such as Bazooka, Jell-O, and Post Cereal in addition to the O-Pee-Chee and Venezuelan Topps issues throughout the decade. Killebrew is featured on many *League Leader* cards, since he always seemed to be in the home run chase, but he is showcased on some multi-player cards as well. His most popular multi-player card, entitled *Super Stars*, pictures the slugger next to Mickey Mantle and Willie Mays in the 1968 Topps set.

Before the decade was over, Killebrew also found himself a part of some of the toughest Topps

test issues ever created. He was included in the nearly-impossible 1967 Stand-Up set, the oddball 1967 Punch-Outs issue, and on a condition-sensitive 1968 Topps Plaks Checklist card (#1). As we round the corner and head into the home stretch of Killebrew's career, the fan favorite added to his career card total in a big way. Some of the more interesting Topps issues to include Killebrew were the 1971 Greatest Moments and a few tough test sets like the 1970 and 1972 Candy Lids, 1973 Comics, and 1973 Pin-Ups. Killebrew's final mainstream hobby appearance came in the 1975 Topps set (card #640), one of the most popular sets of the decade.

The HARMON KILLEBREW CARD

In 1955, Topps produced one of its best-looking sets ever, and that is saying something considering that their previous three standard issues are all considered so appealing. The combination of color and artwork made for a spectacular visual. It was also the first time that Topps issued an entire set using a horizontal design. At the center of this beautiful set are three key rookie cards capturing the debuts of Roberto Clemente, Sandy Koufax, and Killebrew. While Killebrew doesn't quite have the name power of the other two legends, keep in mind that the slugger was one of the early members of the revered 500 Home Run Club. Like many of the cards in the set, the Killebrew rookie has tremendous eye appeal. The two most challenging, inherent condition obstacles are subpar centering and print defects that can impact the bright yellow background around both of Killebrew's images.

"The Killebrew rookie has tremendous eye appeal."

ONE CARD TO WATCH

In 1959, American Motors produced an unnumbered 20-card set to help bring attention to the new television program *Home Run Derby*. Hosted by Mark Scott, this fun competition pitted many of the best sluggers in the league against each other. The participants came away with a cash prize, with the winner receiving $2,000 and a chance to return the following week. As one of the show's participants, Killebrew was included in the set along with the likes of Hank Aaron, Mantle, and Mays. The black-and-white cards had blank backs and were oversized, measuring approximately 3¼" by 5¼". This desirable Killebrew issue is one of his most difficult and valuable cards, but beware of reprints and counterfeits.

JUAN MARICHAL

WHEN I MADE IT TO THE MAJORS, it was a thrill to face Juan Marichal during spring training. The Red Sox were in Scottsdale, Arizona, and the Giants played only 15 miles away in Phoenix, so we played them a lot, both home and away. They were a great hitting team with Mays and the rest. Marichal was a great competitor. He didn't throw real hard but he had a killer curveball that came over the top and sidearm. His breaking pitch was excellent and he had great control. Marichal would go way down and almost hit the ground with the ball before he threw it. With his really high leg kick, he could be so tough. That kick hid the ball and before you knew it, the ball was on top of you. That's why his fastball looked faster than it really was. I could hit him pretty well at the beginning of spring training, but as we got closer to Opening Day, he became tougher and tougher.

Juan joined us near the end of his career, in 1974. Even though he pitched pretty well, his velocity was not there and he had a hard time throwing strikes. He signed with the Dodgers in 1975 but decided to retire early in the season, which was really the best thing for him.

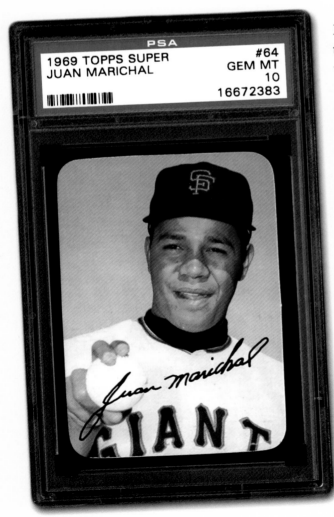

I remember Luis Tiant and Marichal pitched in a doubleheader that year he was with the Red Sox. Two great pitchers with unusual windups. Juan was a really good guy who mostly kept to himself, but we developed a nice relationship. Marichal liked to bust my chops about weakly popping out when I faced him in the 1967 All-Star Game. At least he didn't strike me out! I was curious about where he came from and how he got started pitching. Like most of the guys from the Dominican [Republic], Marichal started at a very young age. I was amazed at how poor he was growing up. You know, there were not a lot of Latin players in MLB in those days, and the racism he experienced in the early part of his career made it very rough for him.

Juan told me that the greatest moment of his career was the 16-inning complete game that he threw against the Braves. It was in 1963. Marichal was in his mid-twenties, and he faced the great Warren Spahn, who was near the end of his career. They both threw complete games and finally, in the 16th, Mays homered for the Giants 1–0 win. Can you imagine a pitcher throwing 16 innings today? Of course, the Johnny Roseboro bat incident was kind of a black mark on his career, but he always maintained that he thought that Roseboro was trying to hit him in the head with the ball. I know that he and Johnny eventually buried the hatchet, and years later, Roseboro supported Marichal for the Hall of Fame.

You know, Marichal led his league in complete games and shutouts several seasons. He got the pitching title in 1969 and was an All-Star for years. He wasn't really overpowering but he was sneaky-fast and had great breaking stuff. Juan Marichal was a great one. I'm so glad I got to play against him and with him.

THE CARDS

Juan Marichal started his career during a decade that featured the primes of some of the greatest players to ever step on the field. In other words, it was hard to stand out during a time when so many big names were stealing the spotlight. Hank Aaron, Roberto Clemente, Sandy Koufax, and Willie

Mays were all excelling year after year, while a few legends retired from the game like Yogi Berra, Mickey Mantle, and Ted Williams. All along, Marichal put up spectacular numbers and he did it with flair. The stylistic pitcher appeared on dozens of collectibles and cards during his career, including some rarities.

Once Marichal made his debut for Topps in 1961, he became a staple in their regular sets for the remainder of his career, and he even appeared in some of their more creative productions. This included some tough test sets as well. Beyond the regular issue, Marichal also appeared on a 1961 Topps stamp the same year the perennial All-Star entered the hobby. In addition to Topps stamp issues, Marichal can be found on other mediums like Topps coins and rub-offs from the 1960s. Topps was innovative with their card designs, producing oversized issues like 1964 Topps Giants and introducing the jagged-looking Deckle Edge series in 1969.

For a good portion of his career, you will also see Marichal Venezuelan Topps and O-Pee-Chee (Canadian) cards, which are both much harder to locate than the regular Topps cards issued in the United States. The former star was also included in some of Topps' test issues, in both the 1960s and 1970s. This includes everything from the beautiful 1969 Super set to the extremely elusive 1967 Discs and 24-piece 1970 Candy Lids issue. Throughout his prime years, Marichal was also included in many regional issues such

as Bazooka, Jell-O, Nabisco, Post Cereal, and Wheaties.

Because he ranked amongst the best pitchers in baseball, Marichal did appear on many *League Leader* cards over the years. Marichal's most popular multi-player card was part of the 1969 Topps set. It pictures him next to teammate and fellow Hall of Famer, Willie McCovey, on a card entitled *Giants Heroes*. Marichal's last regular card came in the 1974 Topps set (#330), but there's a twist. Topps also released cards that year that were part of a *Traded* series. These were players that were traded during the season. Marichal appears in this set as well (#330T) because of his move to the Boston Red Sox.

The JUAN MARICHAL CARD

The 1961 Topps set is one of the more popular issues of the decade. It is filled with stars, multi-player cards, and an All-Star run in the high-number series. At the core of the set are three Hall of Fame rookie cards in Ron Santo, Billy Williams, and Marichal. The Marichal rookie card shows the legendary pitcher beaming with an ear-to-ear smile. While Marichal may have been overshadowed by the likes of Bob Gibson and Koufax during the same era, his unique delivery and stellar performance made him popular with fans. Marichal's 1961 Topps rookie isn't overly difficult in high grade, but beware of print defects on the face of the card in addition to centering issues. The print defects usually come in the form of "fish eyes" or "snow" in the dark-colored background. Since one of the more popular collecting themes is based on postwar Hall of Fame baseball rookies, this Marichal should always be a desirable addition.

"Marichal's 1961 Topps rookie isn't overly difficult in high grade, but beware of print defects on the face of the card ..."

ONE CARD TO WATCH

Topps owned the market in the 1960s. Yes, others tried their hand at manufacturing, but no one could unseat the dominant player. With that kind of position, Topps decided to get extremely creative and the collectors benefited from their innovation. In 1964, Topps tried a few new things. One of those experiments resulted in the 1964 Topps Stand-Up set, an issue chock-full of superstars like Aaron and Mantle. The set contained 77 cards, but 22 of them were short prints, including Mr. Marichal. These die-cut cards were designed so collectors could pop the player image out from the backing, giving it a 3-D look. Most importantly, the cards are booming with color. The yellow/green borders, however, can reveal the slightest touch of wear or chipping. Inconsistent centering can also pose a threat to those seeking high-grade examples. The 1964 Topps Stand-Up Marichal is not nearly as tough as some of the Topps test issues noted earlier, but the appeal of the set and relative scarcity keep the value of this card on par with his rookie.

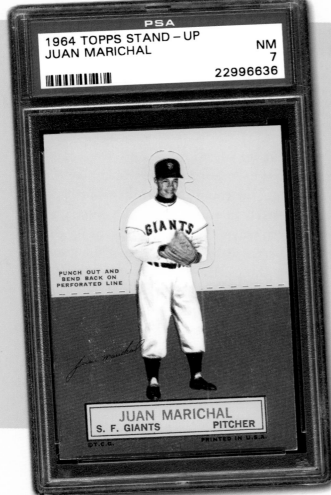

WILLIE MAYS

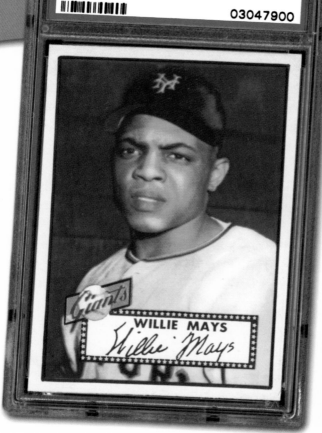

IN MY OPINION, WILLIE MAYS is arguably the best outfielder to ever play the game. He could do it all. He could hit for average, hit for power, he was a great RBI guy, a tremendous fielder, had a great arm, and he was a hell of a baserunner. Willie was a super-superstar. He and I chatted many times. He had that high voice and was always flapping good naturedly. Willie had a great sense of humor and was always very cordial. We talked a lot in Arizona. The Giants were only 15 miles from us, so we played them quite a bit during spring training.

I liked to pick Willie's brain and tried to get his perspective on the game, but I finally realized you just had to have that kind of ability to do the things he did. His approach to the game was simple in his mind: work hard and it will all come into place. It was similar to Ted Williams' approach. It may have been simple for them, but it was a bit more difficult for the rest of us! Mays was amazing. I never saw a guy hit a ball so hard in my life. He just crushed it. The ball would explode off his bat. It sounded like a bazooka going off. He could slam them anywhere on the field: right-center, left, anywhere.

Willie was a happy-go-lucky guy. When he first came up, he struggled a bit and got a little down on himself. Leo Durocher told Willie that he was his centerfielder and to not worry about anything. That gave him a lot of confidence, and from that point there was no stopping him. Actually, Willie was scouted by the Red Sox before he joined the Giants. In those years, there was still bias and racism in baseball. Unfortunately, a lot of owners did not want to sign the African-American players. Some of the greatest ballplayers of all-time were denied the opportunity to play. Both Mays and Robinson were scouted by the Red Sox but didn't get signed, which was a big mistake.

We played the Giants in spring training for several years until we moved to Winter Haven, Florida, and they stayed in Arizona. Willie would play three innings, but as spring training wore on, he would crank it up towards the end. That's when you could see how immensely talented he was. Of course, Ruth could do it all, but of the more modern players, I rank Mays right up there as number one. Ted Williams was a better hitter overall, but Willie was much better defensively and could do more things. They talk about the five tools; I think he had ten! Mays was just tremendous. He really revolutionized the individual player concept. He was the guy you would look for and compare other players' stats with.

When I made the All-Star team, I would see Willie around the batting cage chirping away and joking with the other greats there like Aaron and Clemente. There's no doubt that Mays hung on a little too long, but he really wanted to get back to New York. He got that opportunity with the Mets, but his legs gave out and he couldn't do it anymore. I never held that against him though.

He was a great player and it was an honor to play against him.

THE CARDS

For 22 seasons, Willie Mays racked up the accolades as only the five-tool player could. His immense popularity and extended career ensured that collectors would have a hoard of collectibles to choose from. Mays not only appeared on numerous cards during his playing days, but several of those cards rank amongst the toughest and most important of the era. Collecting all of Mays' cards is not for the faint of heart, but it does take the collector on an impressive journey that touches just about every brand and type of collectible imaginable during the period.

It all started in the 1951 Bowman set, when Mays made his cardboard debut. Thankfully for collectors, this is his only true rookie card, but that is where the simplicity ends. Immediately following Mays' first hobby appearance, he was included in various mainstream, regional, and test issues as the decade progressed. In addition to his inclusion in Topps' release in 1952, Mays can be found in sets like Berk Ross, Coca-Cola Playing Tips (test), and Red Man Tobacco. One of Mays' more underrated cards is his 1952 Bowman, which is overshadowed by his first Topps appearance that same year. Mays was included in every Bowman and Topps set during their rivalry, except for the 1953 Bowman set.

Before the decade ended, Mays was included in some other great sets, like the 1958 Hires Root Beer, 1959 Bazooka, and 1959 Home Run Derby. The Hires issue is collected with or without the large tab intact, with the intact version being much tougher to find. As we venture into the 1960s, the Mays cards really start to pile up. The mediums to include Mays were not limited to cards either. Mays appeared on collectibles such as coins, decals, faux currency, peel-offs, pin-ups, rub-offs, stamps, stickers, tattoos, and transfers. He was a part of several multi-player cards, which date back to the 1950s for Mays, and his most desirable issue of all is the 1962 Topps *Managers' Dream* card where he is pictured with Mickey Mantle. In addition, along with Roberto Clemente and Sandy Koufax, Mays was an anchor in the 1963 Fleer release.

In 1966, Mays was selected by Topps to take the #1 card slot in their annual set. In addition to being subjected to the usual wear and tear associated with cards at the top of the stack, the Mays card is often found with a tilt to the picture, which can produce undesirable centering. From the late-1960s through the end of his career, Mays appeared in more Topps test sets like the 1967 Punch-Outs, 1968 Plaks (Checklist #2), and 1972 Candy Lids. He also found himself in new regional issues like Kellogg's and Milk Duds as his career wound down. Although a handful of Mays cards were produced in 1974, Mays' last regular Topps card was released in 1973 (#305).

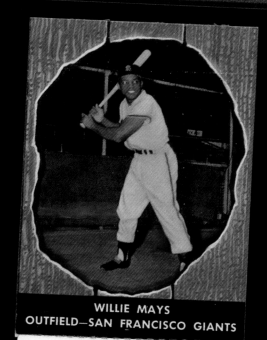

The WILLIE MAYS CARD

Like fellow superstars Mantle and Whitey Ford, Mays made his debut in the 1951 Bowman set. While there were a few hundred Mays collectibles produced during his playing career, his only official rookie card is the one that garners the most attention. Mays' first Topps issue (1952) is also desirable, but it never surpassed the importance of his true rookie. The opposite, of course, is true for Mantle. Mays also appeared on some incredibly-tough regional and Topps test issues, cards that clearly exceed the sheer scarcity of his Bowman rookie, but the popularity of his first card outweighs the rarity alone. When you consider the beauty of the artwork and the power of the three key rookie cards, it's not surprising that the 1951 Bowman set remains one of the most coveted issues of all time. Thus, the Mays rookie card takes the title.

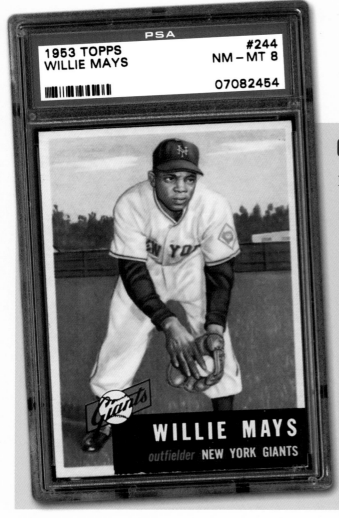

"The image, by itself, exemplifies baseball card collecting."

ONE CARD TO WATCH

Picking the Mays card that rises above all others was easy compared to selecting one of his cards to watch. The collector concentration on rookie cards is what puts his 1951 Bowman over the top, but narrowing this section down to one Mays card is another story. In all three decades, Mays appears on many cards that fit the bill. From the virtually impossible 1953–54 Briggs Meats card to the almost never-seen 1961 Topps Dice Game issue to the intriguing 1972 Topps test Candy Lid, the options are seemingly endless. Ultimately, I selected the classic 1953 Topps Mays. The artwork of Mays making a basket catch is stunning. The card was also a short print and is tough to find in high grade due to obstacles like the black bottom border. In fact, it is clearly tougher than the other major key in the set, the Mantle. Beyond its technical attributes, this Mays card possesses a symbolic quality that is superior to those previously-mentioned Mays rarities. The image, by itself, exemplifies baseball card collecting.

BILL MAZEROSKI

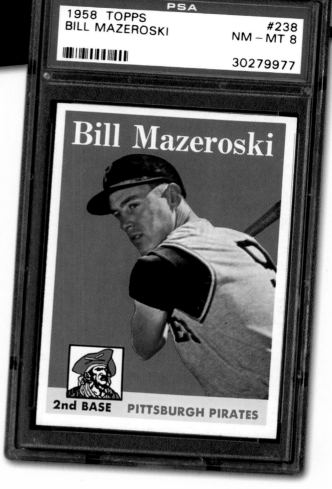

WHEN MAZEROSKI PLAYED, he was noted as the best second baseman in the game. Bill had tremendous quickness and made the double play better than any other second baseman I've ever seen. He won a ton of Gold Gloves and deserved every one of them. His hands were so quick. It was amazing how fast the ball came out of his glove. He was an outstanding fielder and was proficient at flipping the ball. Bill was a good hitter, not a great hitter. Of course, the 1960 World Series home run was the highlight of his hitting career.

Mazeroski was also a terrific guy. We went to Puerto Rico together in 1968, along with some of the other All-Stars, to do a clinic and make an instructional film for MLB. It was called *The Name of the Game is Baseball* and was narrated by Curt Gowdy. We had a blast filming it. Bill was a very funny guy. We had a great time, just talking about general stuff. I asked him how it was to play in Pittsburgh, since their ballpark, Forbes Field, was gigantic.

He told me that it was so far to center field that they kept the batting cage out there during the game. He joked that he would take batting practice in between innings. The ball he hit in the World Series went a distance of about 400 feet. That was amazing because he wasn't a home run hitter, but, you know, every once in a while you catch one.

In those days, if you talked about third base, it was Brooks Robinson and if you talked about second base, it was Bill Mazeroski, period. I watched him closely and learned to work on my hand quickness and first step because of Bill. Early on, the Pirates were fair but they became a really good team when Clemente and the rest of the gang came on board. Mazeroski was so quick that he could flip the ball to make the double play and that saved his pitchers extra throws. Bill and Dick Groat were something to see, an excellent double play combination. Later on, Gene Alley and Mazeroski were a terrific double play combination, too. Actually, Mazeroski was so good that he became the measuring stick for all second basemen. I think that he still holds the record for double plays.

That walk-off home run in Game Seven in the 1960 World Series off the Yankees Ralph Terry is one of the greatest moments in Series history. I put it right up there with Carlton Fisk's home run in the 1975 Series. As a matter of fact, it was more important because it won the Series for Pittsburgh. I haven't seen Bill in years. I know they have a statue of him at the ballpark, which he truly deserves. After all, he played second base for the Pirates for his whole career, 17 years, and they won two World Series during that time. Mazeroski was the complete player. He was not a power hitter but he could get his bat on the ball, he hit for decent average, and he was an outstanding fielder. There was never any controversy about Bill. He was a real team guy and he was well-liked by everyone. Bill's induction into the Hall of Fame came later than it should have.

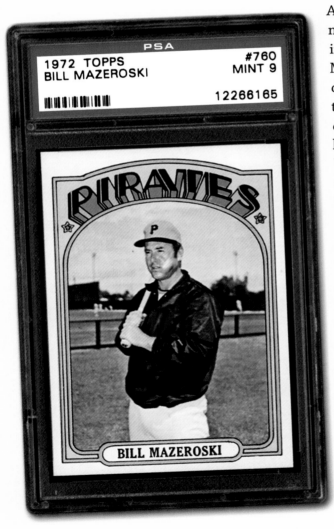

THE CARDS

Since Bill Mazeroski was known much more for his fielding ability versus his skill with the bat, collectors tended to overlook him as he played in an era of super sluggers like Hank Aaron, Mickey Mantle, and Willie Mays. This means his cards are, for the most part, relatively affordable compared to most contemporary stars. That said, Mazeroski's defining moment came with the bat in his hands when he ended the 1960 World Series with a walk-off homer in Game Seven. Fans and collectors will never forget him because of that magical event, and being a part of the beloved Pittsburgh Pirates adds to his appeal.

After making his first mainstream appearance in the 1957 Topps set, Mazeroski would appear on dozens of cards throughout the remainder of his playing career. This included some key regional issues. Kahn's Wieners produced cards over a 15-year period beginning in 1955. From 1957 to 1969, Mazeroski was a staple in this popular series. During the 1950s, he also appeared in two other major regional sets, 1958 Hires Root Beer and 1959 Bazooka. The Hires card can be challenging to find with the large tab intact and the Bazooka issue required careful removal by hand from the box, so high-grade examples are rarely found. Bazooka would make several other Mazeroski cards in the following years.

The next decade produced most of Mazeroski's cards, with Topps clearly in control as the leading mainstream brand. One of the more interesting, yet affordable, Mazeroski issues is his 1961 Topps World Series Game Seven card (#312). It captures the most memorable moment of his career from the previous season's Fall Classic. His famous homer was also captured in the 1961 Nu-Card Scoops set. A couple of years later, Mazeroski joined a group of Hall of Famers in the 1963 Fleer set. The 67-card set (66 individual cards plus one checklist) has a very clean design and the cards were packed with a cookie instead of gum to compete with Topps. It would be their first-and-last major effort of the decade.

Before his career ended, Mazeroski was included in numerous sets outside of the dominant Topps brand such as Exhibit, Jell-O, and Post Cereal. More importantly, Topps produced numerous complementary Mazeroski cards and collectibles in addition to his regular annual issue. The non-card mediums include coins, peel-offs, rub-offs, stamps, stickers, and tattoos. Two of the tougher Mazeroski cards to find are the 1967 Topps test Punch-Outs issue, a card that was intended to act as a game instead of a traditional baseball card, and his 1970 Topps Candy Lid. Mazeroski's last mainstream card can be found in the 1972 Topps set on card #760, which is a set that many collectors feel is the best-looking Topps release of the decade.

The BILL MAZEROSKI CARD

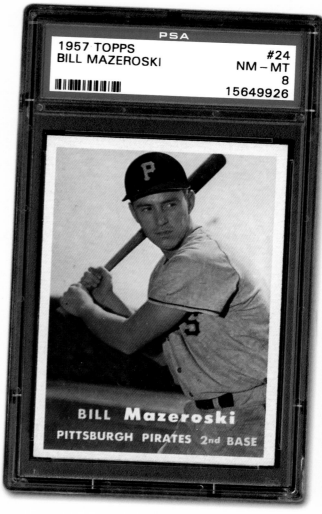

Collectors love rookie cards and there is no exception when it comes to Mazeroski. The slick-fielding second baseman made his debut on card #24 in the 1957 Topps set, one that is filled with important first cards. Joining Mazeroski in the set are rookie cards of Hall of Famers Don Drysdale, Frank Robinson, Brooks Robinson, and Jim Bunning. After incorporating colorful artwork or colorized images into all their annual sets from 1952 to 1956, Topps decided to go with a more simplistic approach in 1957. Photography became the focal point of the fronts, which clearly distinguished this Topps effort from prior releases. Two key condition obstacles to be aware of are subpar centering since the borders are well-defined, and print defects that often tatter the background. Mazeroski's card is one of the most affordable Hall of Famer rookies of the 1950s.

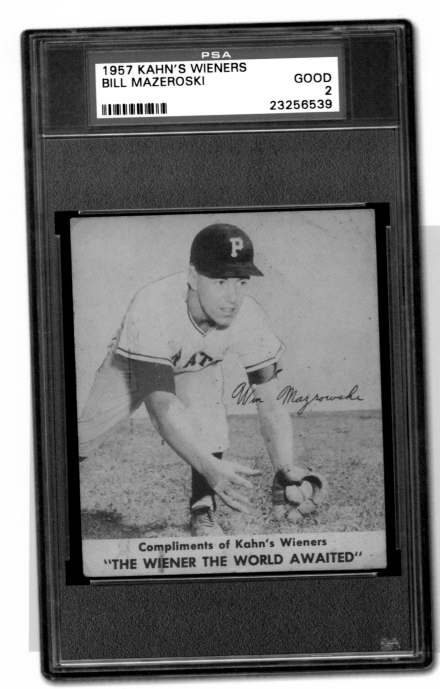

ONE CARD TO WATCH

There was a time when regional cards played a huge role in the hobby. In fact, some of the most important, desirable, and valuable cards made decades ago were of the regional variety, often surpassing the value of many mainstream cards. Kahn's Wieners was one of the brands that consistently produced baseball cards sets in the 1950s and 1960s. It all began in Cincinnati with a six-card set of Reds players in 1955, which expanded to 15 cards the following year. In 1957, Kahn's included a second team, the Pittsburgh Pirates. This opened the door to players like Roberto Clemente and Mazeroski. This is not only one of his earliest cards, matching the 1957 Topps rookie, but it is easily one of his most valuable. In fact, the simple black-and-white issue is far tougher to locate in any grade than his Topps card. Rarely offered for sale, the 1957 Kahn's Mazeroski is one to watch in the future.

BROOKS ROBINSON

I COULD SPEND HOURS talking about Brooks, not only on the field, but off the field. A real gentleman and a class guy, he was friendly and outgoing, and we became good friends. We would joke with each other and have a few laughs when either he was on third base or I was on third base. Brooks was such a great third baseman. He had that first step. He was so quick and his anticipation was amazing. Brooks had an uncanny ability to go both ways and he was a magician at backhanding the ball. He was also outstanding at handling the bunt. Frank Malzone, my mentor when I made the switch to third, was the only other guy who could field the bunt like Brooks.

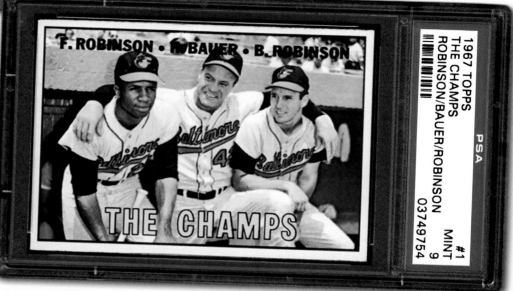

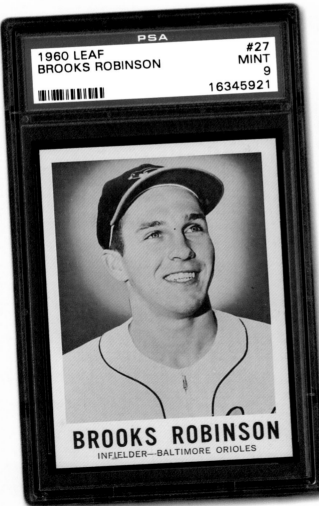

I studied Brooks a lot when I switched positions, hoping to pick up some pointers. When we would play the Orioles and I was in the dugout, I would focus on Brooks, closely watching his every defensive move. Did he have that first step because he was anticipating, or was it a God-given ability? Brooks was a solid hitter and had a great stance. He had that sweet swing and could hit the ball to all fields. At the plate he could go the opposite way. He'd take a fastball, low and away, and go the opposite way. He was also a clutch hitter and got some big home runs. Brooks was actually a better hitter than he gets credit for. Everyone talks about his glove, and can you blame them? He saved so many runs for his team defensively that it was mind boggling. I have Brooks in the top two third basemen of modern times, along with Mike Schmidt.

Off the field, we did a few fantasy camps together. There was one fantasy camp that the Red Sox did jointly with the Orioles. Brooks and I talked a lot about the present day players. He loved Mike Schmidt. When we travelled to Puerto Rico with the All-Stars in the 1960s, his wife Connie and my wife Elsie hit it off and we all had a great time together. Especially after we got to know each other better in Puerto Rico, he would always ask about the family when we were shooting the breeze on third base.

I'll never forget when Tom Phoebus, the Orioles pitcher, threw a no-hitter against us. That was in April of 1968. We were the defending champs and Phoebus had been the AL Rookie Pitcher of the Year in 1967, so we were expecting it to be a battle. Brooks robbed me of a hit in that game. I hit a line drive in the eighth between short and third. Brooks extended himself parallel to the ground and made an absolutely spectacular catch to save the no-hitter for Phoebus.

Brooks Robinson truly deserved to be a first ballot Hall of Famer. As an MVP, perennial Gold Glover, and All-Star, he was one of the best. I am not ashamed to say that I admired him as an opponent and as a man. Both on the field and off the field, he was a great ambassador to the game. I was proud to know him and his wonderful family. I still wish that ball I hit got by him though!

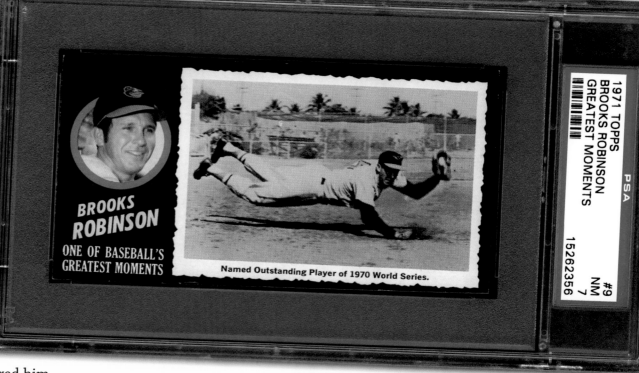

THE CARDS

It would be hard to name a player who is as well-liked by fans and collectors as Brooks Robinson. Robinson's personable nature only elevates his standing in the hobby after having such a terrific career. That 23-year career led to the production of dozens of Robinson cards, from the mainstream staples to the esoteric obscurities. The perennial Gold Glover checks all the boxes that help make a player a favorite in the collecting world, from his AL MVP in 1964 to his world championships in 1966 and 1970 to his reputation as a human being away from the field. What's not to like?

Robinson made his first hobby appearance in the 1957 Topps set, a set that veered away from the general design that collectors had come to know from Topps. Instead, simple photography replaced the colorful approach. The Robinson rookie is not only one of the most valuable cards in the set, it is also one of the best looking. Robinson became a regular with Topps, but he was one of only a handful of stars to appear in the 1960 Leaf set. This black-and-white issue never really caught on with collectors, but Robinson is one of the keys. He also made an appearance in the 1963 Fleer set, a relatively small yet popular non-Topps issue of the decade.

The 1960s produced more Robinson cards and collectibles than any other. In addition to the regular Topps sets, Robinson was part of several related sets like O-Pee-Chee (Canadian) and the tough Venezuelan Topps productions. Including Topps and others, various non-card mediums were made with Robinson's image as well. They included coins, peel-offs, pin-ups, rub-offs, stamps, and transfers. Beyond Topps, Robinson can be found in plenty of other issues, such as Bazooka, Exhibit, Nabisco, and Post Cereal. Several of these issues required the collector to remove the card by hand from a box. Some of the more interesting Robinson cards of the decade include Topps test issues like the elusive 1968 Action All-Star Stickers and the attractive 1969 Super set.

During the last leg of Robinson's career, the cards kept coming for the longtime Oriole. Perhaps one of his most interesting cards of the 1970s is his 1971 Topps Greatest Moments card. This oversized, condition-sensitive, and somewhat scarce issue captures Robinson doing what he did best—fielding. It showcases the star third baseman in full dive mode in honor of his incredible all-around performance in the 1970 World Series when he was named MVP. This was a signature moment in his great career, as Robinson flashed his leather on the big stage. Robinson's final regular card appeared in the 1977 Topps set (#285), but he can also be found in the 1978 Topps issue on a *Record Breaker* card (#4).

The BROOKS ROBINSON CARD

When it comes to identifying the Robinson card that stands above the rest, there's not much to debate. Robinson did play in three different decades and was a fan favorite, so there are plenty of cards to choose from, but few of them can even make a case for consideration. The 1957 Topps set contains several key rookie cards, including those of Don Drysdale, Bill Mazeroski, Frank Robinson, and Jim Bunning. The Brooks rookie (#328), however, is arguably the most desirable of the bunch. Many of the cards within the set possess a rather dull look due to the design. That is not the case with this classic card. The Robinson rookie has a bright appearance. The light-colored background and large portrait of the Hall of Famer make it one of the best-looking cards in the set. That light background, however, can also be a haven for dark print defects, which is one of the condition obstacles for the card.

"The 1957 Topps set contains several key rookie cards . . . the Brooks rookie (#328), however, is arguably the most desirable of the bunch."

ONE CARD TO WATCH

This was tough. Let's get that out of the way right from the start. In the end, it came down to two Robinson cards. The 1967 Topps and 1971 Topps Greatest Moments issues are both desirable but very different. I went with the 1967 Topps Robinson and here's why. Exactly 10 years after Robinson made his cardboard debut and one year after winning a World Series, he found himself in the high-number series on card #600 in one of the cleanest designs of the decade. This visually-appealing Robinson card is the second-most valuable non-rookie in the set, only taking a back seat to Mickey Mantle. Of course, the two key rookies are those of Rod Carew and Tom Seaver. While the set is not considered a condition-sensitive one, subpar centering is common to the issue and the green-colored back is susceptible to chipping. The mainstream appeal of the set and importance within it gave this card the edge as one to watch in the future.

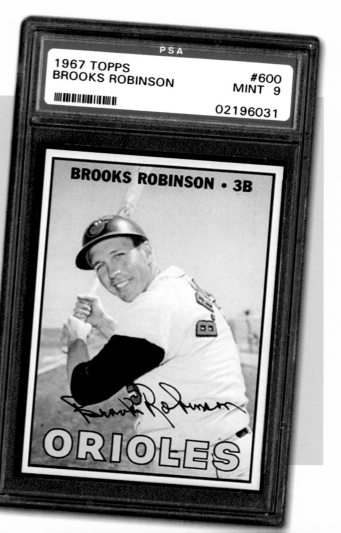

FRANK ROBINSON

WHAT CAN YOU SAY about Frank Robinson? I like Frank. He was a fiery competitor, and man, could he hit. He won the Triple Crown, was the MVP in both leagues, hit almost 600 home runs, and won two World Series. Not a bad resume! After we moved to Winter Haven, and Frank was still with Cincinnati, we played them a lot during spring training because they were close by, in Tampa. Frank was a heck of a player. When he went over to the Orioles, you could see he wanted to prove something. The Reds thought Frank had seen his best years so they traded him to Baltimore for Milt Pappas and a few other guys. I think it's considered one of the worst deals in baseball history. Anyway, that's when Frank started to play with a vengeance.

That first year with Baltimore, Frank crushed the ball. Those Orioles teams were a real pain in the neck for us. With Frank and Brooks, along with Paul Blair, Boog Powell, and their stud pitchers, they were really good. Robinson was a fearless hitter. He stood right on the plate and just dared you to throw it inside. Frank got hit a lot, but he didn't care. He would brush himself off and get you the next time. He was a legitimate home run hitter who also hit for average and RBI, and his clutch hitting was just incredible.

Frank was a little chippy when he played, but he was a real team man who got along great with his teammates and helped them a lot. Frank was the Orioles' "Kangaroo Court" leader and he good-naturedly fined players for any infraction he could think up. They had a lot of laughs. He and Brooks got along great, too. My last year at shortstop, Frank and I dusted up a few times. On a double play, I knew he would come sliding in very hard, but fair, and I perfected the art of jumping over him. Frank was an outstanding baserunner. As a fielder he was adequate. He just wasn't fast enough to get a good jump on the ball.

There is one regular season game that really stands

BIRDIE'S YOUNG SLUGGERS
BAILEY • BIRDIE TEBBETS • FRANK ROBINSON

pieces or body parts that could be punched out and assembled into a full body and used for a board game.

In 1958, Robinson would be included on his first multi-player card in a Topps set. The card was entitled *Birdie's Young Sluggers* and pictured Robinson alongside teammate Ed Bailey and manager Birdie Tebbetts. It would be the first of several multi-player cards to feature Robinson before his career was over. Just one year later, Robinson would be included in in the 1959 Home Run Derby set. American Motors produced this unnumbered 20-card set to help bring attention to the new television program *Home Run Derby*, a show that pitted the top sluggers in baseball against each other. The black-and-white cards had blank backs and were oversized, measuring approximately 3¼" by 5¼".

During the 1960s and 1970s, Robinson was included in many non-mainstream mediums and brands. Topps produced collectibles such as Robinson candy lids, coins, decals, faux currency, peel-offs, rub-offs, stamps, stickers, and tattoos. One of Robinson's most elusive cards was a checklist (#1) produced for the 1968 Topps Plaks set, which was a test issue comprised of miniature plastic player busts. Beyond Kahn's, Robinson appeared in plenty of non-Topps brands like Bazooka, Dexter Press, Exhibit, Jay Publishing, Kellogg's, Milk Duds, Nabisco, and Post Cereal. Robinson's final mainstream Topps single appeared in the 1975 set (#580), but several regional issues were released afterwards with most being collectible discs.

out in my mind. It was at Fenway Park in 1973 and Frank was DH for the Angels. Bob Bolin came in as a reliever. Bob was kind of a nasty pitcher. The first pitch he threw was right at Frank's head. Apparently Frank and Bob had some history in the National League. Anyway, it was one of the best knockdowns that I ever saw. Frank hit the dirt and fell flat on his back. He slowly got up and started jawing at Carlton Fisk, our catcher. He thought Fisk had called the knockdown. Frank wiped himself off and got back in the box, really peeved. Bolin's next pitch was hit so hard, I think it could have hit the CITGO sign in Kenmore Square. It was a rocket. As Frank rounded third base, he started yelling at Fisk again, and Carlton is just standing there saying, "What did I do?" In the meantime, Bolin has this look on his face like, "Nice job, you got me back." That was Frank. Even towards the end of his career, he was still a great competitor.

THE CARDS

When fans search through the history books and try to select a player who they consider the most underrated of all time, Frank Robinson is a name that constantly comes up. Despite putting up numbers that rivaled the best in the business, including the likes of Hank Aaron, Mickey Mantle, and Willie Mays, Robinson was overshadowed by the superstars of the era. The good news for collectors is that his cards and collectibles are still overlooked, which means many Robinson items will not break the bank like those of some contemporary stars.

Robinson made his mainstream hobby debut in the 1957 Topps set, which featured photography on each front. It was the first Topps set to veer from the heavy use of color after the 1952–1956 run. Kahn's Wieners produced cards over a 15-year period beginning in 1955. For several years, Robinson was a staple in this popular series, and technically, his first Kahn's appearance in 1956 predates his Topps debut. That same year, Swift Meats also created a set that contained 18 cards. The cards could be obtained by purchasing a package of their hot dogs or directly through the mail. Each card contained player

The FRANK ROBINSON CARD

Like most Hall of Famers who entered the league in the 1950s, Robinson has a mainstream rookie card that garners most of the attention from collectors. The 1957 Topps set contains several key rookie cards, including those of Don Drysdale, Bill Mazeroski, Brooks Robinson, Jim Bunning, and of course, Frank Robinson. This card (#35) remains one of the most valuable cards in the set, along with some of the other rookie cards and singles like those of Ted Williams, Mantle, and Sandy Koufax. It has also been picking up market momentum in recent years as more collectors are appreciating how underrated Robinson was as a player. In addition to being the official rookie card of this incredible all-around talent, it is also a reminder of the great rookie campaign Robinson had. It still ranks up there as one of the best in history and he was appropriately named NL Rookie of the Year for his performance. The background on the card can be a haven for print defects that are often referred to as "snow," which is one of the condition obstacles for the card.

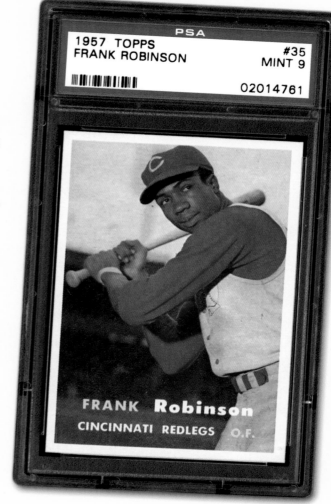

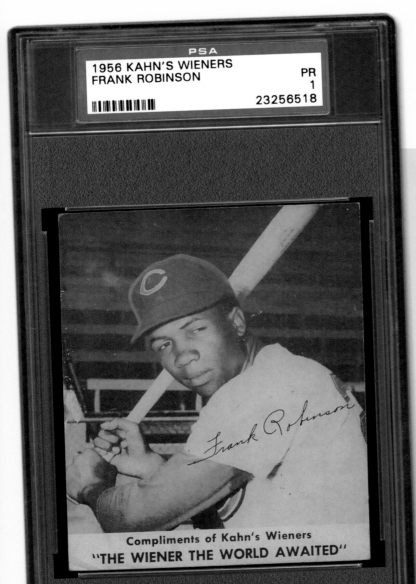

ONE CARD TO WATCH

There was a time when regional cards played a huge role in the hobby. In fact, some of the most important, desirable, and valuable cards made decades ago were of the regional variety, often surpassing the value of many mainstream cards. Kahn's Wieners was one of the brands that consistently produced baseball cards sets in the 1950s and 1960s, with Robinson appearing in many of them. It all began in Cincinnati with a six-card set of Reds players in 1955, which expanded to 15 cards the following year. It was that year when Robinson made his debut on an unnumbered card that was released slightly earlier than his 1957 Topps rookie. In fact, the simple black-and-white 1956 Kahn's issue is far tougher to locate in any grade than his Topps card, easily the key to the set and rarely offered for sale. It's not quite as valuable as the 1959 Home Run Derby card or as scarce as the 1968 Topps Plaks Checklist card, nor does it possess the mainstream appeal of his 1957 Topps rookie, but it offers a combination of intriguing attributes that make it one to watch.

RON SANTO

A VERY, VERY GOOD THIRD BASEMAN, Ron Santo was not quite in the same category as Mike Schmidt or Brooks Robinson. Other than those two, Santo was right up there with some of the best, and he is possibly the greatest third baseman in Cubs history. Ron was a good clutch hitter and could spray the ball all over. He hit for power and was a real RBI machine. Defensively, he was sure-handed, winning a slew of Gold Gloves over the years. As much as Ernie Banks was Mr. Cub, Ron Santo was definitely next in the pecking order. Cubs fans loved him. He was such a good all-around player, year after year, for the Cubs. Santo was never controversial and he always exemplified professionalism.

I really admired Ron for that professionalism. He had Type 1 Diabetes but he kept that a secret for many years. Thankfully, he was able to control it.

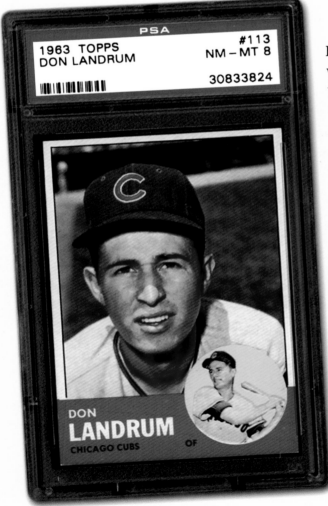

Keep in mind that treating diabetes was more difficult back then with the blood testing and all that went with it. To watch Santo play, you would never know he had a medical issue. He was professional all the way. Ron and I spent a lot of time talking down in spring training. You know how it goes when two paisans get together. We talked about Chicago, our Italian heritage, and of course, food. He had to be careful what he ate, especially because he loved pasta.

It's interesting that Ron was instrumental in my move to third base. The Red Sox told me they eventually wanted to move me to third, but they wanted me to stay at short for a while longer. During the winter meetings our manager, Eddie Kasko, was looking for a third baseman. He was particularly interested in Ron Santo. Then I got a call from Eddie. He said the Cubs were not going to give Santo up, and he asked if I would make the move to third base the next year, 1971. He said he thought we could get Luis Aparicio. In his opinion, Aparicio could still do a good job at short, and he could help us out. Of course, I said no problem. After all, Luis was the best in the league. I was more than happy to make the move in order to get Luis on the team, and the rest is history. It sure would have been fun to play short with Ron on third, though.

Santo knocked in a lot of runs in his career and he was very competitive on the basepaths. He wasn't afraid to rough it up with you if he had to. I could never figure out why it took so long for him to get into the Hall of Fame. His numbers were not spectacular, but they were better than some players who were already in the Hall at that time. Although his batting average was a little above average, he had over 2,000 hits and over 300 home runs, and he was an All-Star so many years. After Santo was done as a player, he did color for the Cubs for a long time and he was very entertaining. As the years went on, the diabetes began to catch up with him. When Ron passed away, I was genuinely sad. He was such a great guy and a great competitor.

THE CARDS

If you are a collector already, then what I am about to tell you isn't going to be news. The general rule in the hobby is that the Hall of Fame blessing is often crucial to the value of a player's cards and collectibles, since so many hobbyists create themes around those who are part of the hallowed halls. There are exceptions, however, like Shoeless Joe Jackson, Roger Maris, and Pete Rose. Furthermore, the longer it takes a player to get in, the more it seems to impact the value. The result for someone like Santo is that most of his collectibles are reasonably priced, despite being a Hall of Famer, which is good news for collectors.

Around the time Santo entered the league, several cards were made bearing his image. Beyond his mainstream rookie card in the 1961 Topps set, Topps also produced a Santo stamp that same year. Bazooka, Post Cereal, and Wilson also joined the action in 1961, in

addition to Jay Publishing who produced collectible black-and-white photos. Following his debut, Santo continued to appear in Topps and regional sets throughout the decade. In 1963, Santo was one of the stars included in the modest-sized Fleer set. The 66-card issue, plus one checklist, offers a clean design that remains popular with collectors.

Interestingly, Topps made an error in 1963 by using an image of Santo on a card intended for Don Landrum (#113). Santo does have his own 1963 Topps card (#252), but the Landrum is a great conversation piece. As the decade progressed, Santo was included on various mediums, including coins, decals, discs, pins, and transfers. These collectibles were of the mainstream and regional variety. In 1964, Topps produced a handful of complementary sets to their base issue. Two of Santo's most interesting cards were included, the seldom seen 1964 Topps Rookie All-Star Banquet card and the colorful 1964 Topps Stand-Up.

"*Interestingly, Topps made an error in 1963 by using an image of Santo on a card intended for Don Landrum (#113).*"

Before the decade was over, Santo found himself in various sets including Exhibit, Jell-O, Kahn's, Nabisco, O-Pee-Chee, Venezuelan Topps, and Wheaties. Santo can also be found in some Topps test issues like 1967 Punch-Outs, 1968 Action Stickers, and 1969 Super. The toughest Topps test issue, and maybe Santo's most valuable card of all, is his 1967 Topps Stand-Up card. As we turn the corner into the 1970s, brands like Kellogg's and Milk Duds included Santo to their releases. Santo's final Topps card (#35) can be found in the 1975 Topps set. Keep in mind that a mini version of the same card was released the same year and is popular with collectors.

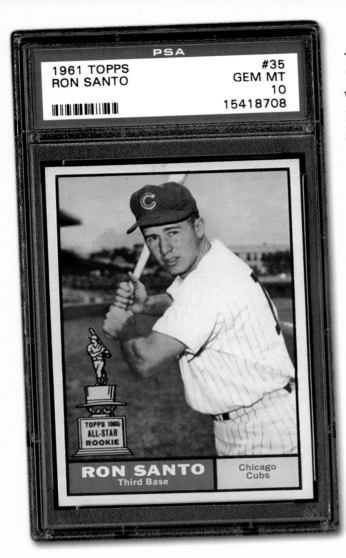

The RON SANTO CARD

When it comes to vintage cards, the pattern is usually consistent. In most cases, a player's debut card stands alone. At worst, it might share the limelight with one other card made during the same year. In the case of Santo, the opposite is true. During his rookie era, several cards were made of the slugging third baseman. The card that garners most of the attention, however, is his mainstream Topps rookie card (#35). Santo shares the rookie limelight with fellow Hall of Famer and former teammate Billy Williams, in addition to Juan Marichal. The 587-card set is not known to be a condition-sensitive issue, but finding well-centered copies absent print defects can be challenging. The Santo card is one of the most affordable Hall of Fame rookies of the period, which is partially a result of the time it took for him to enter Cooperstown. Regardless, of all the Santo cards produced during his playing career, this is the one most collectors pursue.

ONE CARD TO WATCH

Throughout the 1960s, Topps produced several test issues that were never intended for distribution, but they eventually made their way into the hobby over time. In 1967, Topps created a 24-card set that contained color photos of each player against a black background. The color headshots were designed with a die-cut so they could be popped out. Once that occurred, each card could stand up on its own. In addition to the die-cut versions produced on thick stock, proofs were made without the die-cut feature on thinner stock. The diminutive set contained several big names like Hank Aaron, Willie Mays, and Mickey Mantle, in addition to Santo (#22). That star power combined with the card's incredible scarcity and unique design make this issue, arguably, Santo's most intriguing card outside of his 1961 Topps rookie. Santo appeared on dozens of cards throughout his playing career, but his stand-up card truly stands out.

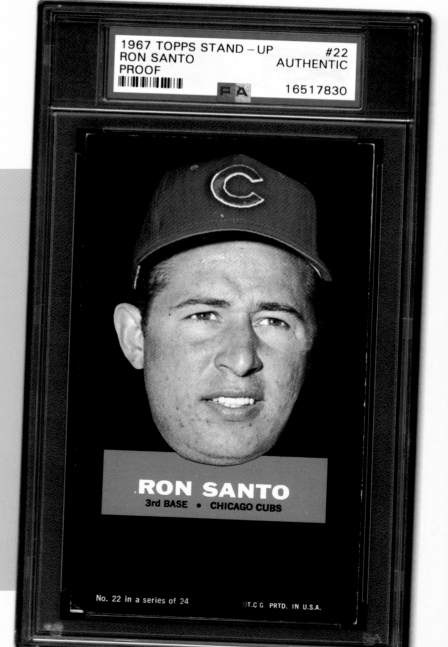

JOE TORRE

JOE TORRE AND I GO WAY BACK, all the way to sandlot ball. He played for the Cadets in Brooklyn, a very good amateur team that played in a very good league and drew a lot of major league scouts. Most of the better ballplayers in the area wanted to play for the Cadets. I was fortunate to play for them three or four years later. By that time, Joe had signed. I remember the first time I saw him. I was trying to get on the Cadets team and had gone to a game to meet with their manager. Joe was the Cadets catcher and was a big guy who looked way older than his age. That day, I watched Joe step up to the plate and nail a pitch to right-center field. I'd say that ball traveled at least 400 feet. The scouts were in the stands and they were all over him.

I connected with Joe several years later in spring training, when he was with the Cardinals. He was a really friendly guy off the field. We hit it off because we are both Italian and we both grew up in Brooklyn. So, besides baseball, we talked about Brooklyn, our neighborhoods, and growing up Italian with a lot of the same traditions. Joe had a tougher time at home with some family issues that are well-documented, but the food was the same. Sometimes when a family situation is difficult, a person can go off the rails a bit. Joe never did. He was like a gentle giant, always friendly and level-headed. He never panicked in tight situations. Joe was always very well-respected by his teammates and the fans.

Joe and I played against each other in the 1967 All-Star Game, but ironically, neither one of us got a hit. He was an outstanding catcher and an excellent RBI guy who could hit the ball to all fields and had some power. I remember, in 1971, he led the league in RBI and batting average. That was the year he was the NL MVP. Off the field, Joe and I sometimes talked about things like different counts and how he would shorten up with two strikes just to make contact. I didn't choke up. I should have! As I recall Joe hit .363 one year for the Cards.

Joe and I bumped into each other quite a bit at Fenway when he was managing the Yankees. We would shoot the breeze and I always wished him good luck—against every team except the Red Sox. He wasn't such a successful manager at first, but so what? The same thing happened to Tito. Their teams just didn't have the talent. They both did become very good managers. You know, even if you have talent on your team, you still need to manage them.

As a player, Joe had a helluva career. He hit for average, hit for power, and banged out over 2,000 hits. Defensively, Joe was very good, a Gold Glover. He managed for a long time, about 30 years. Joe was not as successful managing the Mets, Braves, Cardinals, or Dodgers, but as manager of the Yankees, he won four World Series. How can you beat that? Joe Torre was the real deal and a great asset to the game. I respect him as a great player, a great manager, and a great human being.

THE CARDS

Technically speaking, Joe Torre entered the Hall of Fame as a manager and not a player, but many people forget just how good of a player he was. When you consider all of Torre's accomplishments, you could argue that he came the closest to having a Cooperstown-caliber career in both the player and manager professions. Since he entered the hallowed halls as a manager instead of a player, most of Torre's cards from his playing days remain relatively affordable even though he was a perennial All-Star. For two decades, Torre appeared on well over 100 different cards and collectibles.

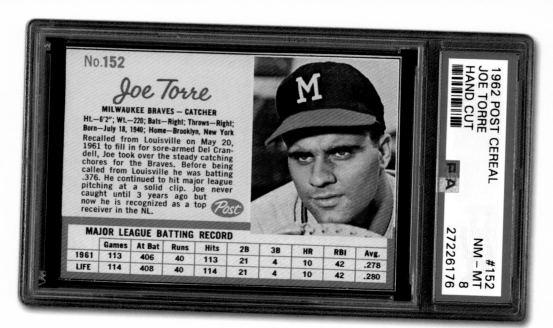

Torre made his mainstream debut in the 1962 Topps set, one of the toughest issues of the decade to complete in high grade. Within the same set, Torre can be seen on a multi-player card alongside teammate Del Crandall entitled *Braves' Backstops*. It was clear that the young talent was identified as the heir apparent to Crandall, an All-Star catcher himself. Like fellow Hall of Famer Ron Santo who made his debut a year earlier, Torre was included on a handful of other cards and collectibles as well in 1962. Two popular regional brands, Jell-O and Post Cereal, produced Torre cards that year, and he even appeared on a Topps stamp and a Salada coin.

As the decade progressed, Torre found himself in various regional issues. This included brands like Ashland Oil, Bazooka, Irvindale Dairy, and Kahn's. The Kahn's cards have always been especially popular with collectors due to their large size and colorful design. Torre, like many other period stars, appeared on various mediums as well such as pin-ups, rub-offs, and stickers. This included a few different coin issues created by companies like Old London, CITGO, and of

course, Topps in 1964. O-Pee-Chee (Canadian) and Venezuelan Topps issued Torre cards throughout the period as complements to the regular Topps cards. Some of Torre's more interesting Topps cards of the 1960s include the rarely seen 1964 Topps Rookie All-Star Banquet card, the eye-catching 1964 Stand-Up issue, and the 1969 Topps Super test card.

After becoming one of baseball's best catchers for the Braves, Torre joined the Cardinals and moved to third base where the star enjoyed his finest season in 1971. The accolades and the cards kept coming. Beyond Topps, brands like Hostess, Kellogg's, and Milk Duds created Torre cards. Two of the toughest Torre collectibles ever made were born in 1973 and created by Topps: the Comics and Pin-Ups sets. Both are rare test issues. In 1976, several Torre discs were released by companies such as Buckmans, Carousel, Crane Potato Chips, Dairy Isle, Isaly's/Sweet William, Michael Schechter Associates, Orbaker's, and Towne Club. Apparently, it was disc mania during disco times. Torre's final mainstream card was part of the 1978 Topps set (#109).

The JOE TORRE CARD

In 1962, Topps decided to change things up by moving away from the traditional white borders used on most of their productions and instead implemented a frame that replicated wood grain. It bore some similarity to Bowman's 1955 effort. The new card frame ranged in appearance from a light tan color to a darker, rich patina depending on the card. So, not only did Topps introduce a completely new look, they also created a 598-card set that is clearly the most condition-sensitive regular Topps issue of the decade. The colored edges reveal the slightest touch of wear, making high-grade copies challenging to come by. Thankfully, some Topps Presentation sets have made their way into the hobby over the years. These premade sets were given as gifts to executives and others, packaged in a similar manner to modern-era factory sets. The Torre card (#218) is one of three key rookie cards in the set, along with fellow Hall of Famer debut singles featuring Gaylord Perry and Lou Brock.

ONE CARD TO WATCH

When it comes to Torre, most of the cards and collectibles bearing his image can be obtained for less than $100 each... even in high grade. There are exceptions to the rule, which include some of the tough Topps test issues manufactured in the 1960s and 1970s. There are also plenty of popular regional Torre cards to choose from, especially those that were released near the beginning of his career. That said, we chose to go with his 1964 Topps Stand-Up here. This 77-card set includes those of standard size, but the design is what separates it from so many others made during his career. These unnumbered, blank-backed cards were die-cut so the images of the players could be popped out from their vibrant backgrounds. The player selection, pound-for-pound, is outstanding. The likes of Hank Aaron, Sandy Koufax, Mickey Mantle, and Willie Mays are all here. Furthermore, 22 of the 77 cards were short prints. In 1964, Torre was really starting to come into his own, posting the first big season of his career. The combination of the set's eye-catching design, star selection, and popularity help make this Torre card one to watch.

HOYT WILHELM

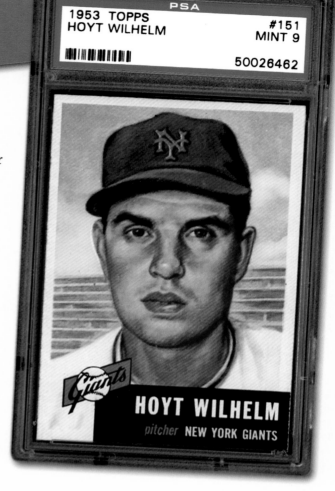

**1953 TOPPS
HOYT WILHELM**
#151
MINT 9
50026462

HOYT HAD AN EXTREMELY TOUGH KNUCKLEBALL to hit because he had some speed on it. You know, with a slow knuckler you have a chance to adjust and follow it down, but with a little faster one like Hoyt threw, it was pretty tough to make contact. Wilhelm was primarily a reliever, and a darn good one. I faced him for the first time in 1965, my rookie year. He was with the White Sox at the time and was considered pretty old because he was in his early forties. The first time I ever got a hit off him, it was in the middle of August and we were at Fenway Park. I had faced him two or three times that season without much success. It was the bottom of the eighth and I led off the inning. Wilhelm throws me a knuckleball. Then he throws another knuckleball, and another. I was getting a little flustered but I was determined to make contact. I didn't want to look like a dumb rookie. The knuckleballs kept coming and the count was 3–2. All of a sudden he throws me a fastball, and for some reason I was thinking fastball.

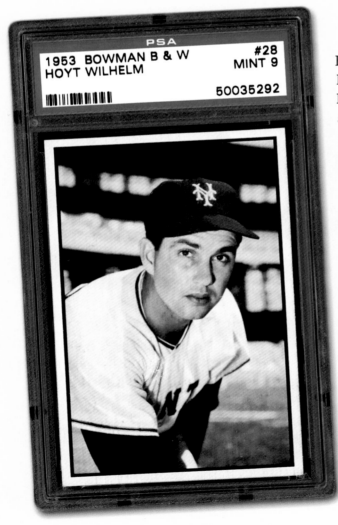

**1953 BOWMAN B & W
HOYT WILHELM**
#28
MINT 9
50035292

I took that ball deep. I hit it up in the net where the Green Monster is now. I'd say it was about an 80 mile an hour fastball. I was running around the bases on cloud nine and Hoyt was swearing at me the whole time. He was calling me names and yelling that, for the rest of my career, I would never get another fastball from him. There I was, a 22-year-old kid, and a future Hall of Famer was swearing at me. I was thrilled.

One thing I found to be interesting about Hoyt was the way he held his head when he was on the mound. His head would always be tilted off to the side. When I faced him, I would try to hold my head like that, too. I figured that way I could see the ball straight! That didn't really work very well for me, but I had to try it. The knuckleball that Wilhelm threw was a lot tougher than most other pitchers. When you face a knuckleball pitcher for the first time, you normally take a pitch to see what he's got, to see the movement. When Hoyt was on, his knuckleball had so much movement it was almost unhittable. By comparison, Wilbur Wood, who pitched for the White Sox right after Hoyt, could make the knuckleball trail away from the hitter or come in on the hitter, but it was slower, which allowed you to wait for it and time it better, especially if it was a hanger.

Wilhelm was a good one. At that time, he was considered one of the best relievers to ever play the game. He was a perennial All-Star, and even though it took him a while to get into the Hall of Fame, he deserved it. He was actually the first relief pitcher ever voted in. I have always been intrigued by knuckleballers. Their motion does not create as much wear and tear on the arm. Hoyt was able to continue pitching, and pitching well, until he was almost 50 years old. Imagine that? He was a tough one.

THE CARDS

The hobby has its preferences, that's for sure. Collectors seem to gravitate towards certain types of players and this is true in every sport, not just baseball. There are quarterbacks and then there are offensive linemen. There are power hitters and then there are defensive specialists. Crafty pitchers are often overlooked compared to their power-pitching brethren. Hoyt Wilhelm is one of those pitchers. The knuckleball wizard helped redefine the role of the relief pitcher long before the concept of the closer came along, but he never captivated fans the way that fireballers like Sandy Koufax or Nolan Ryan did. Despite pitching for 21 seasons, there are relatively few Wilhelm cards to choose from considering his time in the league.

Wilhelm's first card appeared in the 1952 Topps set, and it was his only rookie card since the Hall of Fame pitcher was not included in the 1952 Bowman issue. Bowman was Topps' chief competitor at the time and remained so through 1955. After his cardboard debut with Topps, Wilhelm cards were produced

by both brands until 1955 when Bowman issued his sole card for the year. In 1953, Bowman changed directions by abandoning the colorful artwork that defined their previous few sets and instead made photography the focal point of the design. Their main set contained 160 colorful cards, one that did not include Wilhelm, but the manufacturer also created a smaller, 64-card black-and-white set. These cards are identical in design to their counterparts, absent the use of color. Wilhelm is one of just a handful of Hall of Famers included in the black-and-white issue, which was produced in far fewer numbers than the 1953 Bowman Color set.

During the decade, some regional Wilhelm cards were produced as well. The most popular of the bunch would be cards from the Red Man Tobacco series. Wilhelm was included in their 1953 and 1955 sets. These oversized 3½" by 4" cards are booming with color, and keep in mind that most collectors prefer examples that have the bottom tab intact versus those that have the tab removed. As we venture into the 1960s, Wilhelm continued to be a staple in all the regular Topps sets, and he was also one of the few stars to be included in Leaf's lone effort in 1960. Wilhelm appeared on his first multi-player card in the 1960 Topps set alongside Roy Face on one entitled *Fork & Knuckler*. The duo appeared together again a couple of years later in the 1962 Topps set on a card called *Rival League Relief Aces*.

Before the decade came to an end, Wilhelm's image could be found in several issues aside from the regular Topps releases, with the most notable regional brand being Post Cereal. As Wilhelm's long career headed into the home stretch and entered the 1970s, the durable pitcher made several more cardboard appearances. His 1971 Topps Greatest Moments card is, perhaps, Wilhelm's most interesting of the period. This oversized 2½" by 4¾" horizontal issue contains 55 black-bordered cards, and the Wilhelm is easily one of his most valuable outside of his rookie. Wilhelm's final mainstream appearance came in the 1972 Topps set on card #777 as part of the high-number series (657–787).

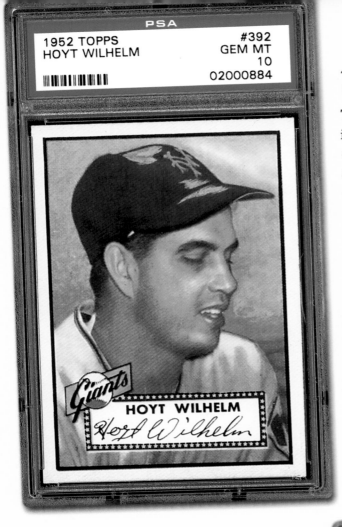

The HOYT WILHELM CARD

To say that Wilhelm picked a great year and set to make his debut in is an understatement, because the importance of the 1952 Topps set cannot be overstated. Topps' full-fledged entry into the market was a game changer for collectors. This 407-card issue is part baseball card set, part pop-culture art. The symbolic power of the Mickey Mantle card alone transcends the hobby. The Wilhelm card (#392) is not only one of two major rookies in the set (along with Eddie Mathews), it also resides in the tough high-number series (311–407). Like a lot of the stars who made their first appearance on cardboard during the Bowman and Topps rivalry, Wilhelm only has one official rookie card...and this is it. In 1953 and 1954, Wilhelm did appear in both the Bowman and Topps sets, but his Topps rookie stands alone. Without a shadow of a doubt, this card is far and away Wilhelm's most desirable as a result of its connection to such a groundbreaking issue.

"This 407-card issue is part baseball card set, part pop-culture art."

ONE CARD TO WATCH

After appearing in both Bowman and Topps sets in 1953 and 1954, Wilhelm was noticeably absent in the 1955 Topps issue. Bowman, on the other hand, produced his only mainstream card that year. The same would be true of the biggest star in the game—a guy named Mantle. This would end up being the final effort from Bowman during an eight-year run (1948–1955), and their 1955 design may have been the brand's most interesting of all. Made to look like miniature television sets, these cards are

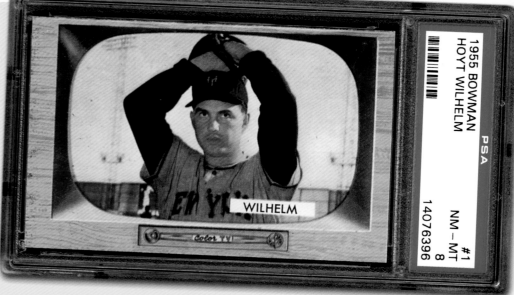

surrounded by wood grain borders, which ranged in color from light tan to dark patina. These colored borders resulted in the issue becoming one of the most condition-sensitive sets of the era, as the edges will reveal the slightest touch of wear. To further the challenge, Wilhelm was chosen for the #1 spot in the set. Many first and last cards were subject to handling damage as they were often exposed on the top or bottom of the stack. The 1955 Bowman set never reached the popularity level of the Topps issue, but its unique design and inherent challenge make this Wilhelm a key for any collector trying to assemble the set.

BILLY WILLIAMS

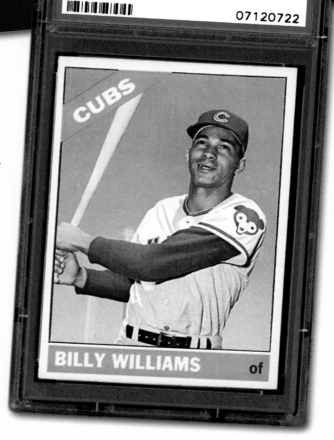

OF ALL THE HALL OF FAMERS that I either played with or against, Billy Williams was probably the one that I had the least contact with. I got to know a lot of the National League players during spring training, but that didn't work out with the Cubs. They did play in Scottsdale, Arizona, but not until the year after we left for Winter Haven, Florida. Even though we were both All-Stars, we never got to face each other in an All-Star Game, either. I finally met Billy towards the very end of his career when he came over to the American League to play for Oakland. I never got to talk to him much, though, because he was kind of a shy guy who kept to himself most of the time. In 1975, he faced us a few times, but I don't remember him doing any real damage in a game.

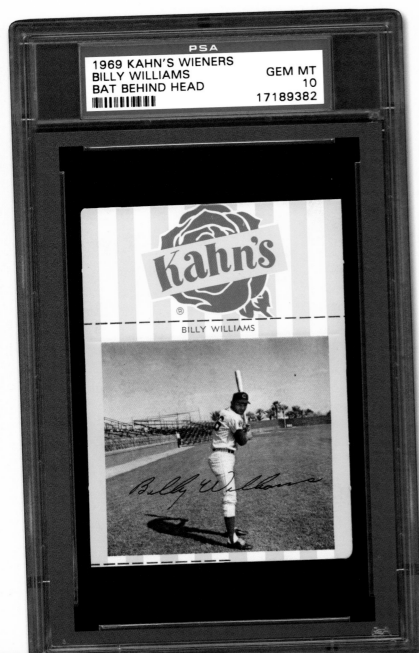

I did appreciate those Cubs teams of the late 1960s and early 1970s with Billy, along with Ernie Banks, Ron Santo, and Fergie Jenkins. They really tried to make a run for it, and for several years in a row, the Cubs finished second or third in the league. Williams was a heck of a hitter who could hit for both average and power. I remember in 1970, he was almost unstoppable. He led the National League in just about every offensive category. Billy had a nice fluid batting motion. They called him "Sweet Swingin' Billy" because he made hitting the baseball look so effortless. I think he was overshadowed by some of his teammates because he was such a quiet guy. Billy wasn't flashy and he didn't try to make headlines, but he was consistent and dependable. He was a real professional and did his job efficiently, without any fanfare. Honestly, Williams was one of those guys that everyone wanted on their team. He was a quiet leader who spoke with his bat.

When I look at a player like Billy, I feel bad that he never played in a postseason game as a Cub. Although we did not win it until many years after I retired, we had the honor of playing in a few World Series. When he was with Oakland, Billy played against us in the 1975 American League Championship Series.

It was near the end of his career and he was Oakland's DH. We beat Oakland in the ALCS and then faced the Big Red Machine in a thrilling World Series. I think Billy only played one more season after that. I would not put Billy Williams in the top tier of the greatest Hall of Fame outfielders, because that class is very special with guys like Ruth, Cobb, DiMaggio, and Ted Williams, but in my opinion, Billy is up there with the next tier of great outfielders. He was a consistent force for the Cubs from the early 1960s to the mid-1970s and he was voted to the All-Star team multiple times. When you look at his numbers, he had over 400 home runs and over 2,700 hits in his career, and he finished up with a .290 average. All in all, Billy was a

great player and he left his mark on Major League Baseball.

THE CARDS

For a team that failed to win a World Series in the 1960s and 1970s, the Chicago Cubs were sure stacked with stars. For most of his career, Williams called the "Friendly Confines" his home, but so did other Hall of Famers like Fergie Jenkins, Ron Santo, and perhaps the most popular Cub of all, Ernie Banks. Maybe Williams was overshadowed by his more popular teammates or never quite given his proper due since his team never won a World Series championship. No matter the reason, collectors can rejoice that most Williams cards are relatively affordable compared to other stars of the period.

Williams made his hobby debut in the 1961 Topps set, but the sweet-swinging lefty also appeared in a stamp set released by the manufacturer that same year. Regardless, the card is the inaugural Williams issue that collectors clearly care about the most. Being part of a non-card medium like stamps was a sign of things to come for Williams. Within the first few years of his career, Williams was included in a few different coin sets produced by Salada-Junket and Shirriff (1962) and Topps (1964). He would appear on even more coins as his career progressed, but Williams was also a part of sets based on other mediums like candy lids, decals, faux currency, pins, rub-offs, tattoos, and transfers. Several of these interesting sets were made by Topps, but others were of the regional variety.

Some of the toughest and most valuable Williams cards were created by Topps during the 1960s. In 1964, the obscure *Rookie All-Star Banquet* card and colorful Stand-Up issue were both released. Williams is one of the short-printed cards in the Stand-Up set along with several other Hall of Famers. Some of the intriguing Topps test issues contained Williams as well, such as the 1967 Punch-Outs, 1968 Action All-Star Sticker, and 1969 Super sets. These Topps sets and more were complemented by the O-Pee-Chee (Canadian) and Venezuelan Topps sets during the decade. Popular regional issues like Bazooka, Jell-O, Kahn's, and Post Cereal featured Williams in their sets as well.

As we journey into the 1970s, Williams started to appear in even more regional sets, such as those released by Kellogg's and Milk Duds. One of the more noteworthy Williams collectibles of the decade is his 1971 Topps Greatest Moments card, a black-bordered beauty with centering problems that is rarely seen in PSA NM-MT 8 or better condition. Topps continued to create test issues with Williams in mind. This includes some of his toughest items, including the 1972 Candy Lid, 1973 Comic, and 1973 Pin-Up issues. Williams' final mainstream card was released as part of the 1976 Topps set (#252) while he was a member of the Oakland A's.

"Williams made his hobby debut in the 1961 Topps set"

The BILLY WILLIAMS CARD

When it comes to Williams, the card that garners most of the attention is his only mainstream rookie card, 1961 Topps #141. Williams shares the rookie limelight with fellow Hall of Famer and former teammate Santo, in addition to Juan Marichal. Amazingly, all three Hall of Famer rookie cards are currently valued about the same. The 587-card set is not known to be a condition-sensitive issue, but finding well-centered copies absent print defects can be challenging. The Williams card is one of the most affordable Hall of Fame rookies of the era, which is due in part to its availability in high grade and the fact that Banks overshadowed the fantastic hitter for a large portion of his career. There are tougher Williams cards to collect and ones that challenge or surpass his rookie when it comes to strict monetary value. That said, of all the Williams cards produced during his playing career, this is the one most collectors pursue.

ONE CARD TO WATCH

Outside of his 1961 Topps rookie, there are two Williams cards that offer a great combination of popularity and difficulty in high grade: the 1962 Topps #288 and the unnumbered 1964 Topps Stand-Up. Both are part of attractive sets and hard to find in PSA 8 or better condition. In the end, we chose to focus on the 1962 Topps Williams because of its overlooked nature. Williams' second Topps card is even tougher than one would think. The 598-card set was designed with borders that resemble wood grain. The brown borders on the Williams card are very susceptible to chipping along the edges and corners. The card is also challenging to find well centered and without pesky print defects along its face. The 1962 Topps Williams isn't one that immediately comes to mind when you think about tough cards, but ask yourself, when was the last time you saw one offered in high grade?

The Changing of the Guard

(to 1989)

Ellen and I are having dinner with Rico and his lovely wife Elsie in a nice little Italian restaurant in Sarasota, Florida. It seems that Italians communicate best with each other over a nice dish of pasta or some great pizza. The wives order a brick-oven mushroom-and-pepperoni pizza and a Caesar salad to share, and the guys go for the ravioli and stuffed shells. The sauce is actually pretty good. In my opinion, a little sugar is the key to good sauce. It should not be too acidic, otherwise you're going to develop a good case of agita. The girls are not crazy about the pizza, but we take no prisoners with the ravioli and shells. The only thing missing is an additional loaf of hot Italian bread. Over dinner we start chatting about some of the

guys Rico played with and against who continued on and retired in the 1980s. What a roster of great baseball talent.

JOHNNY BENCH

1969 TOPPS #95
JOHNNY BENCH
ALL-STAR ROOKIE GEM MT 10
PSA
27396698

JOHNNY BENCH IS PROBABLY THE GREATEST

catcher of all time. At least, in his era, he is certainly the best.
Our guy, Carlton Fisk, was right up there, but Bench had that
natural ability. He was extra special. Bench was so tremendous
at blocking balls and calling a game, and he had a cannon for
an arm. Johnny's hands were gigantic, and man, was he good
at framing pitches. He was also a very good hitter. He was a big
man and very strong, so he could hit home runs, he could hit
the ball to all fields, and he was a good RBI guy.

Bench was very personable and friendly. One thing I liked
about Johnny was he didn't talk much when I was at the plate.
He had that deep voice and would say a few words, but there
was none of the distracting yapping that some of the other
catchers did. Fisk would talk to players once in a while and
Munson did quite a bit, but Johnny was all business.

PSA
1971 TOPPS #250
JOHNNY BENCH MINT 9
11516124

Johnny and Carlton always got along and had great respect for each
other. Fisk and Munson, on the other hand, were known to butt
heads. When we were in Winter Haven, the Reds were in Tampa,
so we faced each other quite a bit during spring training. We really
never had the chance to talk much in Florida, but I loved watching
Johnny play. He was such a talented guy.

That 1975 World Series was quite a contest. Some say it was the
greatest World Series ever. When you look at a catcher, you always
look at his defense first. The hitting is usually gravy. In Johnny's
case, the hitting was a big plus. He really had the whole package.
I'm not sure if Johnny hit for a high average in the 1975 Series, but
I do remember him hitting a rocket off our starter, Rick Wise. As
I recall, he also had a key hit in Game Four. That Big Red Machine
team was so good with Johnny, Rose, Perez, Morgan, Foster, and
Griffey. Their pitching was their Achilles heel, but Johnny had a lot
to do with the Reds success. I had a good World Series. Everything
was going right for me. The rainout couldn't have come at a worse
time because I was doing really well. Thinking back, that Series
was the most fun I ever had in the big leagues.

Johnny was a heck of a golfer. I love the game and still play as
often as I can, but he was on another planet. Johnny actually

started playing on the Senior PGA Tour in the 1990s. With all of his All-Star appearances, his MVP Awards, the teams he played on, his hitting, and his defense, how could you say that Johnny wasn't the greatest of his era? I rank him first, followed by Fisk, and then maybe Carter and Munson. Yogi was great, but he really played before that time. It was a pleasure to play against Johnny Bench and to get to know him. He had great respect for the Red Sox organization and was always very cordial to me. During that 1975 World Series, it was a privilege to play with, and against, two of the greatest catchers of my era.

THE CARDS

Johnny Bench's career began right at the tail end of the 1960s, a decade when Topps dominated the market and experimented with various concepts. By the time Bench's playing days were over, the hobby landscape at the manufacturer level had already started to change as legitimate rivals emerged to challenge the longstanding champion. The perennial All-Star had his career cut a little short as a result of injuries and the general wear and tear associated with being a backstop, but before it all came to an end, hundreds of Bench collectibles were made.

In 1967, Bench did play in 26 games, although it was not enough to qualify as a full-fledged rookie under the rules. In his first full season, Bench was named the NL Rookie of the Year. That same year, a handful of sets that contained Bench were released. This included his first mainstream rookie card in

the 1968 Topps set and the much tougher Venezuelan Topps version of the same card. There were also a few others, but there is one card that dates to the prior year in 1967. The Reds issued a small set of photo postcards that year and each one measures approximately 3½" by 5½". A bold facsimile signature graces the front of these black-and-white postcards.

As we head into the 1970s, the decade that Bench became a household name, the Hall of Famer was included in dozens of collectible sets. Of course, Bench was a regular with Topps. Some of his more interesting Topps cards, however, were not of the mainstream variety. From the black-bordered 1971 Greatest Moments condition rarity to the inherently scarce 1973 Pin-Ups test issue to the jagged-looking 1974 Deckle Edge card, some of Bench's most valuable collectibles were made during this era. Bench was featured in many regional issues, too. Bazooka, Hostess, Kellogg's, Milk Duds, Pepsi-Cola, and Wendy's are just some of the non-Topps brands to issue Bench cards while the star was leading the "Big Red Machine" to pennants.

In 1981, the hobby was changed forever. After

Topps secured the market as the only mainstream card manufacturer for years, two new competitors started an annual battle with the hobby giant. Donruss and Fleer became staples during a time when the industry transformed from a relatively small hobby into a nationwide phenomenon. Topps held their ground, but as the years went by, their competitors found pockets of success and gained market share. Bench's final year in the hobby commemorated his exit in creative ways. All three brands paid tribute to Bench with special cards. Each of these cards include Carl Yastrzemski, while one (Topps) included Gaylord Perry as well. Interestingly, only Fleer made a solo card of Bench (#462) in their 1984 set.

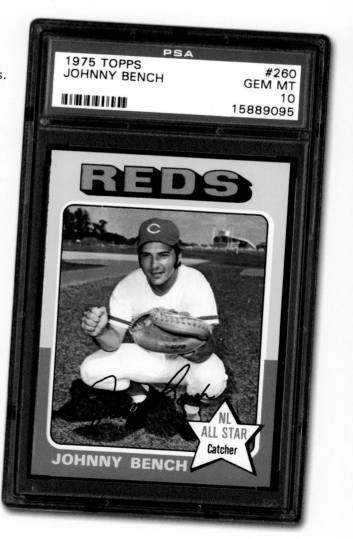

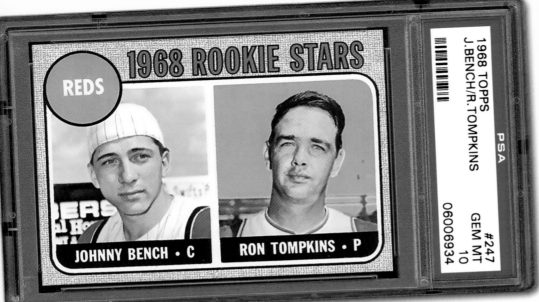

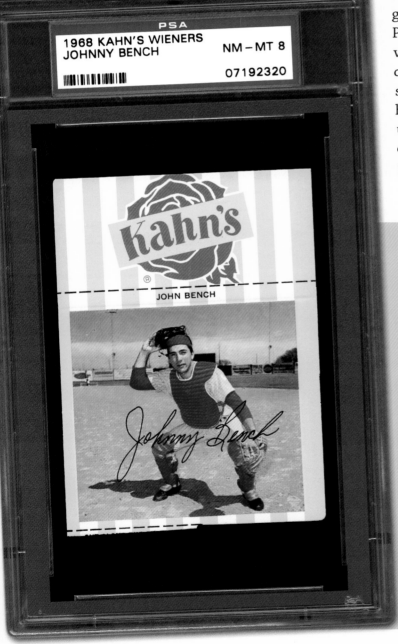

The JOHNNY BENCH CARD

During the 1960s, Topps started to produce rookie cards that featured more than one player. Some of the biggest names in baseball history had to share the limelight with at least one other person when they made their hobby debut. Bench was one of them. In 1968, Bench is featured on a horizontal Topps card along with teammate and pitcher Ron Tompkins. Tompkins never reached stardom, but his batterymate earned enough accolades for both of them. The Bench rookie card (#247) is certainly not considered a condition rarity, but it is the Bench issue that generates the most attention from collectors. For those seeking PSA Mint 9s or higher, keep in mind that the centering does vary on this card, and the pattern along the edges and corners can mask wear. Furthermore, the solid orange/yellow backs are susceptible to chipping. A very young Bench is pictured with his cap on backwards, something catchers often did prior to the universal use of the plastic helmet. Along with a debut single of Nolan Ryan, this Bench card is one of two key rookies in the popular 598-card set.

ONE CARD TO WATCH

There is no doubt that Bench's only mainstream rookie card is his 1968 Topps issue. That said, another Bench card was produced that same year. In this case, the card is larger, more colorful, and much tougher to locate than his regular Topps rookie. Kahn's, the Cincinnati-area meat company, produced small regional sets for many years before Bench came along. These oversized cards measure approximately 2¹³⁄₁₆" by 4⁹⁄₁₆" and each one was designed with an advertising tab that could be removed by hand. They even included a dotted line to help guide the collector. Today, most collectors prefer that the cards remain intact, since the Kahn's logo adds visual appeal. The blank-backed set only contains 38 subjects, but there are numerous variations throughout. When it comes to Bench, however, there is only one version. The eye-popping card pictures Bench removing his catcher's mask and the image is draped with a facsimile signature. The 1968 Kahn's Bench card is a perfect tribute to the man that would become the greatest catcher in baseball history.

ROD CAREW

1969 TOPPS #419
ROD CAREW
ALL-STAR NM-MT 8
14221488

I PLAYED AGAINST ROD CAREW for most of my career. That's when he was with Minnesota. Rod was one of the greatest pure hitters of all time. He could hit to all fields, hit with a little power, and boy, could he hit for average. No wonder he was the league batting champ so many times. One time we even tried to hit him in the rear end, but it was like trying to hit a moving target. When I played shortstop, he would frustrate the heck out of me. If you played him in the hole, he'd hit up the middle. If you played in the middle, he'd hit through the hole. His bat control and eyesight were unbelievable. Rod would wait until the last second, and you could almost see his eyes follow the ball right through the swing. To me, it looked like the ball stood still at contact. He could hit it anywhere.

Rod was just a terrific guy. We talked a lot about hitting, and he even explained his approach to hitting a baseball to me, but to hit like him was almost impossible. Nobody could hit like him. Carew had his own unique style. Later on, I'd say Tony Gwynn and Wade Boggs came the closest. We used to joke about how I would try to defend him.

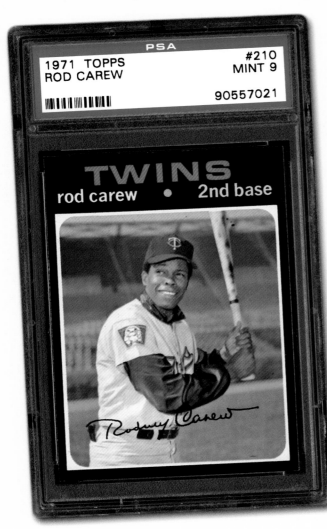

1971 TOPPS #210
ROD CAREW MINT 9
90557021

I told him that when he came up to bat, I might as well just go to the bench and sit down. We had a good laugh about that. He was an expert at fouling off the tough pitch. Whether it was low and away, or up and in, he had the uncanny ability to hang in with those pitches.

I had the honor and pleasure of playing with Rod in both the 1967 and 1969 All-Star Games. He was at second and I was at short. I looked it up and it was pretty funny, Rod and I were a combined 1-for-10 in those two games. Of course, Carew was just starting out with the Twins in 1967, and he was Rookie of the Year that year. We beat that Twins team on the last day of the season, and later on in the afternoon, clinched the American League pennant when California beat Detroit.

When Rod was on third base, you had to watch out because he had the talent to steal home. He stole home so many times in his career. I remember in the late 1960s Carew stole home seven times one year. He had such a great career. Rod's batting average was .328 and he had over 3,000 hits. He was an All-Star every single year he played for the Twins, and after Rod joined the Angels in 1979, he was an All-Star every year except his last. When we played against each other, I always admired his willingness to share some of his batting secrets, not just with me, but with other players. He was a good instructor after he retired, but really, nobody could ever hit like him. He's had a tough go of it recently with his heart transplant and some medical issues, but he's doing well now. What a terrific guy and a terrific player. For Carew, it seemed effortless. Man, he would have looked good in a Red Sox uniform!

THE CARDS

Over his 19-year career, Rod Carew continually put up the kind of numbers you would expect from a Hall of Famer. With a flip of the wrist, Carew appeared to have the ability to place the ball wherever

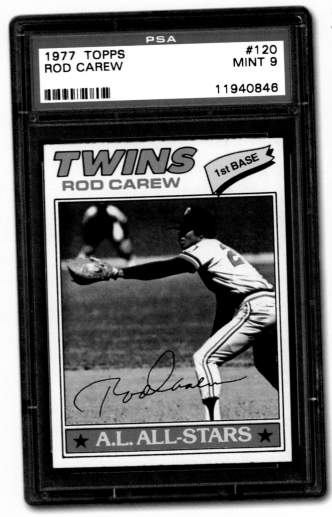

he wanted en route to several batting titles. Despite amassing over 3,000 hits and countless individual awards during his playing days, most of Carew's cards are relatively affordable. This is most likely a product of playing for the Minnesota Twins and California Angels versus one of the big market teams. With more national exposure, things might have been different for the legendary hitter and his collectibles.

It all started in 1967 for Carew, the year he entered the league and the hobby. While a team-issued photo was released that same year, the Carew collectible that generates most of the demand is his first Topps card. The multi-player design was one in a long line of similar Topps designs, from the 1963 Pete Rose to the 1965 Joe Morgan to the 1968 Nolan Ryan. Many of the major Topps rookie cards produced during the era featured anywhere from two to four players. In the following two Topps sets, 1968 and 1969, the image used for the Carew card is identical. This was a product of a player holdout, which meant Topps was forced to reuse the same image for many of the cards.

Since Carew began his career in the latter portion of the decade, he was left out of several of the tough Topps test issues that were products of the manufacturer's most experimental period. A couple that Carew did

appear in included the 1968 Action All-Star Stickers and the 1968 Discs sets. Keep in mind that Milton Bradley printed cards in 1968 that are virtually identical to the Topps issue. This set, which included Carew, exhibit a brighter yellow reverse compared to the Topps issue and some cards will occasionally reveal evidence of a white border along the edges. This was a result of the white-bordered football and hot rod cards that became part of the same sheet.

As we head into the 1970s, Carew continued to be included in O-Pee-Chee (Canadian) and Venezuelan Topps sets, which are far tougher to find than their regular Topps counterparts. One of the more interesting Topps creations of the decade was the 1974 Deckle Edge issue. Both gray-back and white-back variations of Carew are known, with the white version being slightly scarcer. Carew was included in several sets in 1986, including all the major brands at the time like Donruss, Fleer, and Topps. This includes some special cards that acknowledged his exceptional career. In fact, that same year, Star Co. issued a small set of Carew cards that recognized many of his career highlights, and new brands such as Sportflics entered the market, producing several Carew cards of their own.

The ROD CAREW CARD

In 1967, Topps released another set in a long line of annual baseball card issues. This time, the manufacturer went with a relatively simple and clean design, which resulted in one of the more attractive releases of the decade. Carew made his debut here on a dual-player rookie. The card (#569) also featured outfielder Hank Allen of the Washington Senators. The Carew rookie is one of the keys to the 609-card set and one of two major Hall of Famer rookies. Tom Seaver's first appearance is the other.

The card, while not considered a condition rarity, does have a couple of obstacles to note for those seeking high-grade examples. The card is commonly found with poor centering, which is magnified by the narrow borders. In addition, dark print defects are often visible in the light-colored background. Finally, it is important to note that the backs of the 1967 Topps cards have a green border that can reveal the slightest hint of wear.

"The Carew rookie is one of the keys to the 609-card set."

ONE CARD TO WATCH

When the hobby moved from the 1960s to the 1970s, the look and feel of the annual Topps sets seemed to change. In some cases, the change was dramatic. The usual eye-catching formats were replaced, at least in some cases, by somewhat lackluster ones. Nevertheless, some of the sets are still regarded as classics today, and for different reasons. The 1971 Topps set is surrounded by black borders and is still the most challenging Topps issue of the decade to assemble in high grade. The 1975 Topps set offers several important rookie cards and a multi-colored design that really grabs the eye. Of all the sets released by Topps that decade, perhaps none of them is more fitting for the time than the 1972 issue. The psychedelic design used for this 787-card set is arguably the most visually appealing of the era. The 1972 Topps Carew (#695) is part of the high-number series and has always been regarded as one of the more desirable cards in the set. This was also the year Carew began a run of winning six AL batting titles in seven years.

STEVE CARLTON

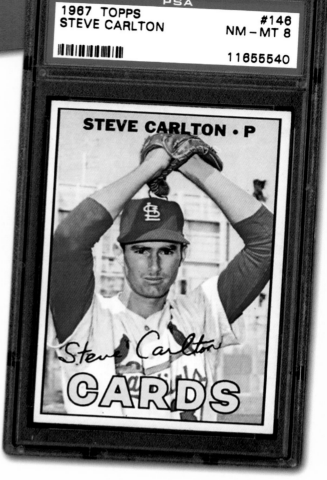

HOW GOOD WAS STEVE CARLTON? The year he won 27 games, the Phillies won less than 60 total games. Can you imagine that? He won almost half their games that year. Steve pitched for the Cardinals in 1967, and we faced him in Game Five of the World Series. He pitched very well, but our guy Jim Lonborg beat him. I think I went 0-for-3 in that game with a couple of fly outs. Lonnie tossed a three-hitter. That year, Steve and I were such young kids, but for Steve in particular, 1967 was a taste of things to come. It was the first double-digit win season for him, and he got to pitch in the Series. Not a bad rookie year.

I also faced Steve in the 1969 All-Star Game. We won't talk about that at-bat, either! I remember he had a contract dispute with the Cards and they traded him to the Phillies in the early 1970s. The Cards actually traded him for my future teammate, Rick Wise, who played on our 1975 Red Sox pennant winners.

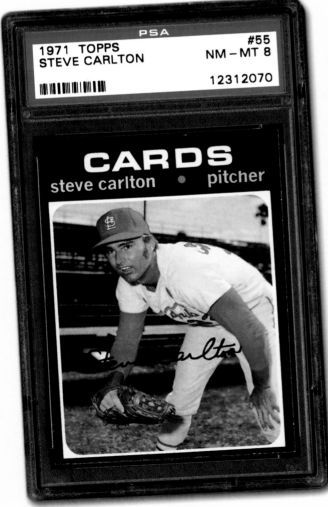

Rick was a good pitcher and great guy, but the Phils definitely got the better of that deal. Once Steve got to the Phillies, he was dominant. By the way, the year he won 27 games was his first year with the Phillies. He did have that one bad year when he lost 20, but after that he was as good as there was in the National League. He had incredible stuff. Carlton could throw hard, he had a great cutter/slider, and he would bore in on right-handed hitters.

At some point in the late 1970s, Steve got ticked off at the media for something and didn't talk to reporters for a long time. In Philly, the press could get really tough, so I don't blame him. Steve was a great competitor and was really focused on winning. He was able to mentally block out distractions when he was on the mound. Maybe it had something to do with his unusual conditioning program. He did martial arts instead of the usual stretching and running routine. Anyway, because Steve won, a lot of the other pitchers decided to try martial arts, too. Did it work for them? Who knows!

The other thing about Carlton was that he pitched ornery. That's probably what made him a great pitcher. He and Nolan Ryan had some epic battles. Of today's pitchers, Chris Sale has a delivery that is kind of like Carlton's, but Steve had more of a three-quarter delivery than Sale. I think Carlton is right behind Warren Spahn for most wins by a lefty. When you look at Steve's whole career, you have to shake your head in amazement. Four Cy Young Awards. That really says it all. And then there were all of those All-Star appearances and his 329 wins. On top of that, Carlton led the league in strikeouts so many times, and let's not forget he won the World Series with both the Cards and the Phillies. Steve Carlton was one of the great ones. I've always said that Gibson, Koufax, and Ryan were the toughest pitchers I ever faced, but Steve Carlton, along with Marichal and a few others, were right behind them.

THE CARDS

When you pitch for a remarkable 24 years at the major-league level, chances are that a lot of baseball cards will bear your name. This is especially true if that career spanned from the 1960s to the 1980s, when the hobby went from a niche endeavor to a nationwide phenomenon. That is the case with Steve Carlton. He appeared on hundreds of collectible cards during his playing days, from the mainstream staples to a host of regional issues that gained popularity in the 1970s. Considering his accomplishments, Carlton is still regarded as one of the most undervalued players in our hobby.

In 1965, Carlton made his cardboard debut on a dual-player card. Having a rookie card to yourself became a rarity during that decade. One such example would be Jim Palmer in the 1966 Topps set. In fact, other Hall of Fame pitchers who entered the league around the same time, such as Tom Seaver and Nolan Ryan, suffered the same fate as Carlton. Interestingly, after Carlton made his first hobby appearance, he was noticeably absent from the annual Topps production the very next year. In 1966, Carlton didn't start the year with a big-league club, which may have been a deciding factor as to why the lefty wasn't seen again in a Topps set until 1967.

As his career headed into the next decade, an explosion of Carlton cards occurred as the Hall of Famer established himself as a premier pitcher in the league. One of Carlton's most elusive and valuable cards was part of a Topps test issue in 1972 called Candy Lids. Topps did create a few different Candy Lids sets in the 1970s. Some were intended for the public, like the 1973 issue, while others were not, including this rare set in 1972. Keep in mind that two different versions of these lids are known. One is an uncut square proof of the player images and the other is the more traditional, modified lid format. In 1973, Carlton appeared in more tough test sets from the manufacturer, including the Topps Comics and Pin-Ups issues.

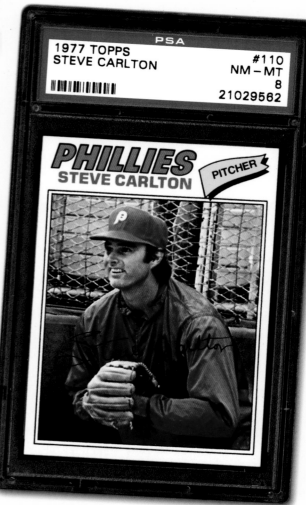

"An explosion of Carlton cards occurred as the Hall of Famer established himself as a premier pitcher in the league."

While not a test issue, one of the more interesting Carlton cards from the period is the 1974 Topps Deckle Edge card. Outside of some of the rare test issues, this jagged-looking card is still one of Carlton's most valuable. Over the next two decades, Carlton was included in many regional issues such as Burger King, Hostess, and Kellogg's to name a few. When we entered the era of the hobby boom in the 1980s, Carlton became a regular with Donruss and Fleer in addition to Topps. Carlton's final mainstream appearance came in the 1988 Fleer set (#7). He was not included in the Donruss or Topps sets, which is most likely a result of the limited innings he pitched (9.2) in 1988.

The STEVE CARLTON CARD

There is no question that the Carlton card that stands above all others in terms of demand is his 1965 Topps rookie card (#477). Like many rookie cards made during the 1960s, Carlton shares the limelight with another player. In this case, it is fellow pitcher and teammate Fritz Ackley. The Carlton card is one of four Hall of Famer rookies that reside in the set, along with debuts of Joe Morgan, Catfish Hunter, and Tony Perez. Amazingly, all four players and rookies are somewhat overlooked in their own way, especially Carlton and Morgan, who remain two of the most underrated players of the period. The Carlton rookie itself, while not overly difficult to find in high grade, does have a few obstacles that are worth noting. The white borders are well defined, so centering is something that can't be ignored if you are searching for PSA NM-MT 8 or better examples. Chipping along the reverse is not uncommon, nor is the presence of print defects in the somewhat dark background on the front.

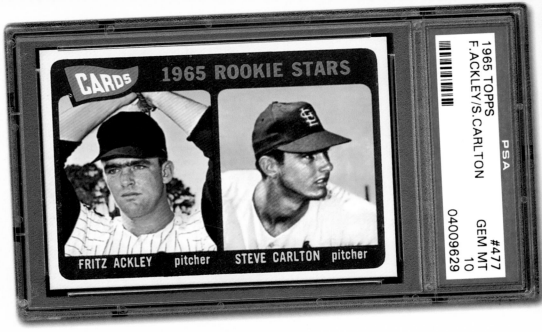

"The psychedelic design, huge star selection, and creative concepts make the 1972 Topps issue a hobby favorite."

ONE CARD TO WATCH

The reality about Carlton's cards is that most of them can be purchased for under $10. In other words, there are only a relative handful of Carlton issues that stand out from the rest based on pure monetary value. One card that tends to fall somewhere in between is his 1972 Topps (Traded) #751. The 1972 Topps set is, arguably, the most popular Topps release of the 1970s. The psychedelic design, huge star selection, and creative card concepts make the 1972 Topps issue a hobby favorite. One of those interesting concepts appeared in the high-number series. A group of seven cards were included with the word "Traded" across the front to denote that the player had just switched teams. This was a significant moment in Carlton's career as he moved from St. Louis to Philadelphia. He would not only have his best individual season and be named the NL Cy Young Award winner as a member of a last-place team in 1972, Carlton would win three more during his stay.

ROLLIE FINGERS

ROLLIE FINGERS AND JOE RUDI were my teammates for three whole days. We were playing in Oakland, and Charlie Finley, the owner of the Oakland A's, sold both of them to the Red Sox for, I believe, a million bucks apiece. In any event, when they walked into our clubhouse, not many of us were there. Keep in mind that the situation was very bizarre. They literally walked from their clubhouse, across the field, to ours. When they came in, I shook their hands and welcomed them to the team. They got their Red Sox uniforms and we took a picture together. They were both thrilled to be playing for us because they hated Charlie and loved Fenway, not to mention that we were a contender that year. Before you knew it though, the commissioner of baseball, Bowie Kuhn, stepped in and squashed the deal because he thought it wasn't in the best interest of the game. Both guys were ticked off to say the least. I knew Rollie wasn't crazy about Finley, and he later told me that he was really disappointed about not playing for us.

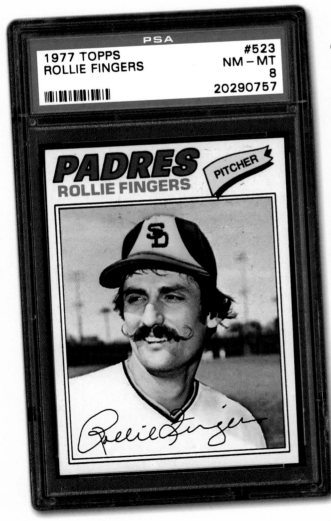

One of my most prized photos hanging in my home is that picture of the three of us in uniform, and we all have big smiles on our faces. I think it is probably the only photo like that in existence. Too bad it didn't work out, because it would definitely have helped the Red Sox. Rollie was a great guy. First of all, he was one of the elite closers of that time along with Gossage and Lyle. He had nasty stuff. He threw in the middle 90s with his fastball, and he had an even better curveball. You could hit off his fastball, but you just couldn't hit his breaking ball. When he came in, he really mixed up his pitches, keeping you off guard. Actually, I hit Rollie pretty well. I remember hitting a home run off him in the playoffs. As a matter of fact, I had some good success against him throughout my career. Rollie was tough. He could go three innings if necessary and then come back and pitch the next day. He really revolutionized the role of the closer in baseball.

It is interesting that Rollie is in the Hall of Fame even though he had a losing record as a pitcher. To me, that's an indication of how good he was. When I look at his ERA and the number of saves he had for that time in baseball history, he is a guy who truly deserves to be in the Hall. Rollie had some great seasons. He was league MVP and a Cy Young Award winner in the same year. Besides that, Rollie was a multi-year All-Star and a World Series MVP. Oakland won the World Series three years in a row, but we beat them in the 1975 playoffs. That Oakland team had some great guys and real characters on it. Rollie, along with Sal Bando, Reggie Jackson, Joe Rudi, Vida Blue, and Gene Tenace were great competitors. I'm not sure how far those teams would have gone without Rollie, though. I liked him and we always got along. He was quite the character with that big handlebar moustache. Rollie remained a great competitor and a colorful character even when he played for the Padres and Brewers. As a matter of fact, he's still quite a character and still has the mustache!

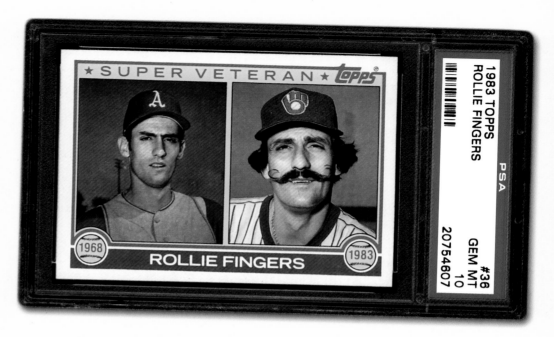

THE CARDS

One of the first closers to ever be enshrined in Cooperstown, Rollie Fingers was a trailblazer in that regard. The concept of the true closer was not fashionable at the time. As a result, the appreciation for what Fingers did is somewhat overlooked by collectors, who are often driven by certain statistics and milestones. Today, the closer is an appreciated and sometimes revered role, but that was not the case in Fingers' day. Despite his impact on the game, his unmistakable mustache, and the fact that he played a key part on

"In high grade, the 1971 Topps Fingers is even more valuable than his rookie card."

the dominant Oakland A's teams of the 1970s, Fingers' cards are relatively affordable compared to his contemporaries.

The card that started it all was born in the 1969 Topps set, one of the most appealing issues of the decade. Including the Fingers debut, the set featured some important rookie cards, like those of Reggie Jackson, Graig Nettles, and Bobby Bonds. It also contained the final card of hobby giant Mickey Mantle, along with some tough White Letter variations found within the range of #s 440–511 that show the team names on the front in white instead of the usual yellow. However, the Fingers rookie was not part of this specific run or subject to the possible variation.

Beyond the basic Topps and O-Pee-Chee (Canadian) sets, Fingers started to appear more frequently in regional releases by the mid-1970s. This was around the time that the Oakland A's ended their impressive postseason run, so perhaps playing on the big stage helped more fans get to know the All-Star reliever, which ultimately resulted in more

cards bearing his image. These regional issues included brands like Burger King, Hostess, and Kellogg's. During the mid-to-late 1970s, collectible discs became a popular medium as all sorts of sets were issued. Perhaps the toughest Fingers disc of all can be found in the 1977 Saga issue. This set was distributed in the Philadelphia area as part of a school lunch purchase program.

From the late-1970s and into the mid-1980s, Fingers continued to appear in numerous non-mainstream issues, from the oversized 1979 Sportscaster series to plenty of obscure regional sets like K-Mart and Squirt in 1982. Fingers appeared on several cards in 1986, which include those made by three of the key players in the business: Donruss, Fleer, and Topps. This would be the last time Fingers would appear on cards from his playing days. The total number of Fingers cards made during his career certainly exceeds 100, but there weren't quite as many made as one would think, considering his stature, longevity, and the period he was active.

The ROLLIE FINGERS CARD

As is the case with most postwar Hall of Famers, the rookie card is the one that generates the greatest interest among collectors. The 1969 Topps Fingers rookie card (#597), like so many from the 1960s and 1970s, features more than one player on the front. In this case, Fingers had to share the limelight with Bob Floyd of the Baltimore Orioles and Larry Burchart of the Cleveland Indians. Interestingly, Fingers' teammate and fellow Hall of Famer Reggie Jackson also made his debut in the 1969 Topps set. In the case of Jackson, the limelight was all his own, which seems fitting today. The Fingers rookie, while not terribly difficult to find in high grade, does have a few condition obstacles to note. Many cards in the 1969 Topps set not only have centering issues, but they are also commonly found with image tilts. In addition, dark print defects are often seen on the fronts of the cards, and the pink-colored reverse will reveal chipping or wear along the edges.

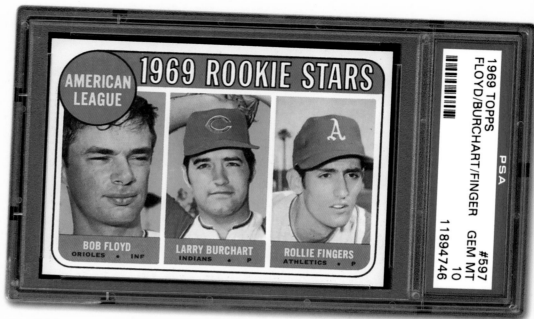

"As is the case with most postwar Hall of Famers, the rookie card generates the greatest interest among collectors."

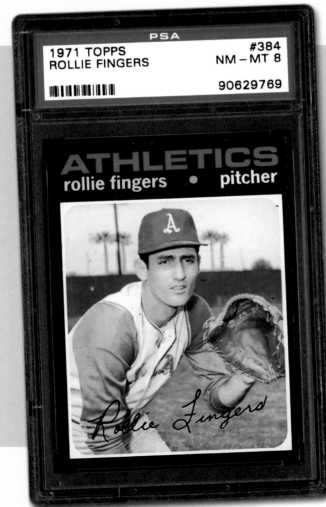

ONE CARD TO WATCH

Other than his official rookie and a handful of elusive issues, there aren't many Fingers cards that immediately come to mind that a hobbyist would deem special or one to watch. In this case, I chose his 1971 Topps card (#384), which is his most valuable regular Topps issue in PSA NM-MT 8 or better. Yes, that's right. In high grade, the 1971 Topps Fingers is even more valuable than his rookie card. The key reason for its superior market value is the fact that this card is tough. To help illustrate the point, at the time of this writing, the card of Hall of Fame teammate Catfish Hunter (#45) had a current population that is nearly four times the Fingers card in PSA 8 condition. The main culprits or condition obstacles are subpar centering and general wear, which is easily seen with the naked eye along those solid-black borders. This is a problem for all the cards in the set, a set that remains popular with those collectors who seek the greatest regular Topps challenge of the decade.

REGGIE JACKSON

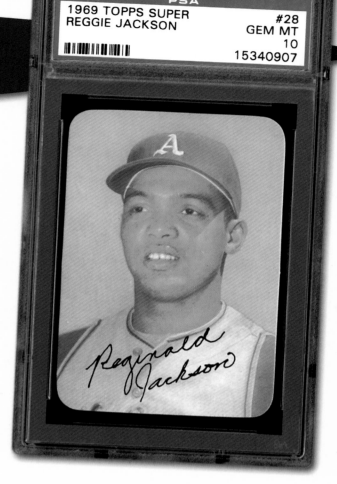

BEFORE REGGIE CAME UP to the big leagues, we had heard a lot about him. There was this real talented kid, a right fielder, coming up through the ranks to Oakland. At that time, I think it was around 1968, Reggie was a decent outfielder with an excellent arm. There is no doubt about it, Reggie had the talent and he enjoyed being in the spotlight. Charlie Finley, the owner of the A's, loved him at first but then things got pretty sour between the two of them. Reggie really helped with attendance, though. As a matter of fact, everywhere he went, attendance figures went up. Overall, Reggie was a talkative and friendly guy. He was well-liked by most of his teammates in Oakland, but he did get into a few jams with some of them. Let's face it, sometimes Reggie went a little over the top. I'm not sure how well-liked he was in New York after he went to the Yankees. There he had some famous run-ins with his manager, Billy Martin, and a couple of teammates.

Reggie hit for tremendous power. Actually his style of play was similar to some of today's power hitters. A lot of strikeouts, and a lot of home runs. I remember there was one game against us in 1969 when he hit two bombs and knocked in ten runs. He killed us! As his career went on, he continued to hit, but his fielding dipped a bit. At the beginning, opposing players thought that Reggie was a bit cocky, but as they got to know him, they realized he probably had to be that way in order to succeed. Reggie was such a great clutch hitter. There is no doubt that, when men were on base, he was a very tough out. You might strike him out, but he was gonna get his swings. Reggie and I were teammates in the 1969 All-Star Game. As a matter of fact, that year happened to be special for me. I was second in the league in slugging percentage to guess who? Reggie. In 1975, we faced the A's in the American League Championship Series. We were running pretty hot by then and were fortunate enough to sweep them. Our three pitchers, Luis Tiant, Reggie Cleveland (with a little help from Roger Moret and Dick Drago), along with Rick Wise kept the A's in check. I have to say, though, that Reggie did his part for the A's. I think he had a pretty good Series, and he also hit a bomb in one of the games.

By the time Reggie got to the Yankees, my career had ended. It was a lot of fun, however, to watch him play for New York. Even though it was like a giant soap opera, it made for some great entertainment. Reggie and I always got along. As a matter of fact, I think he was pretty funny and a lot of what he did was done to motivate himself. Reggie never hit for high average, but he was a power machine and he could bang out those clutch hits. He played on five World Series champions, had a bunch of All-Star appearances, and led the league in bombs several times. He was also the World Series MVP a couple of times. The nickname given to him, Mr. October, was very appropriate.

THE CARDS

Reggie Jackson's illustrious career extended well into the decade when the hobby experienced tremendous growth across the nation. As a result, hundreds of Jackson cards and collectibles were created. Jackson embraced the villain role while he was on the road, and as he aptly said, "Fans don't boo nobodies." The approach inside the hobby was no different. Whether collectors loved him or hated him, they certainly didn't ignore him. His tape-measure home runs and ability to rise to the occasion when it mattered most ensured that collectors paid attention to his cards.

It all started for Jackson in the 1969 Topps set. Well, sort of. That year, a few other Jackson cards were made, including a Topps Decal and a Topps Super, which was part of a test issue. Both items used the same exact Jackson image found on the regular Topps rookie. Even though the Super card is regarded as a test issue, the cards exist in much greater numbers than some of the extraordinarily rare Topps test issues of the period. Interestingly, Jackson was pictured on a 1968 Topps Oakland A's team card a year earlier, yet no individual Jackson card was produced.

As we venture into the next decade, Jackson started to appear on vast numbers of regional cards in addition to the standard Topps issues. This included brands like Bazooka, Burger King, Hostess, and Kellogg's to name a few, but the feared slugger was also featured in more Topps test issues such as 1970 Candy Lids and 1973 Pin-Ups. The Candy Lids set, once again, used the same image seen on the Jackson rookie card. The Pin-Ups Jackson is one of his most valuable collectibles, in any grade, due to its scarcity. Before the decade ended, Jackson was included on various mediums, issued by Topps and others, from coins to discs to stamps. The most valuable Jackson card of all, however, was a card never intended to escape the factory.

In 1976, Jackson moved from the Baltimore Orioles to the

New York Yankees as a free agent. Very early in the manufacturing process, Topps created a Jackson proof that pictured the Hall of Famer on the Orioles. Topps needed to pivot quickly, so they modified the existing card to picture Jackson on his new team before the final printing began. According to most experts, fewer than 10 of the Jackson "Orioles" proofs exist. Not surprisingly, one example sold within the last couple of years for $60,000. As his career turned the corner into the 1980s, huge numbers of Jackson cards were released, including those of the three major manufacturers at the time: Topps, Donruss, and Fleer. In 1988, Jackson made his final appearance on cardboard, which included brands like Fleer, Score, and Sportflics.

The REGGIE JACKSON CARD

During an era where many top prospects had to share the limelight on their debut cards, Jackson had the stage all to himself, which was fitting for a baseball player who loved to perform on the biggest stage. The portrait of Jackson is set against a beautiful blue background on his 1969 Topps rookie (#260), and while it's not a card that is hard to find, it is one that can be challenging in top grades. The 1969 Topps set is plagued by image tilts, and those tilts can impact the technical centering and eye appeal of the cards. Furthermore, dark print defects are commonly found in the light background and along the borders of the Jackson card. The reverse of the card was designed with a solid pink/salmon color and that color extends to all four borders. Those edges can also reveal the slightest bit of wear. Finally, a fair percentage of Jackson rookies possess a rather dull look on the front. In other words, the strength of the color can vary quite a bit and this can impact the overall look.

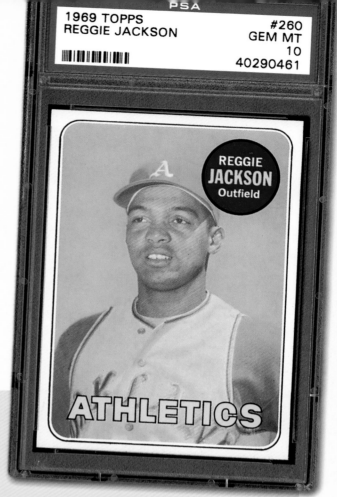

ONE CARD TO WATCH

Jackson had his share of very interesting cards over his 21-year career. Even during his rookie year, Topps produced a 1969 Super, which has always been considered a desirable issue and a great complement to his standard Topps rookie from the same year. Down the road, Jackson appeared in some tough Topps test issues, like the 1973 Pin-Ups, and one of the great rarities in the hobby featured Jackson—the unissued 1977 Topps Baltimore Orioles proof. Each of these and more would be a fine choice, but I decided to go with Jackson's 1971 Topps Greatest Moments card (#47). This oversized 2½" by 4¾" horizontal issue contains 55 cards, and the core of the set is made up of great players who did great things. Ernie Banks, Johnny Bench, Willie Mays, and more are all here in a set designed with vulnerable black borders. If the pesky borders weren't enough to contend with, commonly-found print defects and poor centering add to the collector headache. Along with the #1 card of Thurman Munson, the Jackson card ranks as one of the most valuable in this challenging set.

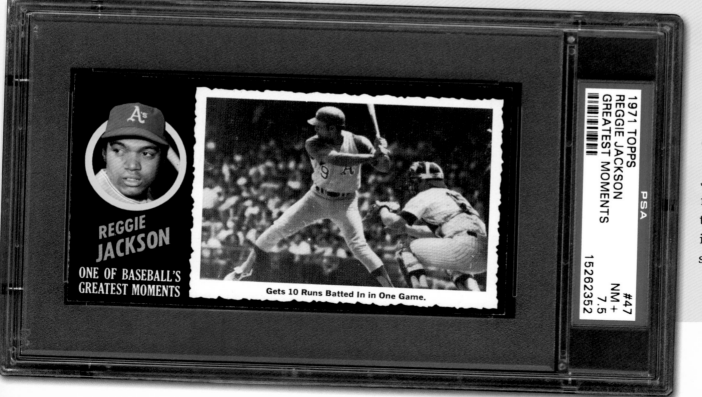

FERGUSON JENKINS

FERGIE'S GREATEST YEARS were with the Cubs. I played with Ferguson Jenkins in 1976, my last year in the big leagues. As a matter of fact, he pitched our Opening Day game and threw a three-hitter, but lost to Jim Palmer and the Orioles. He still had pretty good stuff, but his slider was not what it used to be in his early days with the Cubs. Fergie was in the rotation with Luis Tiant and Rick Wise. I thought that we were going to make a real run for the pennant again, but we finished in third place that year, which was disappointing. I'll tell you though, Fergie was a terrific teammate. Everyone liked him. He was very personable and friendly. Fergie would talk about anything and he was also great about helping his teammates with their hitting. During a game, he would sit with us and explain what the opposing pitcher was doing. Fergie would pick up on things that we didn't see and that made us more aware.

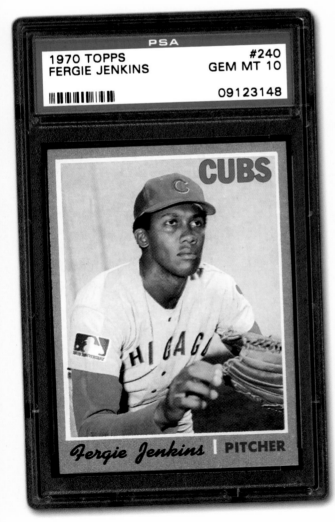

By the time he joined the Red Sox, Fergie did not have tremendous velocity but he still had good control. He could move the ball around and place his pitches, and he could hit that outside corner almost anytime he wanted. When he was with us, Fergie hung with the guys we called "The Buffalo Heads." You know, Carbo, Lee, and a few others. He had some absolutely great seasons with the Cubs. I think he won 20 games about five or six years in a row, and later he won 25 with Texas. Fergie was such a workhorse and he threw a lot of complete games. We played against each other in the 1967 All-Star Game, but the only guy that I faced was Juan Marichal. I remember when Fergie got in that game, he was dynamite. He struck out a bunch of great hitters. In 1974, the year that he won 25 games for Texas, I actually hit him decently. I didn't tear the cover off the ball, but I managed to get some key hits off him, even though he was pretty much lights out. He didn't win the Cy that year, but he was up there in the voting.

One thing that is public knowledge about Fergie is he had some unbelievable tragedy in his life, losing family members. When some of those tragedies occurred, he really could have gone in any direction. Instead he devoted himself to charity work. Over the years, Fergie and I have done several charity golf events for Major League Baseball, and I know he is involved in many charities to this day. Looking at his career, Fergie was on the All-Star team three different times. He won the Cy Young Award, and he led the league in strikeouts. I can't stress enough, though, what a workhorse he was over many years. I know times have changed, and when you think about the way bullpens are used today, it's difficult to get to 200 innings. Fergie pitched over 300 innings several times. That's a competitor! Fergie is very deserving of his place in the Hall of Fame. I was privileged to play with him even for that one year.

THE CARDS

Because Ferguson Jenkins pitched for 19 seasons at the big-league level, from the 1960s into the 1980s, a fair number of cards and collectibles were made bearing his image. Despite his Hall of Fame status, Jenkins was often overshadowed by contemporary stars and teammates. Much like Ron Santo and Billy Williams, both Hall of Famers in their own right, Jenkins never quite reached the level of popularity achieved by former teammate and Cubs icon Ernie Banks. This means that the majority of Jenkins' cards are considered affordable in relation to some of the big names of the day.

Jenkins' entry into the hobby came in 1966. He not only debuted in the 1966 Topps set, but a Venezuelan Topps card was also produced. The Venezuelan Topps cards are much tougher to find than their U.S. counterparts. Soon after making his cardboard debut, Jenkins found his way into some of the more noteworthy regional issues of the era such as Bazooka and Kahn's, an oversized card

that was packaged with hot dogs. In addition to his inclusion in regional sets, Jenkins also appeared on other Topps mediums before the decade was over, which included decal and stamp sets in 1969.

After becoming a star pitcher in the 1960s, Jenkins continued his momentum into the 1970s. Most of his victories and cards date to this period. Beyond the traditional, annual Topps sets that Jenkins was a part of each year, Topps released various other issues during the decade such as the 1971 Super and 1974 Deckle Edge sets. The jagged-looking Deckle Edge card is one of Jenkins' most valuable. Topps also featured Jenkins on some non-card mediums. Some examples are candy lids, coins, and tattoos. While Topps continued to be the dominant force in card manufacturing, Jenkins was included in many other sets. Hostess, Kellogg's, and Milk Duds are just some of the different brands to include Jenkins.

As we head into the home stretch of his career, Jenkins found himself in the middle of the hobby expansion in the 1980s. When Topps was joined by two more major manufacturers, Donruss and Fleer, Jenkins appeared in each brand annually from 1981 through 1984. O-Pee-Chee, the Canadian version of Topps, continued to issue Jenkins cards in the 1980s, which means Jenkins collectors can find O-Pee-Chee cards from all three decades of his career. In 1984, Jenkins can be found in several issues, including two special Topps sets—Nestle and Tiffany. While both Jenkins cards are similar in appearance to the regular Topps issue, each brand was more limited in production.

PSA

1974 TOPPS DECKLE EDGE #59
FERGIE JENKINS   NM – MT 8

40310548

The FERGUSON JENKINS CARD

In 1966, Topps released another eye-catching set, one that has remained popular with collectors today. The design is clean and the imagery is excellent throughout. Like many players of the period, Jenkins had to share the limelight on his first card (#254) with another player. In this case, Philadelphia Phillies teammate and position player Bill Sorrell finds himself next to the future Hall of Famer. The Jenkins rookie is one of three key debut cards in the set. Interestingly, all three keys are rookie cards of Hall of Fame pitchers. In addition to Jenkins, first cards of Jim Palmer and Don Sutton are also included. While the Jenkins card is not overly tough in high grade, collectors should pay special attention to centering and the occasional presence of print defects along the face of the card, especially in the light background of the portraits.

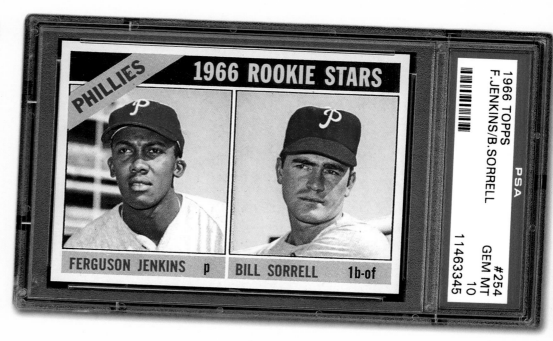

"The Jenkins rookie is one of three key debut cards in the set."

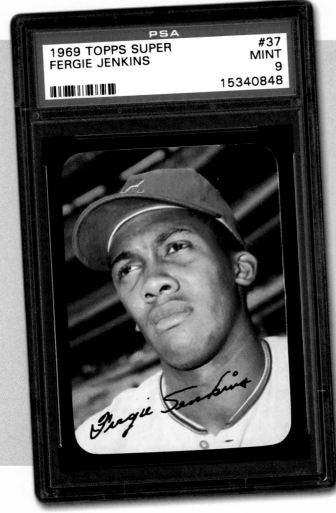

ONE CARD TO WATCH

Over the course of Jenkins' career in cardboard, there aren't too many cards that hobbyists would label as especially noteworthy once you get past his 1966 Topps rookie. One might consider an obscure regional issue like 1967 Pro's Pizza or the aforementioned 1974 Topps Deckle Edge Jenkins to fill this slot. In 1969, Topps created a test issue that remains one of the more attractive designs of the time and one of Jenkins' most desirable cards. The 1969 Topps Super set only contains 66 cards that feature naturally rounded corners, but a healthy portion of the set is devoted to the biggest names in the game. From Hank Aaron to Roberto Clemente to Mickey Mantle, there is no dearth of star power here. The set, while technically of the test variety and produced in far fewer numbers than the regular Topps issue, is attainable and far less scarce than several other Topps test sets of the 1960s and 1970s. The Jenkins card (#37) is clearly one of his most desirable issues, made during the prime of his career and in the middle of a six-year run when the right-hander won 20 or more games each season.

WILLIE McCOVEY

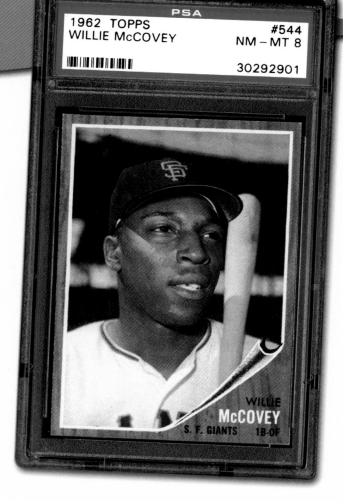

MAN, COULD WILLIE MCCOVEY HIT those home runs. One of the big stars of the Giants, Willie was the prototypical power hitter with home runs and RBI, and he wasn't a bad first baseman either. I played against him in the 1969 All-Star Game and I remember he hit a couple of homers. He was awesome. That year, Willie was the National League MVP. That happened to be my best year as a player, and I got some AL MVP votes myself, which I'm very proud of. Willie though, had a monster year. In my opinion, Willie was really the leader of that Giants team. His teammates looked up to him and went to him when there was an issue.

Willie told me that he was shocked when Bobby Richardson caught the line drive that he hit in Game Seven to end the 1962 World Series. Had that ball gotten through, the Giants would have won it. He hit a rope.

It could have taken Richardson's glove off, it was hit that hard. McCovey was certainly one of the most feared hitters in the major leagues, but he was kind of a quiet guy and he let his playing do his talking. Willie's nickname was Stretch, which was appropriate based on his size. He stood about 6'4" and weighed at least 200 pounds. The thing about Willie was how hard he hit the ball. He was one of those guys who hit line-drive home runs with authority, and talk about a feared tandem, that was Mays and McCovey. I enjoyed following those Giants teams when I was playing. There was a period of time when they were just killing the ball.

There were a couple of years when Willie hit 44–45 bombs to lead the league. In the years when he did not lead the league in home runs, he was always near the top. For me, as a teenager in New York, it was great to watch guys like McCovey, and then get an opportunity to play against them, or with them, later on. It's too bad I didn't get a chance to know him a little better. We did play the Giants in spring training in Arizona, but that ended in 1966 when we moved to Winter Haven, Florida, and they stayed in Phoenix. For the last part of his career, Willie was hampered by all kinds of injuries. He reminded me of Cepeda who basically played on one leg. Willie was like that but he could still hit 20 to 25 homers playing on those gimpy knees.

I know Willie has had health problems for several years now, but he is still active with the Giants. Willie didn't hit for a high average, but with over 500 home runs and more than 2,000 hits, he was certainly a superstar. Heck, they even named the water basin outside of the San Francisco ballpark McCovey Cove. Willie was a class act who very much deserves being in the Hall of Fame. It would have been great to play against him on a regular basis.

THE CARDS

Like teammates Orlando Cepeda and Juan Marichal, Willie McCovey was overshadowed by another Willie, a man who many believe is the greatest five-tool player in baseball history – Willie Mays. McCovey's association with Mays, however, provided the San Francisco Giants with one of the most potent offensive duos in baseball. That association coupled with McCovey's entry into the 500 Home Run Club help keep the slugger in the conversation when discussing the best power hitters of all time. McCovey's 22 seasons ensured plenty of collectibles bearing his likeness for the hobbyist.

When McCovey first came onto the scene, there were a few different

"In 1969, McCovey had his best season and was featured on one of his most appealing cards."

cards released during his rookie era. This included appearances by McCovey in the 1958–1961 Jay Publishing photo set and the 1960 Nu-Card Baseball Hi-Lites issue. Both black-and-white issues are oversized, but neither carries quite the clout that his more diminutive 1960 Topps rookie does. This is the card that most collectors consider to be his official rookie. Technically, there are two different McCovey cards in the set, but the #316 is the one that garners most of the demand.

Shortly into his career, McCovey began to show signs of his slugging prowess and the collectibles followed. Beyond the traditional Topps issues of the time, McCovey was included in a variety of additional Topps sets, not to mention the Canadian (O-Pee-Chee) and Venezuelan Topps versions of the U.S. cards. Interestingly, McCovey can be found on a few noteworthy Topps short prints. McCovey's 1962 and 1966 cards are examples of this, as well as his 1964 Stand-Up. McCovey was also featured on several Topps mediums, from coins to decals to stamps. It didn't stop there either. The slugger was a part of various regional issues as well. Those brands included the likes of Bazooka, Post Cereal, and Wheaties.

Between the 1960s and 1970s, several Topps test McCovey collectibles were created. The 1973 Topps Comics and Pin-Ups rank near the top of his checklist when it comes to sheer scarcity, but perhaps no McCovey collectible is as elusive

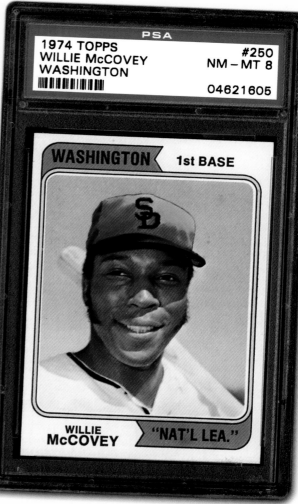

as his 1970 Topps Cloth Sticker, which is far tougher than his 1972 Topps Cloth Sticker. In 1974, in the regular Topps set, the manufacturer inadvertently created an intriguing McCovey variation. Topps assumed that the San Diego Padres were moving to Washington, as did many others. As a result, Topps created 15 different cards with "Washington" noted on the cards in anticipation of the move. Well, the team was purchased and stayed in San Diego. Topps quickly regrouped and issued the same cards with the correct "San Diego" affiliation, but it was too late. McCovey was one of the players affected, creating two different base cards that year. McCovey made his last appearance in the 1981 Fleer set (#434) and was noticeably absent from the Donruss and Topps sets that same year.

The WILLIE MCCOVEY CARD

In 1960, Topps decided to move back to a horizontal design after a few years (1957–1959) of using a vertical format for their annual release. This colorful set, one that ushered in a new decade, contained all kinds of interesting features, from multi-player cards to a high-number All-Star run to finish off the issue. In addition, Topps blended the use of color photography with artwork throughout the 1960 set. One of the cards that featured artwork versus a traditional color photo was the McCovey rookie (#316). Like most other Topps cards in the set, including the Carl Yastrzemski rookie, the debut card of McCovey is often found with print defects and unattractive centering. In most grades, both the McCovey and Yastrzemski rookies are comparable in value. McCovey can be found on another card in the aforementioned high-number series (#554), but while this All-Star card is important, it has never been on equal footing with #316.

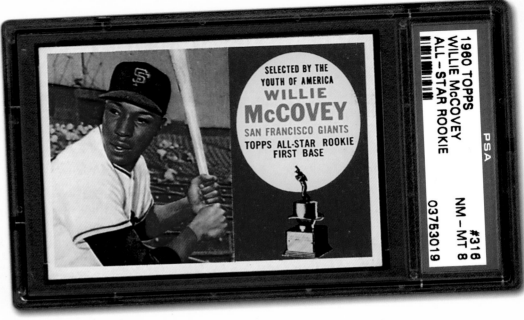

"Topps blended the use of color photography with artwork throughout the 1960 set."

ONE CARD TO WATCH

In 1969, McCovey had his best season and was featured on one of his most appealing cards. During the same year that McCovey won the NL MVP, narrowly missing the Triple Crown, the intimidating slugger was part of a short run where Topps printed the player's last name in white instead of the traditional yellow on the front of each card. This run, which impacted cards found in the #440–511 stretch, included some big names like Hall of Famers McCovey, Gaylord Perry, and Mickey Mantle. This just happened to be Mantle's last Topps card, so the conspiracy theorists have had a field day with this alleged "mistake." Was it an honest printing error or a marketing ploy to get people to buy more packs? We may never know the truth, but one thing's for sure, the McCovey card is one of his toughest to find and most valuable from his career in cardboard. For collectors in search of high-grade examples, beware of image tilts, which are commonly seen in this issue.

JOE MORGAN

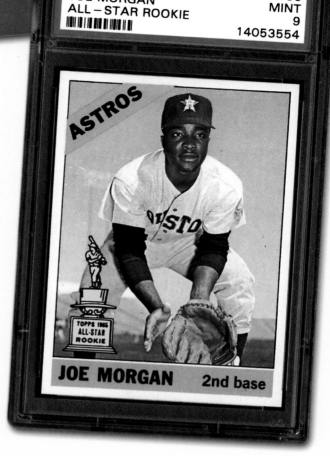

1966 TOPPS
JOE MORGAN
ALL—STAR ROOKIE

PSA

#195

MINT
9

14053554

JOE MORGAN   2nd base

AN OUTSTANDING PLAYER in the minor leagues, Joe Morgan came up to the Houston Colt .45's just a bit earlier than I came up to Boston. In the minors, he played just like he did in the majors. Joe had great range as a second baseman and was great on the double play. He was also an excellent clutch hitter who had some power. I've known Joe really well since we both played in the minor leagues. When he came up he was a little outspoken, and that became kind of a trademark for him. Joe was never afraid to speak his mind about an opposing pitcher or ballplayer. I remember in the 1975 World Series, Joe didn't think that the Red Sox could compete with the Reds. They had a great team, but I think we surprised them a lot. When we played at Fenway and Joe was on base, he complained to me about the ballpark, because his power was to right field and he couldn't take advantage of the close left-field wall. I really think Joe was outspoken because he was so competitive.

1972 TOPPS
JOE MORGAN
TRADED

PSA

#752

NM-MT 8

06066238

JOE MORGAN

Overall as a player, Joe was terrific but his best years were with the Reds. He was the NL MVP twice and he was an All-Star every year he was in Cincinnati. Joe didn't hit for a real high average, but he always made great contact. As I recall, he hit Sandy Koufax well. He could hit the tough pitchers. Joe had that unique elbow jerk when he was up at the plate, kind of a chicken wing elbow. It was just how he learned to keep his elbow up, but I think it threw pitchers off quite a bit. Joe got the winning hit in Game Seven of the 1975 World Series against us. It was a bloop single to center field, but talk about a clutch hit! We had the opportunity to win that game and the championship, but it just wasn't in the cards. Joe was an excellent basestealer and there was always a threat when he was on base. Our guy, Luis Tiant, had a great motion over to first base. Joe always complained it was a balk. That was his way of trying to mess Luis up. Joe was an outspoken, competitive guy, but the thing about him was he could back up what he said with his performance. There's no doubt he was one heck of a ballplayer.

Whenever we bumped into each other in later years, Joe and I would mostly talk about that 1975 Series. It bothered him that the Fisk home run was still talked about and that people seemed to forget the Reds won the Series. You probably already know that Fisk used to tell people that the Red Sox won the

Series 3 games to 4! When I look at the greatest second basemen of all time, I definitely include Joe in the conversation. Besides winning many Gold Gloves, Joe played the game with reckless abandon. When you look at both his offense and defense, I would put him up there with the likes of Robbie Alomar, Rogers Hornsby, and Eddie Collins. Quite frankly, there were a few players who resented Joe's style of play and his outspoken comments. I personally never had a problem with him. For a little guy, he was a big part of the Big Red Machine, and with the talent that surrounded him, he could back it all up.

THE CARDS

With 22 seasons under his belt and a career that stretched into the hobby boom of the 1980s, Joe Morgan was pictured on plenty of baseball cards and collectibles as an active player. One would think that the combination of his individual accomplishments and his connection to one of the greatest teams ever assembled in the "Big Red Machine" would drive the prices for his items out of range for most collectors, but that is not the case. Despite being regarded as one of the best second basemen in baseball history, most Morgan collectibles are fairly affordable, including his rookie card.

Morgan's entry into the hobby came in 1965, and it is important to note that he not only appeared in the regular Topps set, but a Canadian version (O-Pee-Chee) of the same card exists as well. Morgan was paired with another player on that debut card, so he didn't appear by himself until 1966. O-Pee-Chee

and Venezuelan Topps cards were made of Morgan at different times during his career. Morgan became a big leaguer during a period when Topps had become very creative and experimental. Besides appearing on various Topps mediums like rub-offs, pin-ups, and stamps, Morgan found himself in some tough Topps test issues as well, like the seldom-seen 1967 Punch-Outs and beautiful 1969 Super set.

The next decade would prove to be Morgan's finest as a player. After he was traded to the Cincinnati Reds, Morgan became a household name in the game and the hobby. In fact, that moment was captured on cardboard in the 1972 Topps set. Many collectors regard this set as the best regular Topps production of the decade. A group of seven cards were added to the base set with the word "Traded" across the front to denote that the player had just switched teams. Morgan appeared as a member of the Houston Astros on card #132 earlier in the set, but this special run was part of the high-number series, with the Morgan card coming in at #752. It marked a key moment in Morgan's career as he would go on to win back-to-back World Series titles and NL MVP Awards in 1975 and 1976.

One of Morgan's most valuable cards of the decade is his 1971 Topps Greatest Moment card, a card that comes with a host of condition obstacles for those interested in high-grade

examples. As the decade progressed, Morgan was one of many stars to be featured in numerous disc sets, which became a popular medium by the mid-1970s. Before his playing days ended, Morgan would appear on countless regional cards like those issued by Burger King, Hostess, Kellogg's, K-Mart, Mother's Cookies, Pepsi, Tastykake, and Wendy's. His presence in these regional issues extended from the 1970s to the 1980s, a time when the hobby expanded in a big way. In 1985, Morgan made his final appearance in the hobby and all three major manufacturers at the time (Donruss, Fleer, and Topps) honored him with cards.

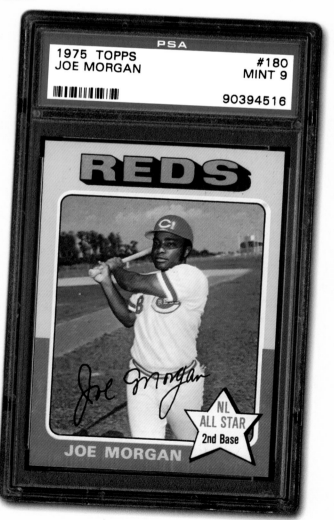

The JOE MORGAN CARD

The 1965 Topps set is anchored by four Hall of Fame rookie cards. Debut singles of Steve Carlton, Catfish Hunter, and Tony Perez are all included, as well as Morgan's first baseball card (#16). As was the case with many rookies of the era, all four of them had to share the spotlight with at least one other player. Morgan was pictured with teammate and fellow Houston prospect Sonny Jackson. There aren't a lot of high-value Morgan cards in the hobby, so his only official rookie stands out even more. The card itself, like most in the set, suffers from inconsistent centering. With somewhat narrow borders on all four sides, a slight shift in any direction can cause eye-appeal issues. Furthermore, dark print defects tend to be noticeable along the face of the

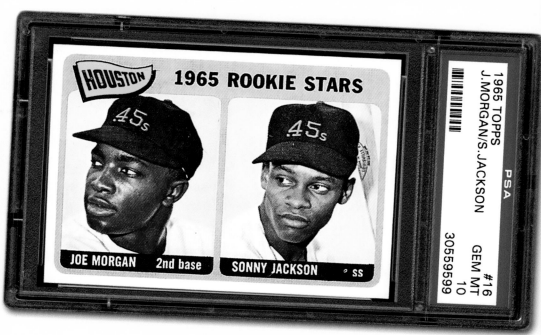

card, which includes a very light blue background behind the headshots of the players. Finally, the reverse has a blue-colored border, making it susceptible to chipping.

ONE CARD TO WATCH

There is no question that many Morgan cards and collectibles were made while he was active, but there aren't many that stand out in dramatic fashion from the rest either as a result of monetary value or significance. The two finalists in this category were Morgan's 1971 Topps Greatest Moments card and his 1972 Topps Traded issue. Both are tough in context and have appealing aspects to them, but in the end, the Greatest Moments card won the day. It combines aesthetic appeal with a true challenge. This oversized 2½" by 4¾" horizontal issue contains 55 cards and the core of the set is made up of great players who did great things. Johnny Bench, Reggie Jackson, Willie Mays, and more are part

of this set, which was designed with vulnerable black borders. To make matters worse, the cards are often found with poor centering. The Morgan, specifically, is often centered low and that is why no unqualified PSA Mint 9s have been graded to date.

PHIL NIEKRO

I NEVER FACED PHIL NIEKRO during the regular season, but I did face him during spring training when he was with Atlanta. Sometimes the pitchers don't ramp it up until spring training is nearly finished. That was not the case with Phil. His speed never changed from the start of spring training until the end, and all he worked on was refining his command. Phil could throw strikes with his knuckler, which is incredible. The way to hit a good knuckleballer is to hang in at the plate, be still, and shorten your swing. For me, a short quick swing was the most effective. I would pray that the knuckleball would hang there and not do very much. If you're locked in, you remain steady and you followed the ball, you could have some success.

Like Wilbur Wood, Niekro was slower than Hoyt Wilhelm, which allowed you to follow the ball a little better. Overall, I had pretty good luck against Phil and some of those other knuckleballers.

Phil once said that he loved pitching for the Braves although some of those teams were pretty weak. Everyone liked Phil, but I remember talking about National League pitchers with a few of the Reds in 1975, and Niekro's name came up as being a pain in the neck to hit. As I recall, Pete Rose found him to be a little difficult.

I'd say of the knucklers that I faced, Phil was the best. Hoyt had more speed, but Phil did throw faster than Wilbur. I remember this clearly because, as a big league hitter, you need to learn to adjust to the speed. When a knuckleballer is good, he can be very valuable to a team, because he can give you a lot of innings. Phil was a real innings eater. He pitched over 300 innings several times and over 200 innings a ton, and he had amazing longevity, pitching until he was almost fifty. I think Phil would have pitched until his arm fell off. Because he was a starter, he ended up pitching way more innings than Wilhelm or Wood.

Phil was an All-Star many times. I played against him in the 1969 All-Star Game, but I did not face him. They brought him in to close out the game but by that time I had already had my at-bats. For a pitcher, Phil was an excellent fielder and I believe he won several Gold Gloves. Winning 300 games is also a tremendous accomplishment, and he pitched a no-hitter to boot! Yes, Phil was the best of the knucklers I faced, especially when you consider the length of time he pitched and that he was in the starting rotation.

In later years, I know Phil spent a lot of time with Tim Wakefield of the Red Sox and was a big help to him. Knuckleballers all help each other. It's not an easy pitch to throw. From Wilhelm to Wood to Niekro to Wakefield to Steven Wright, they seem to be a close-knit fraternity.

THE CARDS

The life of a knuckleball pitcher. Despite being a 300-game winner and Hall of Famer, being a knuckleball pitcher is arguably likened to being the "Rodney Dangerfield" of baseball. As the legendary comedian used to say, "I get no respect!" No, Phil Niekro did not possess a 98-MPH fastball or a braggadocious demeanor, he simply got the job done with the one pitch that a hitter really can't prepare for. As a hitter, you just have to hope you see one that doesn't quite "knuckle." Niekro knuckled his way to 318 victories over the course of 24 years. Perhaps the lack of flash limits the appeal of his cards and collectibles overall, but it also keeps many of them within striking distance for the average collector.

It started for the master of deception in 1964, when Niekro's undisputed rookie card was born in the annual Topps set. Niekro does have a Jay Publishing Photo that arrived during his rookie era, but

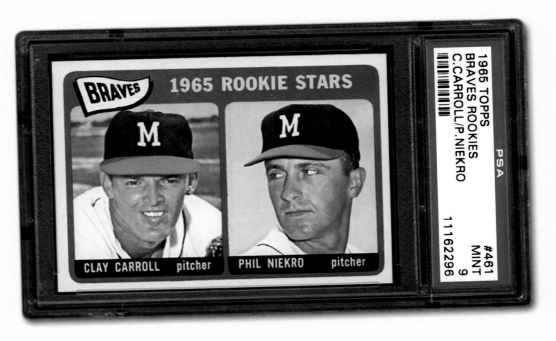

"Niekro knuckled his way to 318 victories."

the 1964 Topps card is considered his true debut. In an interesting twist, not only did Niekro share his rookie card with another player, he had to do it again the very next year. In 1965, Niekro was pictured on a horizontal card along with teammate Clay Carroll entitled *Braves 1965 Rookie Stars*. You can see why new collectors may mistake his 1965 Topps card for his rookie. Why Topps chose to do this remains a mystery. It could be a result of Niekro not playing much his first couple of years, but we'll never know.

Niekro did finally get his own regular-issue Topps card in 1966. In addition to the regular Topps issues, Niekro can be found in an assortment of related O-Pee-Chee (Canadian) and Venezuelan Topps sets along the way. While both are much tougher to find than their U.S. Topps counterparts, the Venezuelan cards are clearly the toughest of the three. Topps became very creative during the 1960s, producing various mediums and test issues at the factory. Strangely, Niekro is noticeably absent from many of these highly-collectible productions. It did take a few years for Niekro

to establish himself in the league, but perhaps this relates to the "No Respect" issue we covered earlier. Or, it could simply be a result of contractual issues.

Once we head into the 1970s, you can find Niekro in several regional sets like those made by Burger King, Coca-Cola, Hostess, and Kellogg's. The most elusive Niekro collectible of all, however, was made by Topps. The 1970 Topps Cloth Stickers test set only contained 15 items and is almost never seen. Niekro is one of a handful of stars who were chosen for the experiment. Niekro's longevity carried him into the hobby explosion of the 1980s, when Donruss and Fleer joined Topps as major baseball card manufacturers. Since knuckleball pitchers are so rare, and Phil and Joe Niekro (Phil's brother) played during the same era, and some years on the same team, a few cards were made like the 1983 Donruss Niekro Brothers and 1986 Donruss Knuckle Brothers honoring the sibling duo. Niekro's final appearance in the hobby came in 1988 on a handful of cards, which included those released by relative newcomers Classic and Score.

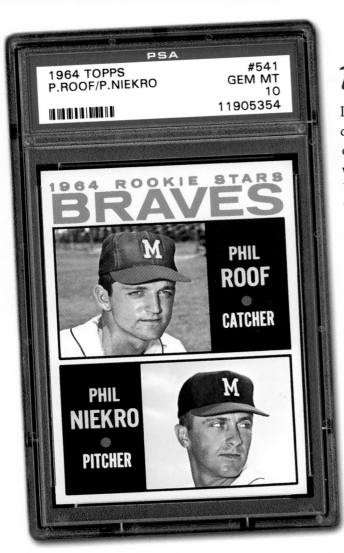

The PHIL NIEKRO CARD

In 1964, Topps released another in a long line of annual baseball card sets. This time, while the set has plenty of appeal, the lack of major rookie cards is evident. Of course, no one ever knows what players will blossom into superstars or become major league busts at the time the cards are made. It is the luck of the draw. The one rookie card that stands out above the rest is the only Hall of Fame player rookie in the entire set, that of Mr. Niekro (#541). There is one other Hall of Fame rookie card in the set, but that is of Tony La Russa, who entered Cooperstown for his managerial excellence. Niekro, like many players of the period, had to share his rookie card with another player. This time, it was batterymate Phil Roof. The card is not known as a condition rarity, but finding a well-centered copy can be challenging, and keep in mind that the reverse is surrounded by a colored border that can reveal wear to the naked eye.

"The 1972 Topps set is also massive at 787 total cards."

ONE CARD TO WATCH

During his career in cardboard, Niekro wasn't included in many sets that would naturally produce standout cards based on their scarcity or overwhelming popularity. So, we must dig further to find a worthy candidate much like Niekro had to dig his fingernails into the ball in order to deliver his hellacious pitch. The 1972 Topps baseball card set has often been referred to as the manufacturer's premier release of the decade. The psychedelic design, terrific star selection, and wide variety of special cards make this one of the most popular period issues. The 1972 Topps set is also massive at 787 total cards. Niekro's card (#620) remains one of the toughest cards to find in PSA Mint 9 or Gem Mint 10 condition due to inherent centering problems. In fact, Niekro's card is clearly worth more than some other Hall of Famers found in the set like Jim Palmer, Willie McCovey, and Frank Robinson in those grades. Relatively speaking, this is one of Niekro's most intriguing cards.

JIM PALMER

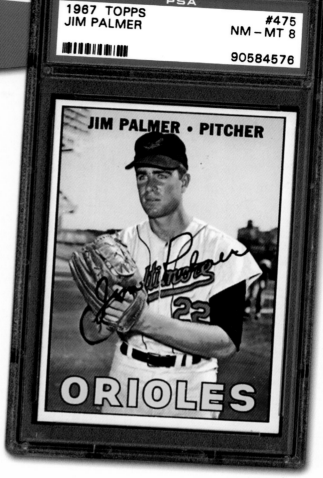

PERSONALLY, I THINK JIM PALMER was one of the classiest pitchers I ever faced. Jim had a very good fastball, curveball, and changeup, and he pitched intelligently. He was one of those guys who acted the same whether he won or lost. Jim pitched in a lot of clutch games and was, without a doubt, Baltimore's most consistent and talented pitcher. In my opinion, when the Orioles had the four 20-game winners, he had the best stuff of all of them. Of course playing with the Robinsons, Powell, and the rest of those guys helped him, but there's no doubt he was the real deal.

I played against Jim for most of my career and I hit him well. There was one game in particular, in 1975, a big game in September against the Orioles. We were leading the division by about four games but Baltimore was on one of their streaks. The pitching matchup for this particular game was Jim against our guy, Luis Tiant. We wound up winning the game 2–0, and I was fortunate to hit a home run. That game really gave us the momentum to go the rest of the way.

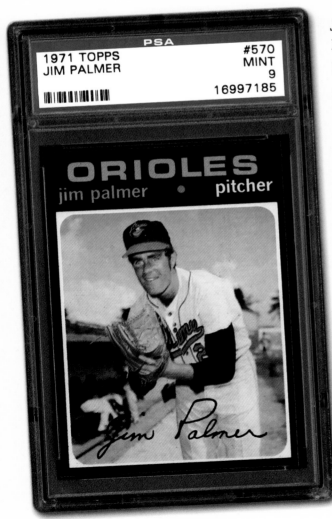

Jim had a high, hard fastball which was difficult to catch up to. I think I had some success off him because I disciplined myself to lay off that particular pitch. Later on, we talked at fantasy camps and Jim would give me the business about being a low-ball hitter. He told me when I laid off his high pitches, he knew he was in trouble. Initially, I started as a high-ball hitter but guys like Palmer started throwing a steady diet of curveballs and low fastballs, and I learned to adjust.

Of the pitchers that I faced over my career, Palmer was definitely in the top ten. I remember after Jim hurt his arm he came back and tried to throw a little eephus pitch followed by slow curveballs, but as he got better, he went back to being his old self. Jim really loved the Orioles and spent his entire career with them. During that time, they were a real juggernaut, with three World Series wins, and they were in the postseason a number of times. Jim won at least 20 games during most of the 1970s and he was dominant, winning the Cy Young Award three times.

Even though he had some classic confrontations on the mound with Earl Weaver, I think Jim genuinely respected Earl.

We have chatted a few times about his off-the-field endeavors, and I'll tell you, Jim was a very good businessman. It started with those underwear commercials and then suddenly he was pitching all kinds of products on TV. He really figured out how to capitalize on his baseball fame. Jim was actually a very down-to-earth guy, and we always got along. He's been doing a nice job as color analyst for the Orioles television broadcasts for many years. As someone who did some color for the Red Sox on both TV and on the radio, I understand the preparation that is involved with that. Jim is very good at whatever he does and he is always prepared, whether it was on the field or in his broadcasting career.

THE CARDS

For nearly 20 years, Jim Palmer donned the same cap. He pitched in six different World Series for the Baltimore Orioles, which helped elevate his status to nationwide stardom. Over the course of his career, Palmer appeared on various cards and collectibles. That said, with his early success and popularity, one would think Palmer would have been included in even more hobby issues. Nevertheless, the good news is there are plenty of Palmer items to choose from and most of them remain affordable for the average collector.

Palmer entered the hobby in 1966, after logging nearly 100 innings at the major-league level in 1965. Keep in mind that in addition to Palmer's Topps rookie, two other versions of the card also exist. The Canadian (O-Pee-Chee) and Venezuelan Topps issues included Palmer as well, with both certainly tougher to locate than his traditional Topps rookie card. Over three decades, Palmer would appear in many O-Pee-Chee sets. Even though he entered the league and the hobby at a time when Topps had become extremely creative and experimental, Palmer was noticeably absent in these

sometimes popular, and often rare, issues that helped define an era.

As we enter the 1970s, Palmer's image can be found on far more collectibles, well beyond the regular Topps sets that hobbyists were accustomed to seeing. Regional issues like Hostess, Kellogg's, Milk Duds, Pepsi, and Wendy's were just some of the brands to feature Palmer throughout the decade. Like many other stars of the mid-to-late 1970s, Palmer was included in a variety of discs sets, which became a popular medium during a several-year stretch. Even within the Topps brand, basic baseball cards weren't the only place that Palmer could be seen. Interesting Topps sets such as Coins (1971) and Candy Lids (1973) made Palmer part of their checklists, too.

Since Palmer was a model of consistency, winning 20 or more games eight times during the decade, you will find the right-hander on plenty of *League Leader* cards alongside other star

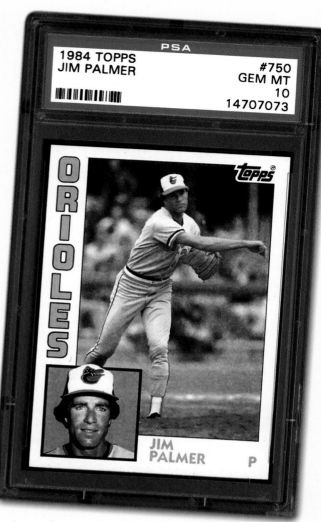

"The Venezuelan Topps Palmer rookie is, by far, his most elusive …"

pitchers of the time. Throughout his career, you will also notice Palmer's inclusion on a handful of cards dedicated to his World Series appearances. In 1982, one of Palmer's more interesting cards was produced. This time, it was an error. That year, Topps issued some of the cards without black ink. The regular cards are missing the expected facsimile signature and the All-Star cards are missing the player names on the fronts. They are referred to as "blackless" variations and can be very tough to find. Palmer's last year in baseball and the hobby, at least as an active player, was 1984. Every major manufacturer included Palmer in their base sets that year, with Topps releasing several complementary Palmer issues.

The JIM PALMER CARD

Throughout the 1960s, many new players were forced to share the limelight with fellow rookies on their debut card. In some cases, it was one other rookie, which was the case for Hall of Famers like Joe Morgan, Tom Seaver, and Nolan Ryan. In other cases, the rookie was one of three or four featured on the face of the card, which was true for stars Tony Perez and Willie Stargell. There were instances, however, where the fresh face was able to secure his own card. That is the case with Jim Palmer, who debuted in the 1966 Topps set (#126). Fellow Hall of Fame pitchers Ferguson Jenkins and Don Sutton also made their debut in the 1966 Topps set, but Palmer's rookie clearly garners the most demand of the trio. In addition, that same year, Palmer was also included in the Canadian version (O-Pee-Chee) of the Topps set and the Venezuelan Topps issue. The Venezuelan Topps Palmer rookie is, by far, his most elusive of the three, but the more common U.S. Topps issue remains the most popular. While it is not considered a condition rarity, the card is commonly found with image tilts, which can impact centering and eye appeal.

ONE CARD TO WATCH

Right in the middle of Palmer's peak years as a pitcher, Topps decided to rekindle an old concept. In 1974, Topps created a 72-card set called Deckle Edge, inserting Palmer on card #45. Even though this star-packed set is technically considered a test issue, it wasn't the first time that the manufacturer used the unmistakable jagged design along the borders. The first Topps Deckle Edge concept was released in 1969, but those cards are much easier to find and smaller at 2¼" by 3¼" in size. The oversized 1974 cards measure approximately 2⅞" by 5". The borderless cards feature a blue facsimile autograph against a black-and-white front. The backs showcase the basic player info in blue script, while a mock newspaper clipping sits beneath it, providing a noteworthy highlight about the player. There are two variations. The more common version has a dull, gray-colored reverse. The backs, however, can also be found in white, and they are the tougher of the two variations.

TONY PEREZ

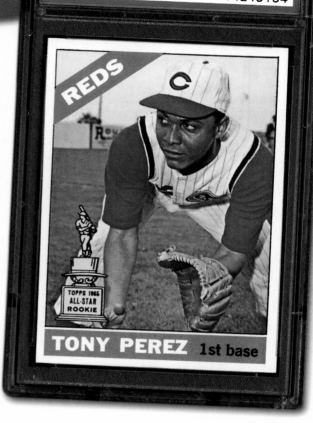

A MANAGER'S DREAM, TONY PEREZ was a big game player, power hitter, and RBI guy. He was also the epitome of a clutch hitter, and Tony held his own defensively. "Big Dog" was a professional hitter. Luis Tiant and I often talked about Tony because they were close friends. We both thought Perez was a great guy, but once he got on the field, he was all business and very competitive. When we faced the Reds in the 1975 World Series, Tony struggled offensively but he hit a few big bombs when it counted. In that Series, Bill Lee got him out on a steady diet of sinkers and slow curveballs. Lee had a big breaking ball he called the "Leephus" pitch. Perez would chase it in the dirt, take a big swing, and miss. Tony managed to keep his sense of humor throughout the Series, and in Game Seven, he finally got his revenge. We were ahead 3–0 in the sixth inning.

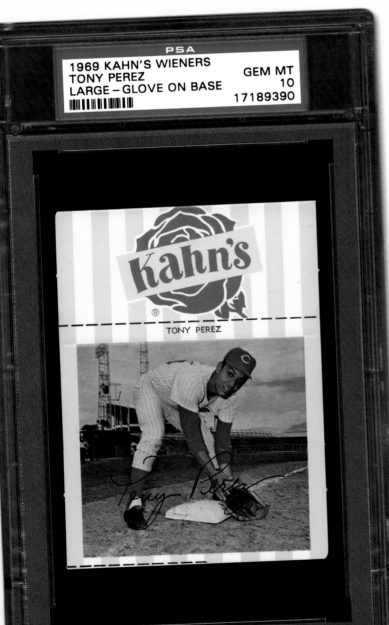

With a 0–2 count and Johnny Bench on base, "Spaceman" threw that big sweeping curve, and this time Tony waited on it and got it. Tony kept his hands back, got the good part of the wood on it, and hit that ball so hard, I think it's still traveling. He was a great clutch hitter, especially when there were men on base.

I've had Tony on my radio show a number of times. He often talks about Cuba and is hopeful that relations will improve between our countries. He was a year ahead of me in the minors and soon after he came up to Cincy, the team was loaded with talent with Bench, Rose, Morgan, Griffey, Perez, and the rest. Tony and I have had many discussions about that team and he has always said that he felt blessed to be playing on it. Believe me though, he more than carried his weight with them. He was a multi-year All-Star, played on two World Series champs and was very well-rounded with the hits to home runs. I remember he got a 15th-inning home run off Catfish Hunter to win the 1967 All-Star Game. He was actually the All-Star MVP that year.

Tony came over to the Red Sox after I retired, and in his first year with the Sox, he was outstanding. I had just finished my color commentary job for the Red Sox, but I still spent quite a bit of time with the team although I was hosting a weekly TV show in Boston called, believe it or not, *Bowling for Dollars*. Tony always greeted me with, "Rico, my friend." That meant a

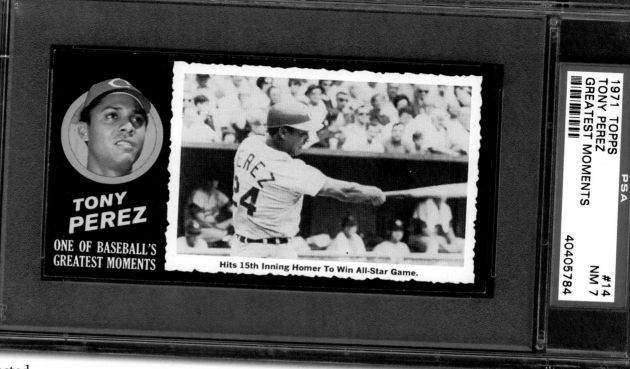

lot to me. I was happy to see Tony with the Sox, and we often chatted about what a blast it was to play in that 1975 World Series. The thing I always appreciated about Tony was that he consistently made the top ten in his league in most offensive categories throughout his career. I was happy that he was inducted into the Hall of Fame the same year my friend Carlton Fisk was inducted. Tony Perez is a great role model for Latinos all over the country, and I am proud to know him.

THE CARDS

Tony Perez played for an impressive 23 seasons from 1964 through 1986, which meant that plenty of cards and collectibles were made for the hobbyist. Perez's career extended into the hobby explosion of the 1980s, which meant that Topps no longer had the stage to themselves as a major manufacturer once they were joined by Donruss and Fleer. Perez was not the flashiest of players and he was often overshadowed by his own legendary teammates like Johnny Bench, Joe Morgan, and Pete Rose, but his eventual induction into baseball's hallowed halls ensured that future generations will appreciate his accomplishments more fully.

Despite the existence of period postcards issued by the Reds team, the Perez card that collectors clamor for is his 1965 Topps rookie. Like

many other rookies of the era, such as Rose and Rod Carew, Perez was pictured on the front along with other prospects. The difference is in the design, and it seemed to reflect the confidence that scouts had in Perez's ability. Perez was positioned in prominent fashion with a larger photo above the other two rookies on the card. This design is unlike the typical rookie cards made at the time, where each player was generally given equal billing.

Near the beginning of Perez's career and before the decade came to a close, the RBI machine made appearances in one of the more popular regional issues of the 1950s and 1960s. Kahn's Wieners released colorful trading card sets featuring Perez from 1967 through 1969, their final year of a 15-year run in the business of baseball cards. Kahn's was a Cincinnati-based meat company that issued small sets of local teams like the Reds, Pittsburgh Pirates, and more during their run. The card designs changed over time, but each of the three sets that contained Perez had similar looks,

which included a defined Kahn's ad tab accompanied by a dotted line. Collectors clearly prefer the cards to be intact. Examples with the tab removed are valued significantly lower than those that are complete.

As his career progressed, Perez started to appear on various mediums like coins, discs, and stamps, but perhaps two of the Hall of Famer's most intriguing cards of the 1970s came in 1971 and 1974. The black-bordered 1971 Topps Greatest Moments are oversized at 2½" by 4¾" and very tough in high grade. The Perez card specifically is very hard to find well centered. In fact, less than 10 examples have been graded PSA NM-MT 8 to date. The oversized and jagged-looking 1974 Topps Deckle Edge test cards measure approximately 2⅞" by 5". There are two versions: a more common gray-colored reverse and the tougher white backs. Perez made his final appearance on cardboard, at least as an active player, in 1987. Interestingly, Fleer was the only major manufacturer to issue a Perez card that year.

The TONY PEREZ CARD

In 1965, Topps put together a set that is still revered today for its clean design and excellent star selection. In particular, while the manufacturer didn't know it at the time, the set would ultimately produce four Hall of Famer rookie cards in Morgan, Steve Carlton, Catfish Hunter, and Perez. Morgan and Perez would eventually join forces as part of the "Big Red Machine" in Cincinnati, the most feared team of the 1970s. Perez was prominently featured on the face of his rookie card but had to share the stage with Kevin Collins and Dave Ricketts, who were pictured underneath the slugging first baseman. The card itself is not known as a condition rarity, but there are a few things that collectors should be aware of. The portrait of Perez is surrounded by a light-yellow background, which can be a haven for print defects. In addition, the card is often found with poor centering and the reverse of the card has a blue border. As a result, the slightest touch of wear will become visible to the naked eye.

ONE CARD TO WATCH

Without a doubt, the 1965 Topps Perez is the one hobbyists focus on as they build their Hall of Fame rookie card collections. This theme is one of the most popular in all of card collecting, so it's hard to unseat an official rookie card of any Hall of Famer knowing that. Monetary value, on the other hand, is a different story. When it comes to value, there is one Perez card rarity that stands above the rest and it's not even close. In 1968, Topps put together one of many test issues that helped define an era for the manufacturer. This time, Topps created a 12-card set and these were no ordinary-looking cards. The images of the players were set against blurred backgrounds on the plastic fronts, creating a revolutionary 3-D effect. There is nothing like it from that decade or before. There are only two Hall of Famers in the set: Perez and Pittsburgh icon Roberto Clemente.

GAYLORD PERRY

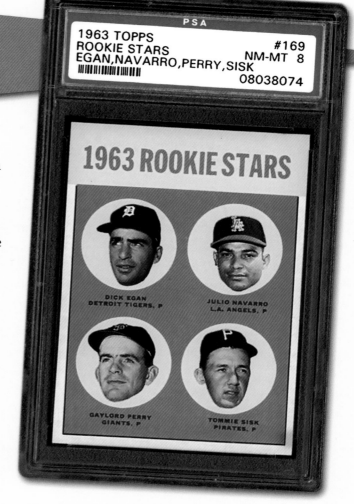

WHEN GAYLORD PERRY CAME OVER to the American League, he had a bit of a reputation for throwing spitballs. In almost every game he pitched, the hitter or the opposing manager would ask the ump to check the ball. Then they would go out and check Gaylord to see if he had any foreign substance on him like Vaseline, spit, or lard, but usually they didn't find anything. Did he throw spitters? Probably now and then. Gaylord also used the rosin bag, and shook it so much that the whole area around the mound would look like it was in a fog. You couldn't see the ball coming out of his hand. He was something else. He was certainly a character, but I'll tell you, Gaylord was a helluva pitcher.

To me, his so-called spitter looked more like a split-fingered fastball. I think he had a couple of pitches that he did something with, but I also think that a lot of it was psychological. The guy was in everybody's head.

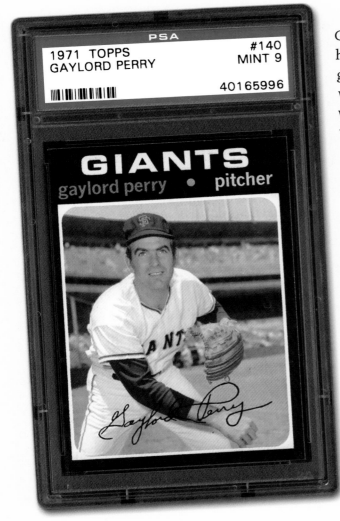

Gaylord could throw strikes consistently with that fastball and he had a nice curveball and a sinker. He was a big, strong "old school" guy, and really tough. In one game, he hit Fisk in the head. He wasn't throwing real hard, but I always had the impression that he wasn't too fond of Carlton. When we first faced Gaylord, everyone was always looking for that spitball. Guys would come back into the dugout mumbling, "Did you see it? Did you see it?" That pitch drove us nuts! I think Gaylord only got busted for it once at the end of his career.

Gaylord is a terrific guy. I've played in several golf tournaments with him, and did some autograph signings also. He has a real Southern drawl and he owns a big farm somewhere in North Carolina. He has a great sense of humor, too. One time I had him on my radio show, and about halfway through our phone interview he said, "I gotta go now and feed the hogs," and he hung up! It was Gaylord being Gaylord. I remember one time riding with Gaylord and Fergie Jenkins to an event for a charity, and he had both Jenkins and me laughing the whole time about a topic which, unfortunately, I cannot divulge.

Even though he didn't throw exceptionally hard, I didn't have much luck with him. I'm of the opinion that Gaylord did, in fact, use a little something to juice the ball now and then, but not as often as everyone thinks. A lot of it was Gaylord wanting you to think that he was doctoring the ball. Maybe he did go overboard periodically but you know something? He was still a great pitcher. The word trade and Gaylord Perry go hand in hand. Gaylord played for eight different major league teams over his career and was successful with each one. The 1970s were his strong years. That's when he won a couple of Cy Young Awards, and he was on the All-Star team several times. As a 300 game winner, doctoring or no doctoring, Gaylord Perry is a bona fide Hall of Famer.

THE CARDS

For 22 seasons, Gaylord Perry baffled major league hitters with his assortment of filth. During that serious showing of longevity,

dozens of cards and collectibles were produced bearing his image. Considering the three decades Perry pitched in, collectors may be even more baffled as to why there weren't more cards made of the tricky hurler. Perry, while a 300-game winner and a Hall of Famer, earned his stripes by being durable as opposed to lighting up the radar gun. In fact, once he finished his stint with the Giants, Perry was often the workhorse for teams that weren't exactly leading the league in fan support.

It all started for Perry in 1962, as a player and in the hobby. Perry's 1962 Topps rookie is not only a great-looking card, but the spotlight was entirely on the master of deception. In a strange twist, Perry was featured on a four-player "rookie" the following year in the 1963 Topps set on his second card. He was pictured along with Dick Egan, Julio Navarro, and Tommie Sisk on a *1963 Rookie Stars* card. This was similar in style to the true rookie cards of Pete Rose and Willie Stargell in the same set. For Perry, however, his only official rookie is his 1962 Topps card.

In a decade where Topps became extremely creative, Perry was noticeably absent in several of their more popular or valuable complementary sets. Throughout the decade, you can find Canadian (O-Pee-Chee) and Venezuelan versions of Topps Perry cards,

although they weren't made every year. In 1969, Perry was part of a short run where Topps printed the player's last name in white instead of the traditional yellow on the front of each card. This run, which impacted cards found in the #440–511 stretch, included some big names like Hall of Famers Willie McCovey and Mickey Mantle as well. The Perry White Letter variation is clearly one of the toughest and most valuable of his career in cardboard.

As Perry's career progressed into the 1970s, we started to see his image on several of the popular regional brands of the period such as Hostess and Kellogg's. In addition to the new regional issues, Perry also found himself on new mediums beyond basic trading cards. Topps produced a variety of Perry collectibles such as coins (1971), candy lids (1973), and stamps (1974), to name a few. Some of the toughest Perry collectibles were Topps test issues. The 1972 Candy Lids, 1973 Comics, and 1973 Pin-Ups included the Cy Young Award winner and rank amongst Perry's most elusive. In 1984, Donruss, Fleer, and Topps released Perry cards in his final hobby bow. This included a special Topps card that commemorated the final season for three legends: Perry, Johnny Bench, and Carl Yastrzemski, who all retired in 1983.

The GAYLORD PERRY CARD

In 1962, Topps produced another in a long line of annual baseball card sets, but this time they veered quite a bit from their recent designs. Each card in their 598-card set is surrounded by borders that resemble wood grain, which vary from a light tan color to dark brown. The darker the border color, the easier it is to see any visible wear with the naked eye, making high-grade copies somewhat elusive and desirable. In fact, this is the toughest regular-issue Topps set of the decade to assemble in PSA NM-MT 8 or better condition. Within the set are three Hall of Famer rookies. The debut singles of Lou Brock and Joe Torre, who entered Cooperstown as a manager despite having a stellar career as a player, both complement Perry's Topps debut (#199). Interestingly, while most of the cards in the set feature standard color photos, Perry's rookie features a painted one, which resembles the kind of artwork used by the manufacturer in the previous decade.

"In 1966, Topps started and ended their set with teammates who both became Hall of Famers."

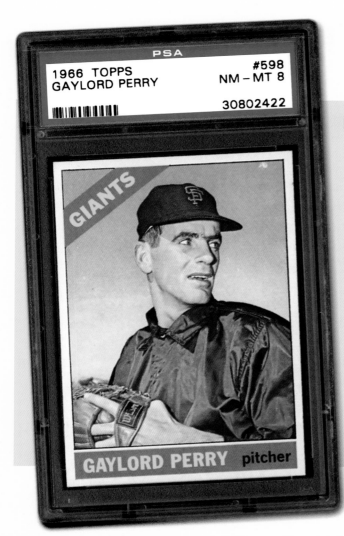

ONE CARD TO WATCH

There has also been a special place for first and last vintage cards with collectors. It harkens back to another time when collectors often assembled sets by hand and subjected those cards to more potential damage than the rest. This was long before plastic sheets and binders were commonly used to protect individual cards. Whether they were sitting atop or at the bottom of a stack bound together by rubber bands or just acting as bookends to the set, the first and last cards always seemed to be in harm's way. In some cases, those cards come in the form of a star. The 1951 Bowman #1 Whitey Ford and the 1954 Topps #250 Ted Williams are popular examples of each. In 1966, Topps started and ended their set with teammates who both became Hall of Famers. Willie Mays led things off at #1 while Perry finished it off at #598. Not only is the Perry the last card in the set, it is also a short print from the high-number series (523–598).

JIM RICE

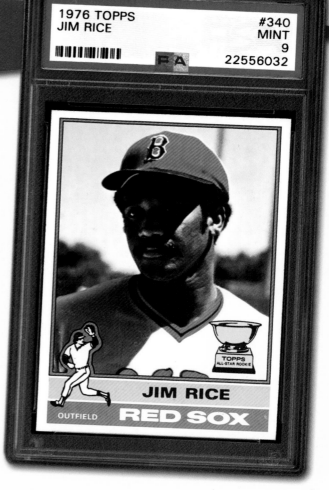

1976 TOPPS #340
JIM RICE
MINT 9
PSA 22556032

THE RED SOX WEREN'T EXPECTED to go very far in 1975, the year Jimmy Rice came up with Freddy Lynn as my rookie teammates. We had a decent ball club, but we figured the two rookies would struggle a bit with growing pains. Man, were we wrong! If it wasn't for those two guys, there is no way we would have made it to the World Series. Jimmy struggled defensively when he started. He had to learn how to play the wall. Johnny Pesky hit him hundreds of balls off that wall. Jim worked his butt off and eventually became very good playing those caroms.

Some people pegged Jim as being aloof. In reality, Jimmy was a nice, personable kid. Here's what happened. An out-of-state writer asked Jim for an interview and started the questioning talking about baseball and playing in the big leagues in Boston.

PSA
1977 TOPPS #60
JIM RICE
MINT 9
21369635

Then he asked Jim about racism in Boston. Jim was very young and it was his first year in Boston, so he just said he really didn't know but he had heard a few things. The article was published as though Jim agreed that Boston was racist. That was definitely not the case. Here was a kid whose comment was taken out of context and several articles came out criticizing him. From that point on, he stopped doing interviews. Can you blame him? Listen, Jimmy was rough on the press, but a lot if it was justified.

Jim was a great teammate and he loved to play the game. To him, it didn't matter who was pitching. To give you an example of the kind of guy he was, I remember when we were in Yankee Stadium, Jim carried a young fan off the field when the kid got hit with a ball. Jimmy did not play in the 1975 Series because of a broken wrist. I'm convinced that we could have won the World Series had he not been hurt. Jim had tremendous numbers and got a lot of key hits for us. He could hit the ball to all fields with power, hit for average, he could run, and he hit all those homers. Actually, playing at Fenway probably robbed Jim of 50 home runs because he hit rising line drives that bounced off the top of the Green Monster.

I only played with Jim in 1975 and 1976, but we have remained close friends for all of these years. We have done a ton of events together and I have never seen him refuse an autograph. He is always so outgoing and respectful of the fans. Jim and I have played golf many times and man, can he hit the ball. One time when Jim was about 170 yards from the pin, he pulled out a pitching wedge. I told him to quit fooling around and to grab the right iron. Bang, he hit it right onto the green! Jim is now working for the Red Sox in the studio as an analyst and he does a great job. We still talk about that rookie season when he and Lynn were known as the "Gold Dust Twins." It was a pleasure playing with those kids that year. I'm so glad that he is in the Hall of Fame. He is a good friend and was a great teammate.

THE CARDS

For a career that resulted in a Hall of Fame induction, Jim Rice seemed to suddenly disappear from the game and the hobby after so many years of excellence. Never one to crave attention, Rice retired with little fanfare, but the mark he left was undeniable. Season after season, Rice reminded fans and pitchers throughout the league how well-rounded he was as a hitter, and the collectibles followed. Rice's image can be found on hundreds of cards. With collectors, numbers can often drive demand and Rice let his booming bat do the talking.

Rice made his major league cardboard debut in both the 1975 Topps regular and Mini set. The Minis measure approximately 2¼" by 3⅛" and are identical in every other respect to their larger counterparts. They are also more challenging to find, yet the price premiums are modest in comparison to the standard-sized cards. In addition to Topps, the lesser-known Sport Star Publishing Company

(SSPC) set included Rice in their 1975 production as well. It is believed that the set was not actually issued until 1976 even though it was created the preceding year. The SSPC issue never really caught on with the collecting community in a major way, as the cards were removed from the market due to legal issues that plagued the company.

Even though the two different Topps cards garner most of the attention from hobbyists, there was a collectible that predates Rice's 1975 appearance by a couple of years. In 1973, Rice was included in a Venezuelan League Sticker set well before his first official Topps rookie card emerged. This obscure issue is, arguably, the most difficult Rice card to locate in any condition. Over the course of the next several years, Rice was featured in various regional issues such as Burger King, Coca-Cola, Drakes, Hostess, Kellogg's, and Squirt.

"In 1973, Rice was included in a Venezuelan League Sticker set well before his first official Topps rookie card emerged."

As we move forward and deeper into the 1980s, the volume of Rice cards increased rapidly as the hobby itself expanded to new levels. Ten years after trying their hand at a smaller version of their base set, Topps decided to experiment with the diminutive design again. The 1985 Topps Mini set was never intended for public distribution, but as is the case with most test issues, the cards eventually found their way into the marketplace. It is believed that only 100 cards of each player in the 132-card set were produced, creating an extreme rarity for Rice collectors. In 1990, several different Rice cards were issued after his retirement in 1989. This included cards from Score, Topps, Upper Deck, and more as a final hobby farewell.

The JIM RICE CARD

In 1975, Topps issued one of its best sets of the decade. The multi-colored design and outstanding star selection keeps this 660-card set on the minds of active collectors. Aside from the 1972 Topps offering, perhaps no other set captured the period as well as the 1975 issue did through the look of the cards alone. The set, which has two cards of the legendary Hank Aaron operating as bookends, contains several key rookie cards. The Hall of Famers who made their debut here include Rice, along with George Brett, Gary Carter, and Robin Yount, not to mention a rookie card of fan-favorite Keith Hernandez. The Rice rookie (#616) showcases the young slugger along with three other outfield prospects, Dave Augustine, Pepe Mangual, and John Scott. Unlike Brett and Yount, Rice had to share the limelight on his rookie much like Gary Carter in the same set. Keep in mind that a mini version of the same card was released by Topps. While the Minis are not rare, they are tougher to find than their regular-sized counterparts. Poor centering, chipping along the colored edges, and print defects are all condition obstacles to be aware of on this card.

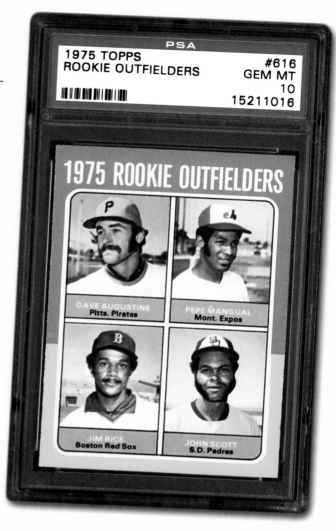

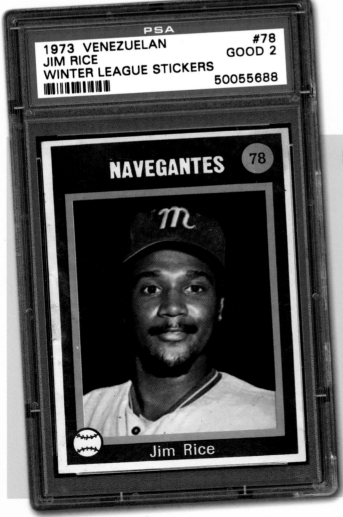

ONE CARD TO WATCH

While hundreds of Rice cards were issued during his playing days, there aren't too many that stand out from the rest of the pack in a major way. One exception to that rule is a card that was technically issued prior to the start of his big-league career. It was very common for players to sharpen their skills in the off season. One way they could achieve this was to participate in winter league baseball. Before Rice stepped into the batter's box at Fenway, he terrorized pitchers in Venezuela. The 1973 Venezuelan League Sticker set featured local talent and some American prospects, like Rice, who were trying to make it to the majors. These stickers were issued with albums so each sticker could be affixed inside, which unfortunately means that many of the Rice examples (#78) have back damage and grade very low from a technical standpoint. For the Rice collector seeking the ultimate challenge, this pre-rookie card is for you.

MIKE SCHMIDT

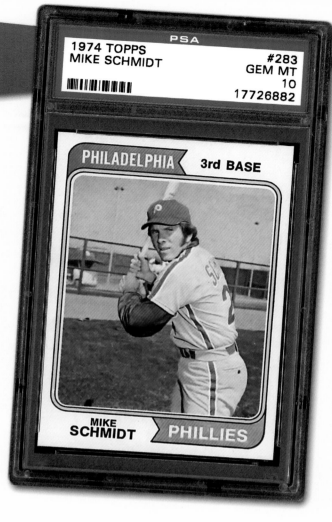

IN MY OPINION, MIKE SCHMIDT is the greatest third baseman to play the game in the modern era. Not only was he a tremendous fielder with great range and a cannon for an arm but he was also a great hitter and RBI guy. All around, I think Brooksie had just as good range and soft hands, but he could not hit as well as Schmidt. Mike had it all and he made it look easy.

Mike and I only played in the majors at the same time for about four years. At the beginning, Mike struck out a lot but then he started to put the bat on the ball and began driving it. I loved the way he was playing, and already hitting for power. Mike once told me the thing that got him on his home run drive was an adjustment he made at the plate. Ted Williams was a disciple of hitting up on the ball and Bobby Doerr preached that you should hit down on the ball. After Schmidt started using the Doerr method, he started getting on top of the ball and the ball began jumping off the bat. He became one of the most feared hitters in the National League. If he had not made this adjustment, Mike told me he would not have had anywhere near as many home runs as he did.

I spent some time with Mike when I was working for one of the networks, and I used to go down to Philly to do the game. The Philly fans got on Mike a little bit at the end of his career as his skills began to diminish somewhat. That can be tough for a player. Even so, the Philly fans consider Mike Schmidt to be the greatest player of all time in the history of their team. Mike was not a very emotional guy on the field, and I think some people thought he was being a little aloof. In reality, Mike was as cool as a cucumber and that was part of his greatness.

Schmidt holds a ton of fielding records and his Gold Glove Awards are in the double digits. He was excellent at coming in on the bunt and making the play. As a former third baseman, I can really appreciate how great a player guys like Mike and Brooks were. I took a look at Mike's stats and they are fantastic. He had 12 All-Star appearances, he won the National League MVP Award three times, and he hit 548 home runs. When I take his numbers and put them all together, Schmidt is my starting third baseman on the All-Time All-Star team, at least in the modern era. I haven't seen Mike in years, but I spoke to him not too long ago on my radio show. He has kept a pretty low profile recently. I know that he has had some medical issues, and I'm glad that he is fine right now. As one former third baseman to another, I tip my cap to him. He was the best at what he did.

THE CARDS

With the top-shelf talent that has come through the major leagues for well over 100 years, it is rare when a player retains an undisputed title as the best at a specific position or skill. Even when you bring up some of the biggest names in baseball, there is usually at least a solid argument to be made on behalf of someone else. Was Ty Cobb or Willie Mays the best all-around outfielder? Was Babe Ruth or Ted Williams the greatest hitter? No matter whose side you take, a decent argument can be made. When it comes to identifying the best third baseman of all time, it's hard to counter the side that takes Mike Schmidt. Fans and hobbyists feel the same way. Hundreds of collectibles were made during the revered slugger's 18-year career.

Before making his mainstream hobby debut in 1973 as part of the annual Topps set, Schmidt was included in an obscure but highly collectible sticker set that captured some U.S. stars who traveled in the offseason to work on their craft. The 1972 Puerto Rican League Sticker features Schmidt while he participated in their winter season. Schmidt, like many future Hall of Famers of the 1960s and 1970s, had to share the limelight with fellow newcomers on his Topps rookie card. So, it wasn't until 1974 when Schmidt had the stage to himself in a Topps set.

For the remainder of the decade, Schmidt found himself in various regional issues like Burger King, Hostess, Kellogg's, Pepsi-Cola, and Wendy's. Starting with his rookie card, Schmidt was frequently included in the Canadian version (O-Pee-Chee) of the Topps set. The connection to O-Pee-Chee continued through the end of his career. In 1977, Topps issued one of the more oddball sets of the era. The 1977 Topps Cloth Stickers set mirrored the basic look of the regular Topps set, but it only contained 55 players. This time, the paper backing could be removed, allowing the sticker to be adhered to various surfaces. The following year, Schmidt even appeared in an Iron-On set issued by Royal Crown Cola in 1978. As you can see, Schmidt's image can be found on mediums outside of trading cards.

Many collectors refer to the 1980s as the hobby explosion and that term best describes the expansion of Schmidt collectibles during that span. Not only was Schmidt a regular with all the major manufacturers, it's hard to name a regional issue the Hall of Famer wasn't a part of during that period. From Drakes to FBI Foods to Tastykake, Schmidt was everywhere. He was also one of the first subjects featured with new manufacturer Star Co., who issued dozens of Schmidt cards by themselves. After retiring in 1989, Schmidt made his last hobby appearance in 1990. Major manufacturers like Donruss, Topps, and Upper Deck all honored him that year.

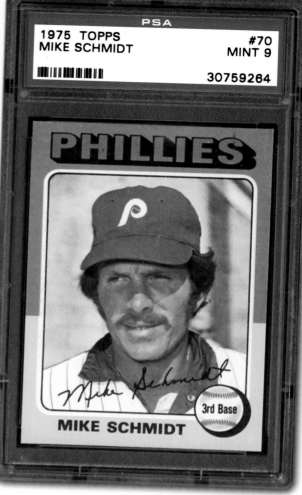

The MIKE SCHMIDT CARD

During the 1950s and 1960s, Topps was known for producing trading card sets that possessed fantastic eye appeal. In fact, in 1972 the manufacturer produced another set that still captivates collectors today based on the colorful design alone. For whatever reason, the very next year Topps decided to go with a bland look, one that doesn't exactly stop hobbyists in their tracks. What the issue may have lacked in aesthetic beauty, however, it made up for in difficultly. The quality of the paper and print, coupled with the black borders on the reverse, can make high-grade examples hard to come by relative to the period. The unquestioned king of the 1973 Topps set is the Mike Schmidt rookie (#615). Schmidt is pictured along with fellow third base prospects Ron Cey, who did have an excellent career, and the lesser-known John Hilton. The somewhat thin borders on the left and right of the card can create eye-appeal issues if the centering is poor. A Canadian version (O-Pee-Chee) of the same card also exists. While it is tougher to find overall, the Topps rookie is the one that garners the most attention from collectors.

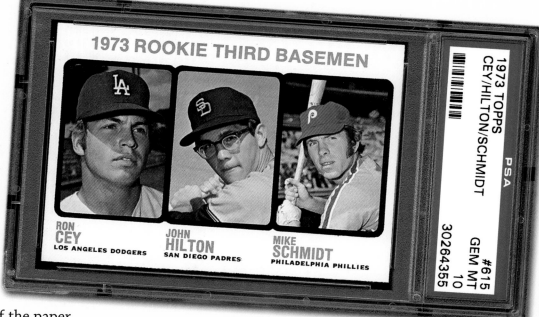

"The unquestioned king of the 1973 Topps set is the Mike Schmidt rookie (#615)."

ONE CARD TO WATCH

Schmidt, like many prospects of his generation, would often sharpen his skills in the offseason by continuing to play. In 1972, a collectible was produced that predates his 1973 Topps rookie card. The 1972 Puerto Rican Winter League Sticker is one that stands out amongst the hundreds of Schmidt cards and collectibles made during his playing career. It is, arguably, the toughest of all Schmidt items to find for collectors focused on the slugging third sacker. The Schmidt (#64) is part of a 231-sticker set and each sticker was intended to be affixed inside an album for display. The stickers, which measure approximately 2¼" by 3", are often found in lower grades due to handling and damage to the reverse. The thin stock used to create these stickers made it difficult to preserve them over time. Each sticker showcases a color photo on the front, while the back contains brief information printed in Spanish.

TOM SEAVER

WE USED TO PLAY THE METS quite a bit during spring training, and that's when I had the opportunity to face Tom Seaver. He was a power pitcher with very good control. Tom could hit the outside corner, the inside corner, and he had a very good breaking ball, too. I always thought Seaver's pitching style was very similar to Nolan Ryan's, in that he used his legs as his power base. I think that's why neither one of those guys ever had any serious arm trouble. The leg strength definitely takes the stress off the arm. Seaver didn't throw quite as hard as Ryan, but it was close. Facing pitchers in spring training is a little different, because they are working on certain things, and at the beginning, they are not throwing hard. Sometimes you know what's coming, so it's not really a good indicator on the stuff the pitcher has. In Seaver's case, he was always tough. His velocity and command always seemed to be a little ahead of the other guys.

From his rookie year in 1967 right up until the year I retired in 1976, Seaver was one of the real dominant pitchers in the National League. He participated in the 1967 All-Star Game with me. That game went 15 innings, and I remember he pitched that last inning. In 1969, I was fortunate enough to be the starting shortstop in the All-Star Game. Tom was on the National League team, but I don't think he got into the game. However, he had a great year in 1969. That year, the Mets won their first World Series ever and Seaver won his first Cy Young Award.

During the 1970s, Tom was one of the most consistent pitchers in baseball. They called him "Tom Terrific," and he was well-liked by his teammates and opponents. He was the kind of guy who wanted everything to be right and he prepared for games really well. Seaver took the time to mentor and share his philosophy with a lot of young pitchers. They came to him for help because he had such a great motion that it was almost perfect, and he had excellent control.

After he was traded to Cincinnati, he continued to have some great seasons. I find it strange that he wound up playing for five different teams over his career. By the time Seaver came to the Red Sox at the end of his career, I had been out of baseball as a player for quite a while. He was over forty years old at the time.

Although he did not pitch for us in the 1986 World Series because of an injury, he definitely contributed to the Sox pennant win.

Tom was elected to the Hall of Fame by a wide margin. That big overhand delivery along with his great command, opened the doors. With all of those All-Star appearances to go along with his Cy Young Awards, over 3,000 strikeouts, and that Mets world championship, Tom Seaver has to be considered one of the top ten pitchers of all time. After he retired as a pitcher, Tom did a pretty good job as an analyst for baseball. I have not seen him in years, but I'll tell you, from all of those times that I faced him in spring training, he was really that good.

THE CARDS

Most young players who enter the league take some time to develop. This is especially true when that player is a pitcher. The ability to pitch combines a gifted arm with a craft that improves with age. In the case of Tom Seaver, success was instantaneous. A young and wildly talented Seaver showed the kind of maturity on the mound that is expected from seasoned veterans. His early rise to stardom meant Seaver became a household name in rapid fashion. It also meant the right-hander would be included in a variety of hobby issues right from the start. This gave collectors more to choose from during the early stages of Seaver's career.

Seaver's big league and hobby debut came in 1967 when he appeared on his first Topps card. The Seaver rookie is clearly his most desirable card and it has long been considered

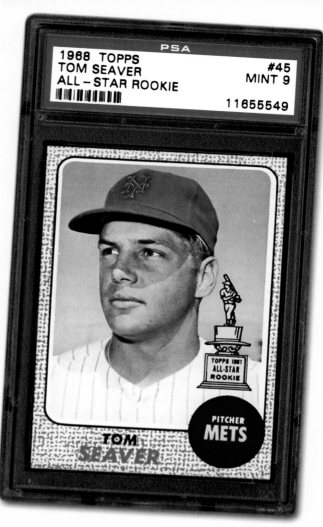

one of the most important hobby debuts of the decade. Since Seaver had to share the stage with another player in 1967, the future Hall of Famer had to wait one more year to get his first solo card in the 1968 Topps set. Tougher Canadian (O-Pee-Chee) and Venezuelan versions of this very same card exist as well, but they are not nearly as popular as the traditional U.S. issue. Keep in mind that the border pattern found on all three cards can mask wear to the naked eye, so keep a loupe handy for closer inspection.

Interestingly, the same exact image of Seaver was used in the 1968 and 1969 Topps regular sets, in addition to the 1969 Topps Super test issue. This glossy and colorful 66-card set includes one of Seaver's most desirable cards. Seaver's early success on the field helped bring him into the regional-card fold almost immediately, as he was already making appearances in brands like Bazooka, Nabisco, and Transogram before the end of the decade. Topps, who dominated the market at the time, also included Seaver in various non-card issues on mediums like decals, stamps, and stickers.

As we move into the 1970s, some of the scarcest Seaver collectibles of all were produced. The Topps Candy Lids of 1970 and 1972, both test issues, are amongst the elite group. These tiny lids measure approximately 1⅞" in diameter,

but they pack a punch with the collecting community due to their rarity and star selection. The popular pitcher made additional appearances in other Topps test issues like the 1973 Comics and Pin-Ups sets. Seaver's longevity carried him well into the hobby boom of the 1980s, which meant large numbers of regular cards and regional issues were made. This included the challenging 1985 Topps Mini Seaver, another Topps test issue with very limited production numbers. An interesting card of note is his 1985 Donruss error, one that mistakenly pictures teammate Floyd Bannister instead of Seaver himself. After throwing his last pitch in 1986, several brands such as Donruss, Sportflics, and Topps issued Seaver cards in 1987 to honor the recent retiree.

The TOM SEAVER CARD

During the 1960s, Topps was known for creating trading card sets with very clean designs. The 1967 Topps set was a great example of that approach. The overall look of the cards is sharp like a well-fitting suit, not complicated or bogged down by frills. In addition to Mickey Mantle, the set is anchored by two Hall of Fame rookie cards in Rod Carew and Seaver (#581), with the latter operating as the key to the entire issue. Both rookies are part of the high-number series (534–609), but the Seaver rookie is the most valuable card in the set by a good margin. Like Carew and many prospects of the era, Seaver shares his only official rookie card with someone else. This time, it was teammate and fellow hurler Bill Denehy. The card, while not known as a major condition rarity, can be challenging to find well centered due to the narrow borders that frame the images of the New York Mets newcomers. In addition, the reverse of the card has a green-colored border that will reveal wear along the edges.

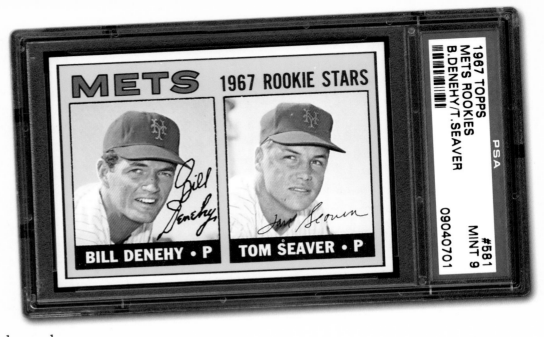

"The 1969 Topps Seaver is one of the tougher cards to find in PSA NM-MT 8 or better condition due to centering problems."

ONE CARD TO WATCH

As we noted earlier, Seaver was a familiar face in several very desirable Topps test issues in the 1960s and 1970s. While each Seaver collectible offers varying degrees of difficulty, nearly all of them are so tough to find that their pursuit is usually limited for the most advanced collectors. Knowing that and the fact that it was so hard to pick a standout from the bunch, we decided to go in another direction. In 1969, Topps issued a memorable set, one that claims Mantle's final cardboard entry. Like the two sets before it, and many sets after it, this Topps set also featured Seaver. However, it's certainly not a rarity like the test cards discussed before. So, what makes this card special? The 1969 Topps Seaver is one of the tougher stars to find in PSA NM-MT 8 or better condition due to centering problems. In fact, to help illustrate the point, the market value for a high-grade Seaver card is higher than those of Hank Aaron, Roberto Clemente, or Willie Mays. It is one of Seaver's best regular-issue cards and it happens to date to the "Miracle Mets" World Series title run.

WILLIE STARGELL

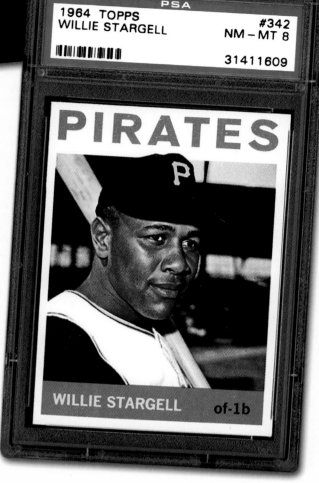

WHAT CAN I SAY ABOUT WILLIE STARGELL? Let's face it, Willie was THE MAN with the Pittsburgh Pirates. He was a great all-around player and he was very well-respected by everybody in baseball. Willie was really the leader of those Pittsburgh teams. I'd say he was to the Pirates what, later on, Big Papi was to the Red Sox. Stargell was a terrific hitter, a home run and RBI guy, and he got a lot of clutch hits. As I recall, in 1979, Willie hit a few big homers against the Orioles in the World Series. I covered the Pirates during that Series for a Boston station and I remember chatting with Willie when the team was down three games to one. I asked Willie his opinion of the Orioles. He said they were a scrappy team but that everybody felt like they were gonna come back against them to win the Series. The thing was, if Willie believed, everybody believed. He was the guy who kept them all close. Willie had confidence in the team and he backed that up on the field with the big hits.

If there was anyone who could lead a sports team, it was Willie Stargell. He was very outgoing and he was always upbeat and positive. That 1979 season was very exciting in the National League and it was a big year for Willie. He was the MVP. The Pirates struggled at the beginning, but as the season went on they really picked up a head of steam. That song "We Are Family" became their mantra. They really were like one big family. In Major League Baseball, Willie had the reputation of being kind of a father figure for the Pirates players. Like many of the African-American players, he experienced racial prejudice in his minor league days but I think he used that as a catalyst to become a leader. I know that the Pittsburgh fans adored him.

Willie and I first became friendly in spring training in Winter Haven. I remember that team was loaded with offensive studs like Clemente and Stargell, along with Mazeroski, Maury Wills, and Gene Alley. The problem with that Pirates team was their pitching was always a little suspect. I actually hit them pretty well. Willie had such great power. He didn't just hit home runs, he launched them. Willie hit some of the longest home runs I ever saw. I remember he hit a shot during a spring training game that I don't think ever landed.

I know Willie really struggled with his health as the years went by. I bumped into him a few times when he was working for the Pirates, but he really had a difficult time towards the end of his life. It's a shame that he passed away at such a relatively young age. Looking back, the thing that really sticks out about Willie was that he was a player's player. He always looked out for his teammates and I never heard a bad thing about him from anyone. When you look at his numbers and the length of his career, Willie left his mark on the game. A multi-year All-Star and great power hitter, he certainly belongs in the Hall. I put Willie Stargell right up there with guys like Robinson, Aaron, Mays, and the rest who led the way for African-Americans in Major League Baseball.

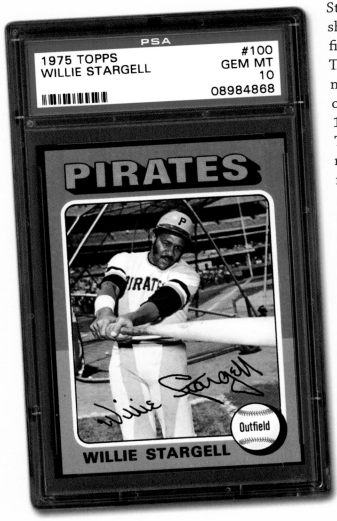

THE CARDS

For 21 seasons, Willie Stargell was a menacing presence in the batter's box for opposing pitchers to face. A great selection of cards and collectibles were produced bearing his image over three different decades. During the first half of his career, Stargell was often overshadowed by his legendary teammate Roberto Clemente, and despite his excellent career numbers, the fact that the big slugger missed entry into the 500 Home Run Club by a whisker may have limited his hobby appeal in some respects. The good news for hobbyists is that many of Stargell's collectibles are within range for the average collector.

Stargell entered the hobby shortly after making his first appearance in 1962. The Stargell card that gets more attention than any other is, of course, his 1963 Topps rookie card. This is the mainstream rookie that most collectors focus on; however, other early Stargell cards also exist. This includes the 1963 I.D.L. Drug Store card, a regional issue devoted entirely to the Pittsburgh Pirates. It contained 27 black-and-white cards with each unnumbered and blank-backed specimen measuring approximately 4" by 5". This Stargell doesn't get nearly the fanfare of his 1963 Topps rookie, but it does picture the Hall of Famer by himself.

Stargell became a regular with Topps, which included appearances in the Canadian (O-Pee-Chee) and Venezuelan versions before the decade was over. Interestingly, in back-to-back years, Stargell was pictured alongside teammate Donn Clendenon on a Topps multi-player card. In 1966, the duo joined forces on *Bucs Belters* and in 1967 on a card entitled *Pitt Power*. Why Stargell never appeared with Clemente on a card remains a mystery. From 1965 to 1967, Stargell was also included in a colorful and popular regional issue called Kahn's Wieners. The Cincinnati-area meat company produced small regional sets for many years, with the design and contents changing over that span. During the period he was featured, Stargell was joined by other stars in the set such as Hank Aaron, Clemente, and Pete Rose at different times.

Throughout the 1960s and 1970s, Stargell was inserted into some very tough Topps test issues that ultimately made their way into the hobby. Some examples include 1967 Punch-Outs, 1972 Candy Lids, 1973 Comics, 1973 Pin-Ups, and 1974 Deckle Edge. Each issue varies in difficulty based on their distribution and popularity as a product of their design. Regional set inclusion continued for Stargell in sets like Hostess and Kellogg's in the 1970s, but the decade produced various collectible mediums, too. Stargell's image can be found on everything from coins to discs to tattoos. After playing his last game in 1982, Stargell made his final hobby appearance in 1983. While this did include brands such as Donruss and Fleer, Topps did not issue a Stargell card that year.

The WILLIE STARGELL CARD

After the hulking prospect made his big-league debut in 1962, Stargell appeared on his first Topps card in 1963. Like most other newcomers, including fellow rookie Rose in the same set, Stargell had to share the spotlight with others. In this case, Stargell was pictured along with headshots of promising outfielders Brock Davis, Jim Gosger, and John Herrnstein. Of course, it was Stargell who became the star of the bunch. The Stargell rookie (#553) is one of the keys to the set, which includes the previously mentioned Rose rookie as well. With the current state of Rose and MLB, the Stargell card remains the only Hall of Fame rookie in the set. The design of the card poses some condition challenges, namely the solid blue border along the top portion of the card, which will reveal the slightest touch of wear. In addition, the bright-colored background can be a haven for print defects and determining centering can be tricky. The card has three very defined borders, but the blue area at the top can be deceptive. Make sure the bottom border is reasonably balanced with the left and right borders if you are looking for examples that qualify for top grades.

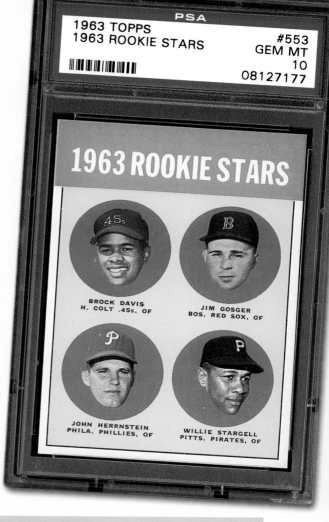

ONE CARD TO WATCH

For 15 years, Kahn's produced baseball cards during an era when regional cards played a significant role in the hobby. Some of the most desirable cards of the 1950s and 1960s are of the regional variety. One of the more popular regional issues was Kahn's Wieners. The Cincinnati-based company manufactured cards for a handful of teams in areas where their meat products were sold. Their first set only included six black-and-white cards. By 1965, their annual set had grown to 45 subjects and one of the players included was Stargell. Now in full color, the 1965 Kahn's Wieners cards measured approximately 3" by 3½" and each unnumbered entry showcased a facsimile signature on the face of its borderless format. Players from the Milwaukee Braves, Cleveland Indians, and Cincinnati Reds joined members of the Pittsburgh Pirates in this attractive set. While the Kahn's Stargell isn't as elusive as some of his Topps test issues, this regional collectible was produced very early in his career and is arguably one of the best-looking cards from his playing days.

DON SUTTON

WHEN DON SUTTON CAME UP to the Dodgers, he joined a team that had just won the World Series the year before. Sure, he was probably thrilled, but think about the pressure he must have had to perform—especially when the other starting pitchers were Sandy Koufax, Don Drysdale, and Claude Osteen. I can't even imagine. They called him "Little D" since Drysdale was "Big D." Well, Sutton just dug in and he became the real workhorse for those Dodgers teams. There was a lot of buzz about Sutton in 1966 because he had 200 Ks as a rookie. I only faced Don in spring training in Florida, but I followed his career very closely. You know, I have always followed the Dodgers since I was a kid in Brooklyn.

The year Sutton came up, the Dodgers made it to the Series. I remember following that National League race because I loved to watch Koufax.

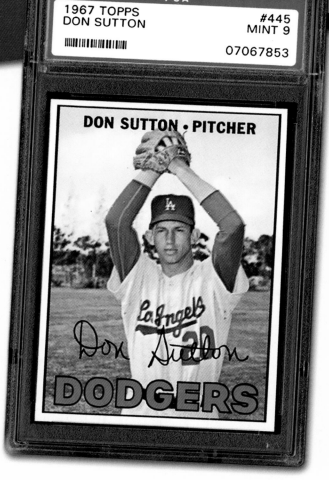

Playing for the Sox in 1966, we struggled quite a bit and wound up in last place, but we accomplished our dream of making it to the Series in 1967. That happened again in the mid-1970s. The Dodgers were in the Series in 1974, and we were in it in 1975. Interesting how those things happen in baseball. I'd say our Series in 1975 got a lot more attention than their contest with Oakland in 1974.

Anyway, Sutton had great stuff—fastball, slider, curveball, screwball— and he had great control. He really came into his own in the 1970s. He was very consistent, and Tommy Lasorda once told me Don was Lasorda's go-to guy when he needed the win. In my opinion, Sutton was always underrated because he was overshadowed by the big gun pitchers during his career. My former teammate and good friend, Reggie Smith, played with Don on the Dodgers in the late 1970s. Reggie told me Don was an unbelievable competitor. Actually, Reggie was part of the reason Sutton had that famous scuffle with Steve Garvey. A story in the paper reported Don thought Reggie, not Garvey, was the one who really carried the team. Apparently Garvey took exception to that. There was a lot more to it, but Sutton and Garvey ended up mixing it up in the locker room at Shea Stadium right before they went on the field to play the Mets. Sutton was always very outspoken. It's probably why he has had a good career as a broadcaster for the Braves.

After I retired, Don moved to the American League where he had some very good seasons even though he was probably close to forty then.

I remember during the 1986 season when the Red Sox made it to the World Series, we played the Angels in the ALCS and Don beat us and our guy, Roger Clemens. Two 300-game winners pitching against each other does not happen very often. I know Don only won 20 games once but what I have always liked about him was his durability. He never missed a start in all those years with the Dodgers and he pitched over 200 innings many, many times. Of course, there was always a lot of talk that Don doctored the balls. He never got suspended or anything like that, but the umpires were always going to the mound to check him for sandpaper. Since he played with Gaylord, I really wouldn't put it past him.

THE CARDS

In many ways, Don Sutton's playing career mirrored his career in cardboard. Over a 23-year period, there wasn't a lot of flash on the mound or isolated, standout moments. Sutton's excellence was defined by his consistency and durability. No one year or performance really leaps out versus another. Sutton gobbled up innings from the moment he entered the league, and as a result, he became a dependable part of the rotation— and every rotation needs someone like that. In the hobby, Sutton's image can be found on dozens of cards and collectibles, but very few come to mind as "special" by collecting standards.

As a bona fide Hall of Famer, the Sutton card that garners the lion's share of the attention is his official rookie card. Produced in 1966, Sutton's Topps rookie pictures

the right-hander next to another Dodgers prospect. Multi-player rookie cards were the common practice during the era, which can frustrate some collectors. In a perfect world or hobby, it would be nice if every player had their rookie card to themselves, but beggars can't be choosers. From Pete Rose to Nolan Ryan to Mike Schmidt, some of the biggest names in baseball history had multi-player rookies and this, unfortunately, includes Sutton.

While there is no doubt that Sutton's standard Topps card is his most appealing rookie, the toughest is the Venezuelan Topps version. Rarely offered, the first 370 cards in the 1966 Topps set were reprinted on dull-looking, darker cardboard. The eye appeal on the face of the cards is noticeably different when compared to the brighter, standard Topps cards. A healthy percentage of the Venezuelan cards are found with back damage as the practice of affixing cards in albums was common in the South American collecting culture at the time. Keep in mind that the Venezuelan Topps cards are often found slightly smaller than the U.S. cards.

Throughout Sutton's active years, there aren't many cards that collectors would identify

as standouts. That said, some of the more intriguing Sutton cards include his 1969 Topps 4-On-1 Mini Sticker, 1974 Topps Deckle Edge issue, and 1985 Topps Mini card. Not surprisingly, all three are Topps test issues. The 1969 Topps 4-On-1 Mini Sticker cards measure approximately 2½" by 3½" and each one contains four individual stickers. Sutton shares his card with Rose, which does elevate its value. Sutton's final hobby appearance came in 1989, a year after making his final pitch for the Dodgers during a one-season return to the team where it all started.

The DON SUTTON CARD

In 1966, Topps issued another eye-catching set, one that has remained popular with collectors today. The design is clean and the imagery is excellent throughout. Like many players of the period, Sutton had to share the limelight on his first card (#288) with another player. In this case, Los Angeles Dodgers teammate and fellow pitcher Bill Singer finds himself next to the future Hall of Famer. You will notice that Sutton's cap appears to have been airbrushed since no logo is present. The Sutton rookie is one of three key debut cards in the set. Interestingly, all three keys are rookie cards of Hall of Fame pitchers. In addition to Sutton, first cards of Jim Palmer and Ferguson Jenkins are also included. While the Sutton card is not overly tough in high grade, collectors should pay special attention to centering and the occasional presence of print defects along the face of the card, especially in the background area of the headshots.

"You will notice that Sutton's cap appears to have been airbrushed since no logo is present."

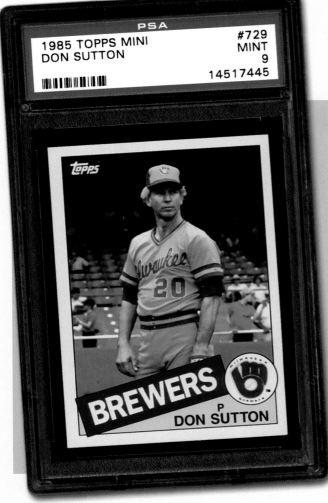

ONE CARD TO WATCH

Ten years after trying their hand at a smaller version of their base set in 1975, Topps decided to experiment with the diminutive design once again. The 1985 Topps Mini set was never intended for public distribution, but as is the case with most test issues, the cards eventually found their way into the marketplace. It is believed that only 100 cards of each player in the 132-card set were produced, creating an extreme rarity for Sutton collectors (card #729). The 132 total cards represent one full sheet and they were printed on white stock, which gave each one a brighter appearance than the regular 1985 Topps cards. In fact, the Topps Minis look more like the Topps Traded or O-Pee-Chee cards from the same year. This makes sense as these cards were allegedly printed by O-Pee-Chee in order to test new printing equipment. The Topps Minis are roughly 10% smaller than their standard-sized counterparts and only a scant number of the subjects on the sheet were Hall of Famers.

CARL YASTRZEMSKI

1962 TOPPS #425
CARL YASTRZEMSKI
NM – MT 8
11928947

CARL
YASTRZEMSKI
BOSTON RED SOX OF

THE FIRST TIME I MET CARL YASTRZEMSKI was in 1961, in the Red Sox dugout at a Yankees game. Bots Nekola, the same guy who signed Yaz, brought me to the game. When I met Yaz, he really encouraged me to sign with the Sox. We were both from New York, and once I joined the team we became fast friends. Carl really took me under his wing when I attended the big league spring training camp in Arizona in 1963. He was very encouraging and almost like a brother to me. He and Carol had me over for dinner and made me feel very comfortable.

I ended up playing my whole career with Carl. He had such pressure on him at the beginning because he was supposed to be the next Ted Williams. How could anybody be Ted Williams? Yaz struggled at the beginning, but he played a great left field and man did he turn it all around! The Red Sox teams were not very good at that time and the burden was on Yaz. When Tony Conigliaro came up, that helped immediately. Actually, Carl, Tony C., Jim Lonborg, and Dalton Jones were my closest friends.

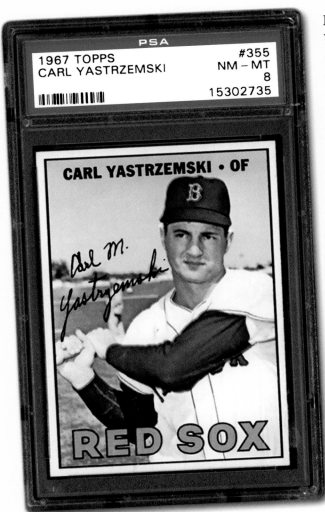

1967 TOPPS #355
CARL YASTRZEMSKI
NM – MT 8
15302735

CARL YASTRZEMSKI • OF

RED SOX

During those first few years, I was like the middle brother between Yaz and Tony C. Sometimes they butted heads but they always worked it out. It was just because they were both competitive and wanted to be great players.

By the time the 1967 season started we felt like we had a pretty good team. Yaz was really energized in spring training. He was enthusiastic about our new manager, Dick Williams, and all of our new young talent. Carl got us to believe that we could make a run. We started off a bit slow, but man alive, everything came together! Carl had a huge year and won the Triple Crown. He carried us right to the World Series. We all loved Yaz. He was a great teammate, and he loved joking around with the guys. Yaz and Luis Aparicio were constantly playing practical jokes on each other after Luis joined the team. I'll never forget Carl's ugly "Columbo" raincoat. We finally burned it! The fans didn't see the fun side of Carl. They saw a fiery competitor who sometimes clashed with umpires, but they loved it when Yaz went crazy during a game. He would cover up home plate with dirt, throw stuff out of the dugout onto the field, and say his piece.

I think Carl was probably the best left fielder ever to play in Fenway Park. He could really play the Green Monster. Then he became a very good first baseman. As he got older, Yaz was able to adjust his swing to keep up with the fastball. He dropped his hands lower and lower as the years went by. If you look at the footage, you'll see that. Yaz is also a very good fisherman and golfer, and a great all-around athlete, but he still tries to stay out of the limelight. We still stay in touch, and over the years, we've spent hours talking about hitting, life, kids, and how fortunate we were. As a player, Yaz had it all. He was a five-tool player, an MVP, and he was an All-Star almost every year. Carl was, and still is, a class act, a good friend, and one of the greatest Red Sox players of all time.

THE CARDS

After 23 seasons manning the Green Monster at Fenway Park, Carl Yastrzemski found his way onto hundreds of cards and collectibles before he took his last swing in 1983. The combination of playing for the Boston Red Sox and becoming a fan favorite, coupled with his entry into the exclusive 3,000 Hit Club, ensures that future generations of collectors will recognize his unique name. The man they called "Yaz" has a special place not only in the hobby, but in pop culture during a time when our industry expanded in a major way. His 1973 Topps card was even referenced on the animated show *The Simpsons* in 1991 on one of their most memorable episodes entitled "Three Men and a Comic Book."

In 1960, Topps decided to return to a horizontal format for their new baseball card set after a few years committed to a vertical design, at least for the most part. The Yastrzemski rookie can be found in both the regular Topps set and within the Venezuelan Topps issue

as well, which is a more obscure but challenging card for the advanced collector. Nearly from the start, Yastrzemski appeared on a variety of mediums. By year two, the slugging lefty had already been featured in coin, faux currency, and stamp sets. In fact, a few different coin issues featured Yastrzemski within the decade, which include brands like Old London, Salada, Shirriff, and Topps. Some of the popular regional trading card issues Yastrzemski can be found in during the 1960s include Jell-O, Post Cereal, and Wheaties.

That decade marked the first time that Yastrzemski appeared in Topps test issues, too. This included two from 1967: Punch-Outs and Stand-Ups. The Stand-Up issue was never released from the factory, not even in limited form, which means only miniscule numbers of each player made it to the market. These cards showcase a large headshot of each player and measure approximately 3⅛" by 5¼". The design allowed for the headshot to be popped out from the black background. Other stars like Hank Aaron, Roberto Clemente, and Mickey Mantle fill this 24-piece set. This extreme rarity is, arguably, Yastrzemski's most valuable card pound-for-pound.

The Topps test issues kept coming in the 1970s, from different mediums like Candy Lids (1970 and

1972) to Comics (1973) to Pin-Ups (1973). In 1974, the Topps test issues continued to emerge with the jagged-looking Deckle Edge cards, but this issue is not nearly as tough as some of the previously mentioned rarities. One of the tougher and more interesting non-test issues from Topps was the 1971 Greatest Moments set. This oversized, black-bordered issue of 55 cards included Yastrzemski along with other stars like Johnny Bench and Willie Mays. After retiring in 1983, Yastrzemski made his final hobby appearance in 1984. In fact, Donruss, Fleer, and Topps each issued a special card picturing Yastrzemski with Bench (who also retired) as a tribute.

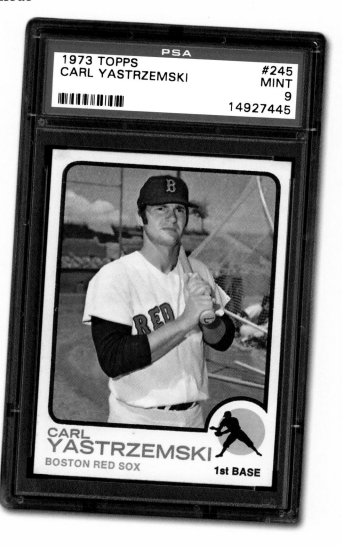

The CARL YASTRZEMSKI CARD

The colorful 1960 Topps set has been a collector favorite for decades and there are two key rookie cards in the set, those of Hall of Famers Willie McCovey and Yastrzemski. In both cases, the players had the spotlight to themselves, as this set predated the manufacturer's inclination to place multiple prospects on many of their rookie cards. The Yastrzemski rookie is not without its challenges for those seeking high-end examples. Centering is an issue that plagues virtually every series and every card throughout the set, but the common presence of print defects is what takes the challenge to another level. The bright-colored background is sometimes tattered with dark, scattered print marks. Their presence can really impact eye appeal. Keep in mind that there is a Venezuelan Topps version of the same card, one that is significantly harder to find, but the U.S. Topps card garners the most attention. The Yastrzemski rookie is, without question, one of the most important rookie cards of the decade.

"The bright-colored background is sometimes tattered with dark, scattered print marks."

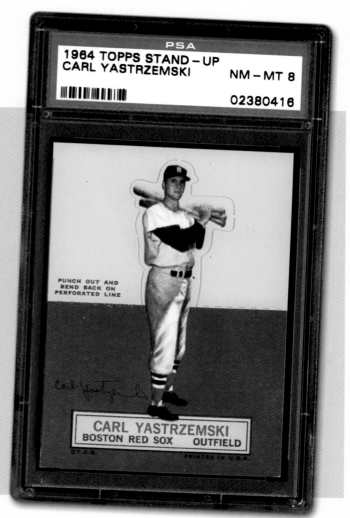

ONE CARD TO WATCH

As the creative juices flowed at Topps in the 1960s, some outstanding sets were designed. Some of these sets never technically made it to the public in any meaningful volume, or at all, and those have been appropriately categorized as test issues. Other creative productions, however, did thankfully make it into the stream of commerce for collectors to consume. One such set was the 1964 Topps Stand-Up issue. This vibrant set contains 77 colorful cards and many of the names are the best in the business. Clemente, Sandy Koufax, Mantle, and more are all here. Each card was designed so the player image could be popped out and stood up from the yellow/green background once folded. The dark green bottom portion of the card is very susceptible to chipping and edge wear. The final player in the set is a short-printed card of Yastrzemski. It is not only one of the most valuable cards in the set, it is also one of Yastrzemski's most valuable non-test issues.

4

The New Young Guns

(to 1999)

We are on a flight to Chicago on the way to the National Sports Collectors Convention. I'm sitting across the aisle from Rico, and Ellen is sitting in front of us. We decided to pass the time chatting about the Hall of Famers that played up through 1999. Since it's late afternoon we decided, why not have a cocktail with some munchies while we talk about some of the greats from the modern era? I order a Tito's Martini, and Rico orders a Jack and Coke. Ellen has a glass of cabernet. As we settle in to enjoy our drinks and chat, I can't help but notice how the guy sitting next to Rico is all ears even though he is pretending to be asleep. I hope he enjoys Rico's take on the likes of Yount, Blyleven, and a guy named Fisk.

BERT BLYLEVEN

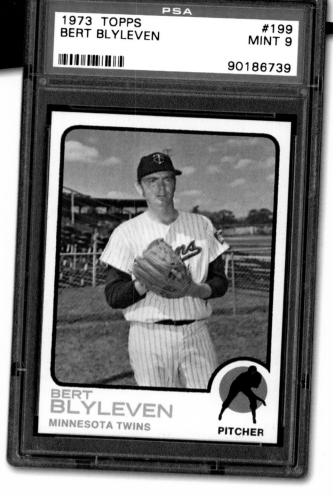

1973 TOPPS   #199
BERT BLYLEVEN
PSA MINT 9
90186739

THE FIRST TIME I FACED BERT BLYLEVEN, he was a 19-year-old kid pitching for Minnesota. We really didn't know anything about him because he had just come up to the Twins. Bert was not an overpowering pitcher. His fastball was about 91 or 92 miles per hour, but man, he had a devastating curveball. His three-quarter curveball was a real biter. It was a sharp breaking ball that came in quickly and would fall off the table. It was an extremely difficult pitch to hit. At the beginning, Bert made a few mistakes with it. But as he matured, he just got better and better. He wasn't afraid to brush you back if he had to, either. Initially, I didn't hit him very well, but as I adjusted to his curve, I did a bit better later on. Bert's biggest weakness was if he could not get the curveball over, he was hittable. From his rookie year in 1970 right through my retirement year of 1976, we had some good battles. He was a terrific competitor.

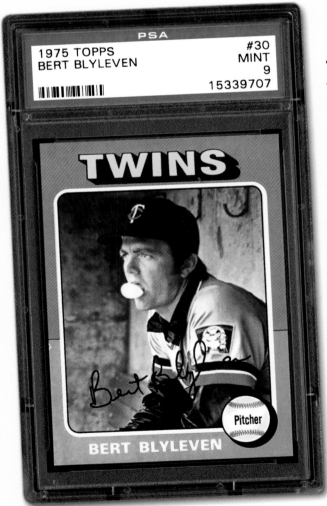

1975 TOPPS   #30
BERT BLYLEVEN
MINT 9
15339707

That one year, when he won twenty games in 1973, he was particularly tough. I didn't get a hit off him until the end of July. Everything seemed to go right for him when I was at the plate that year.

Bert was a real character. I had many friends on the Twins, and they all liked Bert. He always backed up his teammates and he was a practical joker, which helped keep everybody loose. On the other hand, Bert was also a little hot-headed. Every once in a while, he would beef with management over salary disputes or he would spar with fans over one thing or another. By the way, although he grew up in California, Bert came from the Netherlands—a real hot bed for major league ballplayers! I never thought that Bert would leave Minnesota, but like most players, he eventually got traded. He did go back to the Twins near the end of his career, though, and helped them to a World Series win. He also won a Series in the late 1970s with Pittsburgh.

Although Bert played for five or six different teams, he ended up as one of the few at that time to have over 3,000 strikeouts. Even though he led the American League in strikeouts a few times and had those 3,000 Ks, it took Bert quite a while to get into the Hall of Fame. That's probably because he only won about thirty or forty games more than he lost. I'd say that had a lot to do with the weak teams he played on. I liked Bert. He did not like getting too close to the opposing players because he always wanted to maintain that competitive edge, but we got along. When I look at his record, I do agree that Bert belongs in the Hall. I also believe that my former teammate and friend, Luis Tiant, also belongs in the Hall of Fame. Actually, it's kind of ironic that Bert came up to start for the Twins after Luis injured his shoulder. The next year, Luis came to the Red Sox and had some great years in Boston.

THE CARDS

Bert Blyleven may have been a little late to the Hall of Fame party, but the important thing for collectors is that he was invited. Blyleven and his hellacious curveball baffled hitters for 22 seasons. That exceptional longevity led to dozens of Blyleven cards and collectibles over three decades. Despite his Cooperstown status and two World Series championships with the Pittsburgh Pirates and Minnesota Twins, most of the Blyleven collectibles a hobbyist will encounter are relatively affordable. That said, there are always some that are considered standouts.

Blyleven made his MLB debut in 1970 and his mainstream hobby debut the following year, in 1971. That year, Topps and the related O-Pee-Chee (Canadian) sets issued Blyleven rookies that are very condition sensitive. The O-Pee-Chee Blyleven rookie is certainly less common, but the Topps rookie is the version most collectors focus their efforts on attaining. The black borders that provide an attractive frame for each card are very susceptible to chipping along the edges. Any wear will become

noticeable to the naked eye as a result. There were other solid rookie cards in the set, like those of Dusty Baker/Don Baylor, Dave Concepcion, George Foster, Steve Garvey, and Ted Simmons, but Blyleven was the only newcomer in the set to make the Hall of Fame.

In 1974, Topps created a 72-card test set called Deckle Edge, inserting Blyleven on card #47. The oversized 1974 cards, which have unmistakable jagged edges, measure approximately 2⅞" by 5". The borderless cards feature a blue facsimile autograph against a black-and-white front. The backs showcase the basic player info in blue script, while a mock newspaper clipping sits beneath it, providing a noteworthy highlight about the player. There are two variations of the regular card. The more common version has a dull, gray-colored reverse. The backs, however, can also be found in white and they are the tougher of the two variations. Interestingly, even though Blyleven was a successful starter from his very first year in the big leagues, he wasn't included in most of the rare Topps test issues of the era.

"Blyleven and his hellacious curveball baffled hitters for 22 seasons."

As we move forward into the big right-hander's career, Blyleven started to appear in many of the popular regional issues of the period. Those brands included Burger King, Hostess, and Kellogg's to name a few. Before the decade was over, Blyleven's image was included on various mediums as well. From cloth stickers to discs to stamps, Blyleven's hobby presence wasn't limited to baseball cards. Blyleven pitched well into the hobby boom of the 1980s and beyond, which ensured more brands and regionals would be added to the list. This included everything from 7-Eleven to Quaker Oats to Wheaties. Blyleven made his final appearance on cardboard in 1993 on several different cards.

The BERT BLYLEVEN CARD

In 1971, Topps created its most challenging regular set of the decade. In the 1960s, Topps had tried the concept of colored borders. They used a solid wood grain design in 1962, a partial colored border in 1963, and a pattern-style border in 1968. Just one year earlier, Topps framed their baseball cards with a gray-colored border in the 1970 set. All of that experimentation led to their beautiful but brutal 1971 Topps issue, an issue that is surrounded with black edges. Oh, the humanity! If you are a collector who likes high-grade cards and are looking for a fight, this is the set for you. As you would expect, the black edges on the front are easily chipped and reveal the slightest touch of wear. In addition to the fragile borders, the cards are often found with varying degrees of print defects on their face, not to mention less than desirable centering. If the black edges on the front weren't bad enough, the backs are framed in green. The entire set is difficult to find in PSA NM-MT 8 condition or better, but the Blyleven debut (#26) is even tougher than the average 1971 Topps card and it remains the only Hall of Fame rookie card therein.

ONE CARD TO WATCH

Ten years after trying their hand at a smaller version of their base set in 1975, Topps decided to experiment with the diminutive design again. The 1985 Topps Mini set was never intended for public distribution, but as is the case with most test issues, the cards eventually found their way into the marketplace. It is believed that only 100 cards of each player in the 132-card set were produced, creating an extreme rarity for Blyleven collectors (card #355). The 132 total cards represent one full sheet and each one was printed on white stock, which gave the cards a brighter appearance than the regular 1985 Topps cards. In fact, the Topps Minis look more like the Topps Traded or O-Pee-Chee cards from the same year, which would make sense because these cards were allegedly printed by O-Pee-Chee in order to test new printing equipment. The Topps Minis are roughly 10% smaller than their standard-sized counterparts and a scant number of the subjects on the sheet were Hall of Famers.

GEORGE BRETT

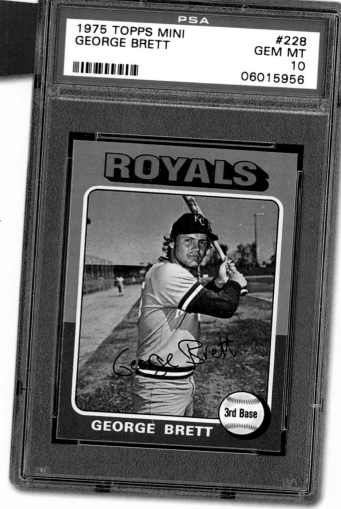

WITHOUT A DOUBT, GEORGE BRETT was one of the toughest outs I've ever seen. George had no weakness at the plate. He could hit the ball to all fields, hit for power, and hit for average. He was outstanding. In the era of Carew, Boggs, and Tony Gwynn, Brett was right up there. I'd say he was one of the best hitters of his time. Brett did an adequate job at third base for Kansas City when he started out. At that time, the AstroTurf made playing at the Royals Stadium very difficult. They had the bases outlined and there was a seam. Oh my goodness, that seam made it extremely difficult. Even if the ball didn't hit the seam, it was still a tough play because you couldn't really charge the ball. Brett adjusted to it and he became a very good third baseman. That Kansas City team with Hal McRae, Willie Wilson, John Mayberry, and the rest of those guys was pretty darn good.

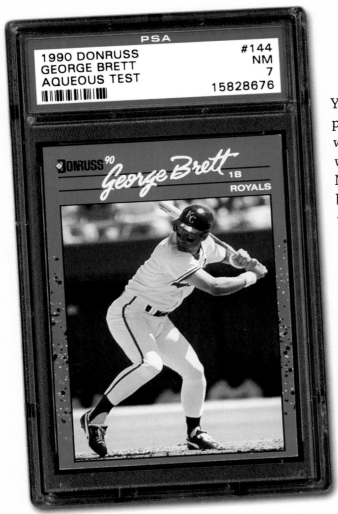

You know, before George came up to the Royals, his brother pitched for us. Ken Brett was probably just 18 or 19 years old when came to Boston, but he had good potential. He was only with us for a couple of years, but he pitched in the 1967 Series. Now, George had a beautiful swing. I played against him at the beginning of his career. It was pretty amazing. He could hit the wall any time he wanted. He was really that good. Brett would either hit doubles or hit the ball out of the ballpark, and what a clutch hitter. If there were a couple of men on base when he came up to bat—*Bang!* He was a tremendous hitter.

George was with the Royals his entire career, and like I said, some of those teams were great. The Royals battled the Yankees for the championship a few years in a row in the late 1970s and early 1980s and they won it in 1985. I remember Brett got close to .400 one year. That was in 1980. We followed him closely in Boston since Ted Williams was the last to hit that number. I believe Brett was MVP that year. What a competitor. He got so many hits—over 3,000—and he was the league batting champ a few times. It seemed like he was an All-Star every year during his prime. The fact that he was voted into the Hall of Fame on the first ballot just shows how talented he was.

That whole pine tar incident was something. Billy Martin was all over it. I was watching the game and thought "Man, the pine tar is way up there." MLB reversed the ruling against Brett's home run after the Royals protested it. We all used pine tar though and I really don't think Brett deliberately applied it where it wasn't allowed. He was so good he didn't need extra pine tar to hit it out of the park. In my opinion, Brett is right up there with the top third basemen of all time. George could do things with the bat that Brooks couldn't do, and was as good a hitter as practically anyone. Like I've said, Mike Schmidt was in a league of his own, but George Brett was really something.

THE CARDS

One of the most popular players of his generation, George Brett's fiery nature and consistent, outstanding performance ensured a strong following in the hobby. By the time Brett's 21-year career was over, hundreds of cards and collectibles were made bearing his image. From mainstream issues to regional obscurities, Brett was included in just about every kind of set imaginable over the three decades he stepped between the lines. While most of them are relatively easy to acquire, there are a few Brett issues that are considered challenging.

As a player, you would be hard-pressed to pick a better set to make your mainstream debut in than the 1975 Topps issue. This super-colorful Topps design was a welcomed surprise after two consecutive years of somewhat bland formats in 1973 and 1974. It is important to note that Brett also has an O-Pee-Chee (Canadian) and mini versions of the same card. The 1975 Topps Mini issue measures slightly smaller than the standard 2½" by 3½" cards, coming in at 2¼" by 3⅛" instead. Both the O-Pee-Chee and Topps Mini cards are tougher to find than the regular Topps issue, but neither generates the kind of interest created by the more common Brett rookie. Other Brett cards were issued during his rookie era such as SSPC, but none of them carry the hobby weight of his Topps debut.

A few years later, one of the toughest Brett collectibles to locate in any grade was created. In 1977, Brett was included in an obscure Venezuelan Baseball Stickers set. This set, which was primarily made up of local, winter league players, also includes a few dozen MLB players. These blank-backed stickers are thinner reproductions of their 1977 Topps card counterparts but have slightly different dimensions at approximately 2⅜" by 3⅛" in size. A custom album was produced to affix each sticker in, and as expected and unfortunately for collectors, a significant percentage of the known examples today exhibit back damage.

From the 1970s through the end of his career, Brett was featured in countless regional issues. A small sampling includes Drake's, Hostess, Kellogg's, Jiffy Pop, Nestle, Pepsi-Cola, Wendy's, and Wiffle Ball. This included several non-card mediums like coins, decals, iron-ons, patches, scratch-offs, stamps, tattoos, and a host of discs. In 1982, a few Brett error cards were created. That year, Topps issued some of the cards without black ink. For example, the regular cards are missing the expected facsimile signature and the All-Star cards are missing the player names on the fronts. They are referred to as "blackless" variations. A couple of Brett's most intriguing and limited cards from late in his career include the 1991 Topps Desert Shield and 1993 Finest Refractor issues. A year after he retired in 1993, Brett appeared on quite a few different cards in 1994 as a hobby farewell.

The GEORGE BRETT CARD

In 1975, Topps issued one of its best sets of the decade. The multi-colored design and outstanding star selection keeps this 660-card set on the minds of active collectors. Aside from the 1972 Topps offering, perhaps no other set captured the period through the look of the cards alone, as well as the 1975 issue did. The set, which has two cards of the legendary Hank Aaron operating as bookends, contains several key rookie cards. The Hall of Famers who made their debut here include Brett (#228), along with Gary Carter, Jim Rice, and Robin Yount, not to mention a rookie card of fan-favorite Keith Hernandez. The Brett rookie featured the young prospect by himself, unlike the multi-player rookies of Carter and Rice. Keep in mind that a mini version of the same card was released by Topps. While the Minis are not rare, they are tougher to find than their regular-sized counterparts. Poor centering due to image tilts, chipping along the colored edges, and print defects are all condition obstacles of which to be aware.

"The 1976 Topps Brett (#19) is one of the most sought-after cards of the decade in high grade."

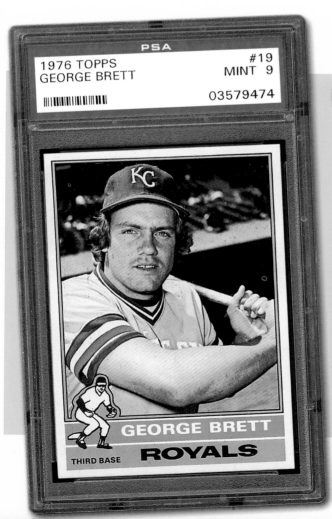

ONE CARD TO WATCH

One year after Brett made his first Topps appearance in 1975, the Hall of Famer once again found himself in the manufacturer's annual set. The 1976 Topps set is unlike the company's previous offering in that it doesn't generate quite the collector interest or boast the overall rookie card power found in its 1975 release. In fact, the only Hall of Fame rookie card in the set belongs to Dennis Eckersley. The 1976 Topps Brett (#19) is one of the most sought-after cards of the decade in high grade. It is considered more valuable in PSA NM-MT 8 or PSA Mint 9 than his rookie. It is very rare for a second-year card of any player to be worth more than that player's rookie in these grades, but that is precisely the case with Brett. Why? The 1976 Topps Brett is usually found off-center from left to right, preventing many examples from achieving high-grade status. At the time of this writing, no copy has been assigned a grade of PSA Gem Mint 10 as a result.

GARY CARTER

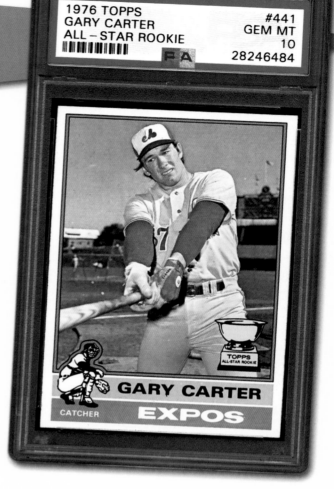

1976 TOPPS
GARY CARTER   #441
ALL – STAR ROOKIE   GEM MT 10
PSA   28246484

WHEN GARY CARTER CAME UP TO MONTREAL you could see he had the tools. He was an exceptional all-around catcher. Gary could hit, hit for power, and hit to all fields, which is very unusual in a catcher. Pitchers loved to throw to him. He was a real leader, his teammates respected him, and he was a very personable guy. Gary was just outstanding. He was one of those guys who liked to chatter when you stepped up to the plate, and he was actually pretty funny. He'd make comments like, "Is that glare out in center field bothering you?" or "What about that paper flying around the field?" Gary was in the Bill Freehan mold when it came to yapping. I remember Freehan once told me they were going to throw at me. I said, "What? What are you talking about?" and he just laughed.

I got to know Gary in spring training. The Expos practiced in Daytona and we played them several times.

PSA
1983 TOPPS   #370
GARY CARTER   GEM MT 10
                    21686606

Carter was just starting out when I was wrapping up my career, so there were only a couple of seasons that we both played in MLB, but we also played in some exhibition games and had a few laughs. When Gary went over to the Mets, he changed their whole way of thinking. They had some pretty good players, but they needed that one guy who would be a leader, and that was Gary. Getting a catcher with Gary's ability was an incredible stroke of luck for the Mets. In 1986, Gary and the Mets beat the Sox in an unbelievable World Series. He had a spectacular Series, and yes, he broke not only my heart, but the hearts of the entire Red Sox Nation. Gary started the Mets rally in Game Six with a two-out single in the 10th inning, which led to the winning hit by Ray Knight and forced Game Seven. I had a glass of champagne in my hand ready to celebrate, and wound up pouring it down the drain.

Defensively Gary was very special. Offensively he was a clutch hitter and a catalyst for the team. He did not hit for a really high average, but he hit over 300 home runs and had over 2,000 hits. Gary was the epitome of a leader, and I always respected him for that. He supported his teammates, was a fan favorite, and was always respectful to the opposition. Gary called an excellent game and really handled his pitchers well. In my opinion, as a player, Gary was pretty close in all-around ability to Carlton Fisk. Looking at his career, with the All-Star appearances, World Series championship, Gold Gloves and batting awards, Gary is one of the top catchers of all time. Actually, for the modern day Hall of Fame catchers that I played with, I have him right behind Bench and Fisk.

The other thing I liked about Gary was that he helped many people behind the scenes. He had a foundation that assisted children in need, and he really put his whole heart into helping people. The guy always had a smile on his face. It was really unfair that Gary died at a fairly young age after suffering from a brain tumor. I remember he once said baseball had been very good to him and that he was blessed to be able to play. Gary was a class act through and through.

THE CARDS

After Johnny Bench ended his run as the premier catcher in the National League, Gary Carter picked up where Bench left off. Beyond his excellent performance, Carter possessed a likable nature that endeared him to fans and collectors. Despite his accomplishments, memorable moments, and affable demeanor, the perennial All-Star was often overshadowed by other names in the game, including the closest thing to Carter in the American League—Carlton Fisk. Carter's extraordinary longevity at the position enabled him to play in three decades, a period when hundreds of cards and collectibles were made bearing his image.

Carter's mainstream debut came in the colorful 1975 Topps issue. After two consecutive years of somewhat bland formats in 1973 and 1974, this super-colorful Topps design was a welcomed surprise. It is important to note that Carter also has an

O-Pee-Chee (Canadian) and mini versions of the same card. The 1975 Topps Mini issue measures slightly smaller than the standard 2½" by 3½" cards, coming in at 2¼" by 3⅛" instead. Both the O-Pee-Chee and Topps Mini cards are tougher to find than the regular Topps issue, but neither generates the kind of interest created by the more common Carter rookie. Other Carter cards were issued during his rookie era by brands such as SSPC and TCMA, but none of them carry the hobby weight of his Topps debut.

It wouldn't be until 1976 when Carter would get a Topps card of his own, since he had to share his rookie with other newcomers, just as fellow Hall of Famer Jim Rice did in the same set. The multi-player rookie card was a very common practice by Topps at the time. Before the end of the decade, Carter found himself in some of the popular regional issues of the era such as those released by leading brands Hostess and Kellogg's. Carter would appear in more Kellogg's sets in the 1980s as the hobby expanded in dramatic fashion. In 1981, Topps was joined by Donruss and Fleer, creating new competition at the major manufacturer level. Later in the decade, the trio would be joined by others like Score and Upper Deck as the industry continued to grow at a rapid pace.

This period would produce the widest variety of Carter cards and collectibles, which included various

mediums. Carter can be found on non-trading card items like coins, faux credit cards, discs, stamps, stickers, and tattoos. Near the end of Carter's career, one of his most intriguing cards was made. In 1991, Topps issued a special version of their base set entitled Desert Shield, which showcased a distinct gold-foil emblem on the face of each card. The cards were designed for the specific purpose of being sent to the Persian Gulf as a gift to those serving in our armed forces. It is believed that only several thousand of each card was made. After retiring in 1992, Carter took his final hobby bow as an active player in 1993 when the future Hall of Famer was pictured on several cards, including those issued by Topps and Upper Deck.

The GARY CARTER CARD

Topps issued one of its best sets of the decade in 1975. The outstanding star selection and colorful design still keeps this 660-card set on the minds of active collectors. Except for the 1972 Topps offering, probably no other set captured the period—through the look of the cards alone—as well as the 1975 issue did. The set, which has two cards of the legendary Hank Aaron operating as bookends, contains several key rookie cards including Hall of Famers Carter (#620), George Brett, Rice, and Robin Yount, not to mention a rookie card of fan-favorite Keith Hernandez. Unlike Brett and Yount, the young catcher had to share the spotlight along with three other prospects: Marc Hill, Danny Meyer, and Leon Roberts. It's important to note that a mini version of the same card was released by Topps. While the Minis are not rare, they are tougher to find than their regular-sized counterparts. Poor centering due to image tilts, chipping along the colored edges, and print defects are all condition obstacles of which to be aware.

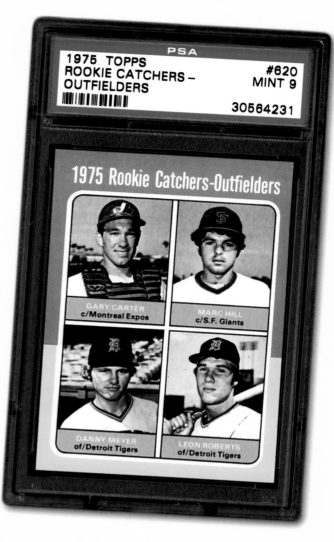

ONE CARD TO WATCH

Ten years after their first Mini issue, Topps decided to experiment with the diminutive design again. For Carter, it was the 10-year anniversary of his Topps debut. As is the case with most test issues, the 1985 Topps Mini set was never intended for public distribution, but the cards eventually found their way into the marketplace. It is believed that only 100 cards of each player in the 132-card set were produced, creating an extreme rarity for Carter collectors (card #230). The 132 total cards represent one full sheet and each one was printed on white stock, giving the cards a brighter appearance than the regular 1985 Topps cards. In fact, the Topps Minis look more like the Topps Traded or O-Pee-Chee cards from the same year. This makes sense because these cards were allegedly printed so O-Pee-Chee could test new printing equipment. The Topps Minis are roughly 10% smaller than their standard-sized counterparts, and a scant number of the subjects on the sheet were Hall of Famers.

DENNIS ECKERSLEY

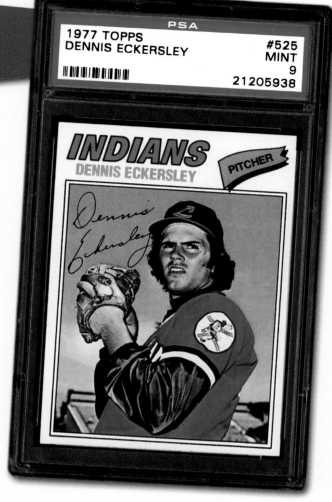

THE FIRST TIME I FACED DENNIS ECKERSLEY was in 1975. Eck was a rookie starter for Cleveland. He had a very good sinker, an excellent slider, and great control. Eck's delivery reminded me of Walter Johnson's. I'd call it a side-arm slingshot. Initially he made a few mistakes, and we got our hits against him, but he soon became an outstanding pitcher. Eck was a free spirit on the mound and was always very animated. He had good success as a starter, but when Tony La Russa decided to put Dennis in the bullpen, he became the best closer in baseball and a real superstar. He saved over 50 games one year for Oakland.

Dennis joined the Red Sox a couple of years after I retired, and he had 20 wins one year for us. In 1979 when I was doing radio color for Boston, I spent a lot of time with Eck. He was well-liked and he would fool around in the clubhouse to keep everyone loose. He was a real professional. If he got hit, he would not even change his expression. Eck is also a very self-deprecating guy.

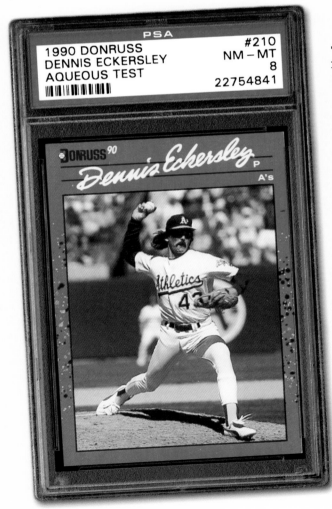

Just recently, while he was on the air doing a Dodgers game, he referred to himself as the guy who gave up the Kirk Gibson home run. Of course, he was referring to the walk-off home run in the ninth inning that Gibson hit to win Game One of the 1988 World Series. We can all remember that footage of Gibson pumping his fists as he circled the bases. I'll tell you though, in the late 1980s and early 1990s, Dennis was dominant as Oakland's closer. The A's were in the World Series three times, and Eck led the league in saves a few seasons. I think he really changed the way the game is played.

Eck closed out his career with one season back in Boston. Right now, he is doing both the pre-game and post-game show for the Red Sox, and he is sometimes in the booth as the color analyst. Man, is his plate full! Eckersley always uses descriptive words like "cheese" or "gas" for a fastball, or "educated salad" for a pitcher that has good command. We call them Eck-isms. What I've always liked about Dennis is that he's the type of guy who tells it like it is, not to the point of being demeaning to a ballplayer, but he is very frank with his analysis. I had a little dust up with Eck on the radio several years ago that, for some reason, became a huge story. There is no need to go into the particulars, but we resolved our differences and all is good. As a matter of fact, we worked the 2004 World Series together, and we are very good friends today.

One thing I need to mention is that recently Eck was involved in another controversy. This time it was concerning David Price of the Red Sox, and quite frankly, Eck was simply doing his broadcasting job. Red Sox fans and management backed Eck, as did his former teammates. I also supported Eck. When you're in the league as long as Dennis was, you deserve respect. He was a starter with good success for many years and then he went into the bullpen with great success for many more years. What an excellent competitor. His All-Star appearances, Cy Young Award, total saves, and longevity certainly make him one of the greatest closers of all time.

THE CARDS

Dennis Eckersley's life in baseball is a tale of two careers. For years, the Hall of Famer was a solid starter for the Cleveland Indians, Boston Red Sox, and Chicago Cubs, before joining the Oakland A's and reinventing himself as a closer. As a starter, despite throwing a no-hitter (1977), posting a 20-win season (1978), and being named to the All-Star team on two different occasions (1977/1982), Eckersley didn't generate a large collector following. That changed somewhat for the stylish hurler once he established himself as the premier reliever in the game for the Oakland A's. This paved the way for future starters like John Smoltz to make the same transition.

Most of Eckersley's cards and collectibles are considered affordable, but the one exception would be high-grade copies of his Topps rookie card. It is important to note that an Eckersley card was technically made prior to his inclusion in the 1976 Topps set. SSPC created an Eckersley card during the year he made his debut (1975), even though it wasn't released until the following year. In 1975, the pitcher racked up quite a few innings for the Indians. The card sells for a fraction of the 1976 Topps rookie card due to its limited following even though it predates the Topps card. In 1976, a Canadian (O-Pee-Chee) version of the same card was also issued. It is

much tougher to find than his Topps card, but it doesn't generate near the collector interest that the U.S. version does.

That same year, Hostess and Kellogg's Eckersley cards were issued as well. Kellogg's, with their immediately recognizable 3-D design, became one of the most popular regional issues of the decade and continued to create cards into the 1980s. The cards are generally found in nice shape, but beware of warping and cracking on the plastic surface. Before the decade was over, Hostess and Kellogg's were joined by a number of disc sets that issued Eckersley collectibles. The disc medium became extremely popular in the 1970s. Some of the disc brands include Chilly Willee, Dairy Isle, Holiday Inn, Pepsi-Cola, and Wiffle Ball. The 1977 MSA Customized Sports set is one of the tougher disc issues of the era to feature Eckersley, and while somewhat obscure, this disc is one of his more valuable issues.

Once we journey into the 1980s and beyond, that is when the great majority of Eckersley's cards were released. The hobby went through a major expansion as several new manufacturers entered the fold. By the 1990s, cards produced in limited numbers became the craze as collectors started to chase scarcity. Examples of Eckersley cards that carry premium value include his 1990 Donruss Aqueous Test, 1990 Leaf Preview, and 1993 Finest Refractor cards. After making his final pitch in 1998, Eckersley appeared on a few cards the following year, which included those issued by hobby giant Upper Deck.

The DENNIS ECKERSLEY CARD

The 1976 Topps set is unlike the company's previous offering in that it doesn't generate quite the collector interest or boast nearly the overall rookie card power found in its 1975 release. In fact, the only Hall of Fame rookie card in the set belongs to Eckersley (#98) and his Topps debut remains one of the keys along with cards of Hank Aaron, George Brett, Pete Rose, and Nolan Ryan. This set would be Aaron's final appearance on cardboard as an active player after 23 seasons of home run hitting. For those looking to assemble a high-grade set, the problem for many of these cards is centering, which alone prevents many examples from PSA Mint 9 or Gem Mint 10 eligibility. This is no different for Eckersley's first Topps issue, which is a lot like the 1979 Topps Ozzie Smith in that regard. In addition to the challenging centering, the Eckersley rookie is often found with a smattering of print defects along the face of the card to complicate matters.

"Hand-cut card issues can be some of the most challenging to collect."

ONE CARD TO WATCH

For five straight years, Hostess added baseball cards to their packages of tasty treats. In 1976, the sweet snack manufacturer issued their second annual set of cards. These cards came in the form three-card panels on the bottom of each box. The individual cards, if removed correctly from the panels, measure approximately 2¼" by 3¼" around the dotted lines, which were provided to guide those who wished to cut them by hand. Some collectors, however, prefer to keep the entire panel intact. Hand-cut card issues can be some of the most challenging to collect. Not only can it be difficult to find them, as many of the boxes were discarded, but the cards were often extracted in a less-than precise manner. Sometimes the cards were cut with uneven borders, causing eye-appeal issues, or well inside the provided lines. If the latter is the case, the cards are precluded from numerical grade eligibility by PSA standards. The Eckersley card (#137), while not nearly as popular as his Topps rookie, is far tougher to find in any condition and a nice complement or alternative to his more prevalent debut.

CARLTON FISK

TO THIS DAY, CARLTON AND I are close friends. I liked him as a player and as a man. When he first came up to the big leagues in Winter Haven, they said he would be the next big Red Sox catcher. Well, he caught a game and he was pretty bad. Fisk had trouble blocking balls. He was striking out and chasing balls in the dirt. I thought, "Are you kidding? This is our catcher of the future?" Fisk obviously wasn't ready yet so, after spring training, he was sent to Triple A.

In September, Fisk was one of the call-ups and I couldn't believe my eyes. He was so polished. Fisk was blocking balls, had a gun for an arm, and man, could he hit. Darrell Johnson must have worked with him a lot in Triple A. Pudge was so good, he took Rookie of the Year honors, and he soon became the best catcher in the American League. On the field, Fisk had an ongoing battle with Thurman Munson, but off the field, they respected each other.

Carlton had big, square shoulders and when he walked, he looked like he was strutting. We teased him about it, but some opposing players thought he was being cocky. In reality, it was just the way he walked.

A superb athlete and real leader, Fisk was an All-Star almost every year he played with us. One of the things I loved was how he recapped every game after it was over. We would talk about what we did right and what we could have done better. Carlton was firm with our pitchers but they respected him. When Bill Lee was pitching and Fisk would head out to the mound, Lee would turn and walk almost halfway to second base because he knew Carlton was going to get all over him. Fisk would wait patiently on the mound until Lee came back. They were really great friends and Fisk knew how to handle Spaceman during the game.

Pudge got more big game clutch hits than anyone on the team. One season we were on the *Game of the Week* about eight times, and I think he hit a homer in all eight games. In Game Six of the 1975 Series, I was in the dugout when Pat Darcy, a sinkerball pitcher, came in to face Carlton, a low-ball hitter, in the bottom of the 12th inning. I thought, "This is going to be interesting." When Fisk hit the ball, we knew it could be a home run, but from the dugout, we couldn't tell if it was fair or foul, so I watched Carlton. He was waving at the ball, telling it to stay fair. When the ball was fair, we all went wild. We thought we had the momentum to win it all. Cincinnati had a great team, though, and they came back to take the Series.

I was shocked when Fisk went to the White Sox over a contract issue. He had many great years in Chicago, playing into his forties. Talk about longevity! I see Carlton a couple of times a year now. He still lives in Chicago but he comes to Fenway every now and then. Hands down, Carlton Fisk is one of the greatest to ever play the position. He never backed down, always protected his teammates, and he was never afraid to mix it up with the opposition, especially the Yankees. He is a great friend and a Hall of Famer in the truest sense of the word.

THE CARDS

When you think of the word "longevity" in relation to the catcher position, Carlton Fisk is the name that immediately comes to mind. Playing a position that generates more bumps and bruises than any other on the field, Fisk somehow piled up 24 seasons of big league service. Through all the trials and tribulations of being a backstop, Fisk excelled and left the game with one of the most memorable moments the sport has ever seen when he waved his walk-off home run fair in Game Six of the 1975 World Series. Hundreds of cards and collectibles were made of Fisk over three decades, giving hobbyists plenty to choose from before he retired.

It all started for Fisk in 1972. It

was the year he became the starting catcher for the Boston Red Sox and the year of his hobby debut on cardboard. Fisk's 1972 Topps rookie is a key in a set filled with established legends like Hank Aaron, Roberto Clemente, and Willie Mays, but it wasn't the only card made of the star backstop that year. O-Pee-Chee, which is the Canadian version of the Topps series, also issued a Fisk rookie. While the Topps and O-Pee-Chee Fisk rookies are virtually identical on the front, the O-Pee-Chee cards feature a brighter-looking paper stock on the reverse and information in both French and English. The O-Pee-Chee Fisk is more elusive, but the Topps version garners more collector interest.

The following year, Fisk would not only get his own basic Topps card, but he was also featured in one of the manufacturer's more popular non-card mediums. The 1973 Topps Candy Lids are not nearly as tough to find as their 1972 test-issue predecessors, but they are still highly collectible. These lids measure 1⅞" in diameter and were placed at the top of a bubble gum product. The 55-lid set is absolutely loaded with stars, including a young Fisk. The very next year, Fisk was a part of another intriguing Topps issue called Deckle Edge. This jagged-looking test issue contained 72 black-and-white cards. This oversized 2⅞" by 5" Fisk card comes with either a gray or white back, with the latter considered slightly tougher to find.

As Fisk's career continued, the Hall of Famer would

find himself in numerous popular regional issues such as Hostess and Kellogg's, but the hardest Fisk collectible to catch may be his 1977 Venezuelan Sticker. This set, which was primarily made up of local, winter-league players, also includes a few dozen MLB players. These blank-backed stickers are thinner reproductions of their 1977 Topps card counterparts but have slightly different dimensions at approximately 2⅜" by 3⅛" in size. A custom album was produced to affix each sticker in, and unfortunately for collectors, a significant percentage of the known examples today exhibit back damage. Fisk's final season and last appearance on cardboard as an active player was 1993, when a few dozen cards were issued during his hobby farewell.

The CARLTON FISK CARD

The 787-card 1972 Topps set remains one of the most popular productions from the decade. Collectors are attracted to the eye-catching design, one that is fitting for the period, and the tremendous star selection throughout. With all the big names contained therein, the only Hall of Famer rookie is that of Fisk (#79). Like many rookie cards of the day, Fisk shared the spotlight with other prospects. This time, teammates Mike Garman and Cecil Cooper were pictured along with the future Cooperstown member. Even though Fisk made brief appearances in 1969 and 1971, he would be named the AL Rookie of the Year in 1972, after playing in 131 games for the Red Sox. He also won his first-and-last Gold Glove that year as well. The card, while not overly difficult to find in PSA NM-MT 8 condition, is somewhat challenging to locate in PSA Mint 9 shape and extraordinarily tough in PSA Gem Mint 10. Condition obstacles include less than optimal centering and the presence of print defects on the face of the card.

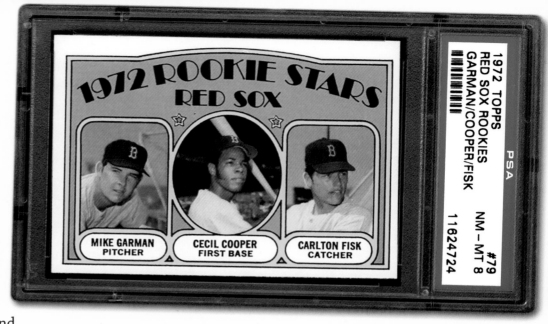

"The 1993 Topps Finest Refractor provides the perfect hobby walk-off for the man that, arguably, hit the most famous walk-off of all time."

ONE CARD TO WATCH

The 1990s ushered in a new era of baseball card production. No longer were the cards from the base sets considered the cards to own. It was the time of the parallels. For better or worse, manufacturers started focusing their energy on creating more and more limited-edition cards, those that would end up being described as "chase" cards later in the decade. The granddaddy of these sets is the 1993 Topps Finest Refractor issue, which contains one of Fisk's last cards (#125). There was a time when no other modern-era set generated more demand or attention than this trailblazing creation. Each card in the set had a reported print run of 241, which meant that about one Refractor was inserted into every Topps box. The cards are surprisingly tough to find in PSA 10. This is a result of marginal centering and a vulnerable surface. This 199-card set was made during Fisk's final season. The 1993 Topps Finest Refractor provides the perfect hobby walk-off for the man that, arguably, hit the most famous walk-off of all time.

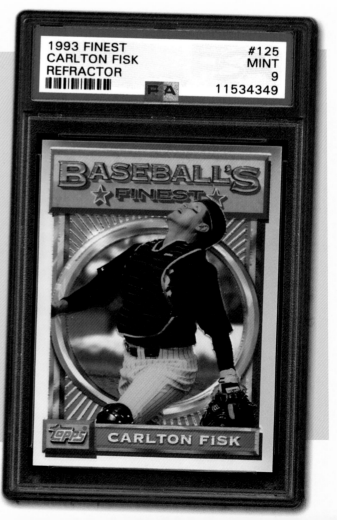

RICH "GOOSE" GOSSAGE

1974 TOPPS
RICH GOSSAGE #542
PSA
GEM MT 10
16474584

WHEN GOOSE GOSSAGE WAS A YOUNG STARTER

for the White Sox, I faced him for the first time. That was back in 1972. Rich had a slider, but that wasn't his best pitch. He threw a fastball that would tail into righties about eight to ten inches. It was a really heavy fastball. A couple of years later, the White Sox made Gossage a relief pitcher and I faced him then as well. A lot of the guys thought Rich was intimidating but I got my hits off him—you know, off the handle, or a few bloops—really nothing major. Once he became a closer, Gossage had great success. He was one of the very first dominant closers in baseball and he pitched a ton of innings. By that time, Rich had one pitch, a fastball. He had tremendous control of that pitch and could top off in the very high 90s. The thing I liked about him was that he worked very quickly when he was on the mound.

You know, Gossage can still throw. I faced him a few years ago in Scranton, Pennsylvania. Some of the old Red Sox and old Yankees got together for a charity event.

1975 TOPPS #554
RICH GOSSAGE MINT 9
PSA
90552183

Even though it was an exhibition game, it was kind of competitive. We went about six innings in front of about 10,000 people. It was great fun to play with Gossage, Bucky Dent, Oscar Gamble, Graig Nettles, Jim Rice, and a bunch of others. I played a little third base. Actually, the best part of the game was watching Mike Torrez pitch to Bucky Dent. Bucky hit one to the warning track and we all had a good laugh. Of course, in 1978 Bucky broke our backs in that playoff game, hitting the home run off Torrez when he pitched for the Red Sox. When I talk with Goose about today's pitchers, he is pretty critical. Since relief pitchers only play one inning now, he thinks they are babied. During his career, Rich typically went two or three innings in relief. He is not a big fan of the pitch count either. Of course, we both agreed that in today's game, you need a great closer to win it all. So many teams come back strong in the ninth inning now.

It's amazing how many teams Gossage played with. I think it was something like 10 or 11. Baseball was a business and Rich clearly understood that. Sometimes he would get traded, and sometimes he would sign with the highest bidder. It didn't matter. Wherever he went, he excelled. His best years were with the White Sox, Yankees, and the Padres. Those were his All-Star years. He led the American League in saves several times during that period, but he was the closer for the Yankees when he pitched in three World Series, so I guess that was probably the highlight of his career. I think the whole thing about him intentionally throwing at batters was overblown. He simply pitched with the attitude that he, not the batter, owned the plate. Goose was actually a very good guy and fierce competitor. I was glad to see him get inducted into the Hall of Fame. It was well-deserved.

THE CARDS

For many Hall of Famers, complete collector appreciation is something that occurs during their active days as a player and long before the star is ever enshrined in Cooperstown. For others, that appreciation takes time to build. Sometimes,

it is a product of how quickly the player reaches baseball's ultimate destination. In other cases, the player was simply overshadowed by other legends of the era, and often what they accomplished on the field wasn't fully appreciated until later. The story of Rich "Goose" Gossage cannot be told without acknowledging each of those factors. Much like the careers of pitchers Catfish Hunter and Don Sutton, the Hall of Fame blessing dramatically changed their hobby appeal.

Before making his mainstream hobby debut in 1973 as part of the annual Topps set, Gossage was included in an obscure but highly collectible sticker set that captured some U.S. stars who traveled in the offseason to work on their craft. The 1972 Puerto Rican League Sticker features Gossage while he participated in their winter season. The Gossage sticker is one of the most valuable in the set, along with those of other young MLB stars like Don Baylor and Mike Schmidt. Some veterans also appeared in the set such as Tony Perez and Frank Robinson, but the recognizable U.S. names are few and far between.

In 1975, Topps created a mini version of their base set. Identical in every other way, the 1975 Topps Mini issue measures slightly smaller than the standard 2½" by 3½" cards, coming in at 2¼" by 3⅛" instead. As his career progressed, Gossage started to appear in some of the more popular regional

issues of the decade such as Burger King, Hostess, and Kellogg's. The hard-throwing righty also became a regular with O-Pee-Chee, which was the Canadian version of the Topps issue. These are much tougher to find in general than their Topps counterparts but not nearly as popular as the U.S. brand. Once we turn the corner into the 1980s, an explosion of Gossage cards came next as the hobby started to expand in a major way.

In addition to Donruss and Fleer becoming full-time competitors of Topps very early in the decade, all kinds of new cards were being made at that time. Various regional issues included Gossage like Coca-Cola and Mother's Cookies. There were even non-card mediums like coins, discs, and stamp sets that featured Gossage. These offbeat collectibles were created both by major manufacturers and regional brands. By the 1990s, the hobby continued to grow, adding more annual issues to the collecting mix from brands such as Bowman and Upper Deck. After throwing his last pitch in 1994, a nice selection of Gossage cards were issued in 1995 to cap his fine career.

"Once we turn the corner into the 1980s, an explosion of Gossage cards came next as the hobby started to expand in a major way."

The RICH GOSSAGE CARD

During the 1950s and 1960s, Topps was known for producing trading card sets that possessed fantastic eye appeal. In fact, in 1972 the manufacturer produced another set that has captivated collectors to this day based on the colorful design alone. The very next year, for some reason, Topps decided to go with a bland look, one that doesn't exactly stop hobbyists in their tracks. What the issue may have lacked in aesthetic beauty, however, it made up for in difficulty. The quality of the paper and print, poor centering, and the black borders on the reverse can make high-grade examples hard to come by relative to the period. Gossage's debut (#174) and Schmidt's first Topps card are the two Hall of Famer rookies in the set. Unlike Schmidt, Gossage had the spotlight all to himself, which was a rarity during the period as many newcomers had to share their rookie cards with fellow prospects. A Canadian version (O-Pee-Chee) of the same card also exists. While it is tougher to find overall, the Topps rookie is the one that gets most of the attention from collectors.

"Goose's epic hair makes the card intriguing all by itself."

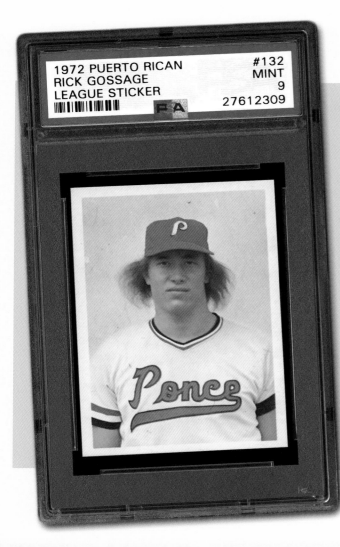

ONE CARD TO WATCH

Gossage, like many prospects of his generation, would often sharpen his skills in the offseason by continuing to play. In 1972, a collectible was produced that predates his 1973 Topps rookie card. The 1972 Puerto Rican Winter League Sticker is one that stands out amongst the hundreds of Gossage cards and collectibles made during his playing career. It is, arguably, the toughest of all Gossage items to find for collectors focused on the flame-throwing reliever. The Gossage (#132) is part of a 231-sticker set and each sticker was intended to be affixed inside an album for display. The stickers, which measure approximately 2¼" by 3", are often found in lower grades due to handling and damage to the reverse. The thin stock used to make these stickers made it difficult to preserve them over time. Each sticker showcases a color photo on the front, while the back contains brief information printed in Spanish and mistakenly lists Gossage's first name as "Rick." Goose's epic hair makes the card intriguing all by itself.

NOLAN RYAN

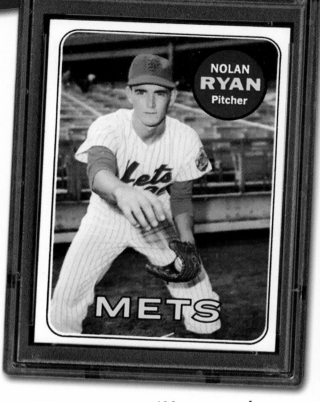

WHEN YOU TALK ABOUT NOLAN RYAN, you talk about a guy that struck out over 5,000 batters. Can you imagine that? By the way, I was part of that 5,000. He was damned tough. He had a great fastball, three-quarter over the top. You would think that the ball was going to be belt-high and somehow it would wind up letter-high. Ryan was unbelievable. Every pitch was 98 or 99 mph and that gave you very little time to react. When he could get his curveball over, Ryan was absolutely unhittable. Sometimes he had control problems, though, and ended up walking guys. Our strategy was to stay close to him, because if his team got a three- or four-run lead, it was going to be very tough to beat him.

I'd say Ryan had the same leg strength as Seaver, and combined with his arm strength, he was extremely tough. Nolan wasn't a little guy, either. When I faced him, I always tried to be positive and tell myself,

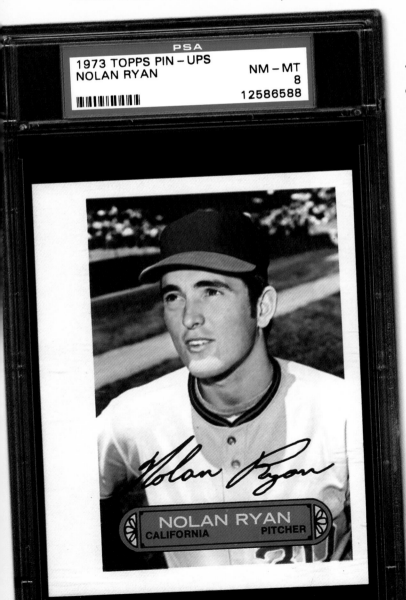

"I'm gonna hit him tonight." Then, of course, I'd have a couple of strikeouts and popups. I remember one game in Anaheim in 1974 when Ryan and our guy, Luis Tiant, went at it. Wow! What a game! With the pitch counts, it's something you just wouldn't see in baseball today. It was a real duel that lasted for about four hours. They battled like warriors. Ryan went 13 innings and Tiant went the distance, pitching into the 15th inning. Finally in the bottom of the 15th, Denny Doyle hit a double to left field scoring Mickey Rivers to win the game for the Angels.

One thing is for sure, Ryan wasn't afraid to come inside. I remember the time he hit our second baseman, Doug Griffin, in the head. At first I thought he was dead. We took him out of the game and brought him to the hospital. Thankfully, he recovered nicely. We didn't face Ryan again until a few months later. Doug stepped into the batter's box, didn't budge, and got two hits off him. We all really respected Doug for that, including Nolan Ryan. As I have said before, Ryan was one of the toughest pitchers I faced. He had nasty stuff. I put him right up there with Gibson and Koufax. Although Gibson had an easier time getting his breaking ball over the plate, he was actually a bit more hittable. When Ryan had his stuff going, he was a beast.

When I look at his numbers, I marvel at how great a pitcher he was. I know he won over 300 games and lost just under 300 games, but if Ryan had played for better-hitting teams, I believe would have won a lot more games. Can you even imagine how many wins he would have if he played for some of the great teams? My guess would be 400, easy. The thing that really stands out in my mind about Ryan was his intimidating mound presence and what a tenacious competitor he was. Ryan was durable, too, pitching into his mid-forties, and you know, he had those seven no-hitters. So, maybe he was the toughest that I faced, but I liked Nolan Ryan. I don't see him too much anymore. I know that he's on his ranch in Texas. Maybe I should go visit and do a little "buck ridin!"

THE CARDS

Nolan Ryan pitched for 27 seasons. Not only is that nearly three full decades as an active player, but that span was one that witnessed tremendous hobby growth. When you combine Ryan's longevity and his immense appeal with the era he played in, it becomes a recipe for a lot of cards. How many? By the end of his career, Ryan was featured on over 2,000 different trading cards and collectibles. No other player from that generation comes remotely close to that number, which is fitting for a pitcher who owns some career marks that may never be approached again. Ryan had more cards issued after the age of 40 than most stars of the period had issued for their entire careers.

With so many Ryan collectibles issued during that era, the icon probably deserves his own annual catalog. For the dedicated collector seeking to assemble a complete master run of Ryan cards, the pursuit is not for the faint of heart or light of wallet. It all started for Ryan in 1968, when the future star

made his Topps debut and ended up with four different versions of his rookie card. Ryan received his first individual card in 1969, an attractive card that pictures the lanky youngster in a throwing pose. Along with becoming a regular with Topps, Ryan became a virtual regular with the related O-Pee-Chee (Canadian) brand as well.

Once we turn the corner and head into the 1970s, we can see the dramatic uptick in Ryan cards begin. In fact, Topps started to include Ryan in various test issues. Some of those test issues rank near the top of the list of Ryan's most elusive and valuable collectibles. From the 1972 Topps Candy Lids to the 1973 Pin-Ups to the 1974 Deckle Edge issue, in almost every instance Ryan is the most valuable component of the set. In some cases, it's not even close, which is most impressive considering that these test issues are often chock-full of contemporary stars. On the 1974 Topps Deckle Edge issue, it is important to note that there are two variations, one with a gray-colored back (standard) and one with a white back, which is considered the tougher of the two to find.

The list of regional issues to include Ryan is simply too vast to present here, but the brands include Burger King, Drakes, Hostess, Jiffy Pop,

Kay Bee, Kellogg's, Kraft, Mother's Cookies, Pepsi-Cola, Ralston Purina, and Woolworth, to name a few. This barely scratches the surface. Ryan was so popular that a few different manufacturers issued entire sets devoted to Ryan in the 1980s and 1990s. Pacific and Star Co. are two examples. Towards the end of his career, some special limited and autographed Ryan cards were issued by various brands. After injuring his arm in 1993, Ryan made his final hobby appearance in 1994 on a host of cards from all the major manufacturers.

The NOLAN RYAN CARD

As is the case with most players, it took Ryan some time to develop into the dominant force that fans and collectors grew to love. While it did take a few years for Ryan to blossom, it seemed like the baseball card world knew what was to come from the flame-throwing righty, as there are four different versions of his rookie card known to exist. In 1968, Ryan made his Topps debut on a card (#177) that he shares with Jerry Koosman, who was a fine pitcher in his own right. The Ryan card is one of two key Hall of Famer rookie cards in the set, along with Johnny Bench. They make up quite the battery. That same year, three other versions of the same card were produced. Milton Bradley, O-Pee-Chee, and Venezuelan Topps issued their own Ryan rookies as well. All three are tougher to find than the traditional Topps Ryan, especially the

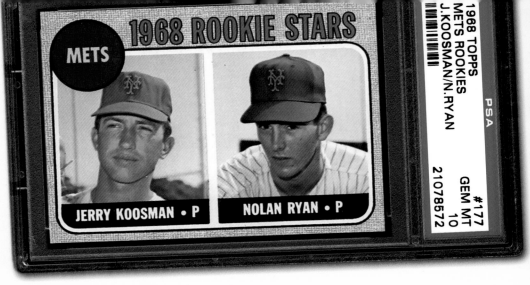

Venezuelan Topps card, but the Topps card is the one that has the most mainstream appeal. Even though all four Ryan rookies have the same general design, there are subtle differences. For example, the Milton Bradley card exhibits a brighter yellow color on the reverse and will sometimes feature a thin white line on one or more edges, which carried over from the white-bordered football and hot rod cards included on the same sheet.

ONE CARD TO WATCH

Well, let me start by saying this isn't technically a card at all, but it's one of many Ryan collectibles that Topps created over the years. In the 1960s and 1970s, Topps really started to let the creative juices flow while coming up with new concepts for the collector marketplace. Today, these Topps productions are referred to as test issues and there are plenty from which to choose. After Ryan came into the league,

Topps continued their quest to innovate beyond the traditional baseball card. In 1973, Topps created two sets in a long line of many test issues: Comics and Pin-Ups. Each set shares an identical checklist, one that contains 24 subjects, from Hank Aaron to Carl Yastrzemski. The Comics, however, appear to be the slightly tougher and more desirable of the two. These miniature comic strips measure approximately 4⅝" by 3⁷⁄₁₆" and each was printed on a waxed paper wrapper. This wrapper was intended to envelop a piece of bubble gum, but most of the known comics today escaped the factory in unused form. On the enormous list of manufactured Ryan collectibles, this 1973 Topps Comic ranks right near the top of collector challenges.

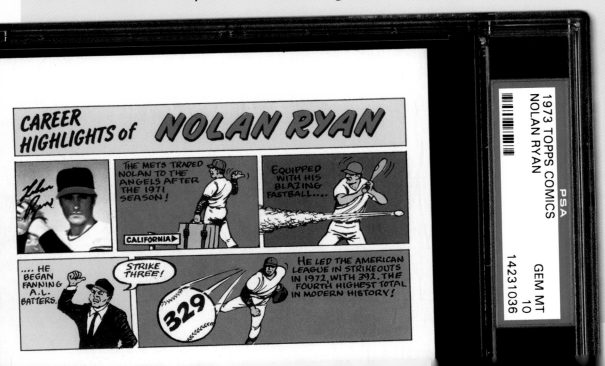

DAVE WINFIELD

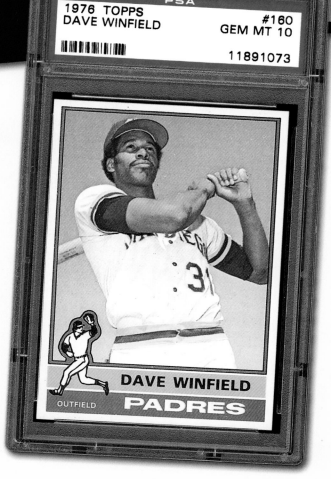

DAVE WINFIELD WAS A SOLID HITTER AND FIELDER

over the course of his lengthy career. We never played against each other, because he didn't come to the American League until after I retired. When I was playing, Dave was one of the bright young stars of the Padres. I always enjoyed watching Winfield. He was a real player's player. This guy hit over 400 home runs, had over 3,000 hits, and won a slew of Gold Gloves in both leagues. In my opinion, Dave was the complete player. Another reason I followed Winfield's career closely was because he was a tremendous overall athlete and he excelled at basketball, too. Dave played basketball in college at the University of Minnesota, and he was so good that the NBA wanted him. You know, I had the opportunity to play Division One basketball, but I chose baseball because that was my first love. I've always wondered how I would have done if I picked basketball instead.

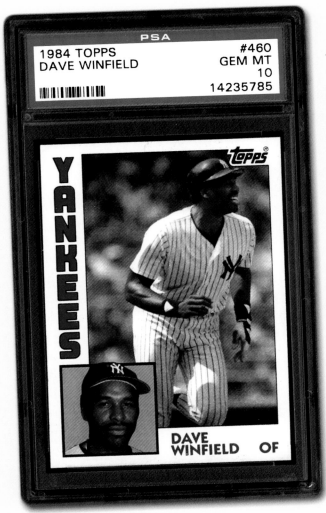

After he left the Padres and joined the Yankees, I think the New York environment really helped Winfield. I believe he was the highest-paid player in baseball at the time and really, in my opinion, he earned it. For some reason, George Steinbrenner was not crazy about Dave despite the fact that he put up great numbers. Winfield and Don Mattingly put on quite a show competing for the American League batting title in the mid-1980s. Mattingly took the title, but it was so close. Although it was not as historic, the Winfield-Mattingly battle kind of reminded me of a contest between two other Yankees, when Mantle and Maris competed to beat the Babe's record in 1961.

From a defensive standpoint, Dave was an outstanding outfielder with a rocket for an arm. I'm not sure that I would put him in the same category as Dwight Evans, but he was pretty close. Offensively, Winfield was very consistent. His power numbers were pretty close every season. You could count on him for 20 or 30 home runs almost every year. He could hit line drives to every field and he was a legitimate threat to opposing pitchers. As he got along in years, Winfield was always productive, but I remember he had an outstanding year when he played for the Blue Jays. I think he was about forty years old when he helped them to the World Series win.

One thing I don't think many people realize is that, right from the beginning, Dave was always giving back to the community.

It's not often that your fellow players pay attention to what you are doing outside of the sport, but Winfield has done some pretty amazing things over the years. His foundation has done a lot of good in this country helping those that are not so fortunate. As I recall, he even received the Clemente Award. I have only crossed paths with Dave once or twice, but I have really enjoyed following his career. For some reason it seems as though he was somewhat under the radar compared to many other Hall of Famers, but with his 12 All-Star appearances, all of those Gold Gloves, and his World Series championship, I'd say that Dave Winfield is up there with some of the greatest outfielders who ever played the game.

THE CARDS

One of the great five-tool players of his generation, Dave Winfield was a terrific athlete. He could hit, hit with power, run, field, and throw. His overall career numbers speak volumes about his all-around ability. Yet even though he played several seasons for the New York Yankees, Winfield never seemed to get the full degree of recognition he deserved at the time. This was due, in part, to the lack of World Series championships the team had. Winfield did win a World Series in 1992 as a part of the Toronto Blue Jays. Despite his impressive resume, most of Winfield's cards and collectibles remain very affordable.

Winfield appeared on hundreds of hobby issues during his playing days, but no card garners anywhere near the attention that his Topps rookie does, even though it wasn't alone that year. In 1974, an O-Pee-Chee (Canadian) version of the same card was issued as well. The O-Pee-Chee Winfield card is much tougher to find than the U.S. version, but it is not nearly as popular with collectors. In addition to the O-Pee-Chee card, other Winfield collectibles were created that year as well. This included non-card mediums like the McDonald's Padre Disc and Topps Stamp. The Winfield image on the Topps stamp, although different, appears to be from the same photoshoot that produced his standard Topps rookie.

As his career progressed, Winfield started to appear

PSA
1985 DONRUSS
DAVE WINFIELD   #51
                 GEM MT 10
                 03200099

DAVE WINFIELD OF

in various regional issues of the period, from popular brands like Hostess and Kellogg's to team sets released by the San Diego Padres. Keep in mind that the hand-cut cards, created by companies such as Hostess, required the collector to remove the card or full panel from the box of their product. In many cases, dotted lines were part of the design to help provide guidance to consumers. On occasion, the collector cut each card well within the provided lines. Today, those cards would not be eligible for a numerical grade from PSA since the company requires that each card or panel retains most of its intended size.

When the hobby went through its dramatic expansion in the 1980s, a major increase in Winfield cards were produced and this continued until the end of his career. In 1982, one of Winfield's more interesting cards was produced. This time, it was an error. That year, Topps issued some of the cards without black ink. The regular cards are missing the expected facsimile signature and the All-Star cards are missing the player names on the fronts. They are referred to as "blackless" variations and can be very tough to find. Perhaps Winfield's most intriguing card from the 1990s is his 1993 Topps Finest Refractor, as each card in the set had a reported print run of only 241. After taking his final swing in 1995, several Winfield cards were issued in 1996 to honor the future Hall of Famer.

The DAVE WINFIELD CARD

In 1974, one year after Winfield made his first MLB appearance, Topps issued a 660-card set that most collectors feel was a slight step up from their previous offering in terms of design, and the issue has some tough variations. Topps made the decision to issue some San Diego Padres player cards with "Washington" instead, since the team was expected to move, but the move never happened. Some of the cards made it into the stream of commerce before Topps could fix it. The set, which features rookie cards of excellent players such as Ken Griffey Sr., Bill Madlock, and Dave Parker, has only one Hall of Famer debut, which belongs to Winfield (#456). There were other Winfield cards and collectibles issued in 1974, but this is the one that most collectors clamor for, and it is easily the most desirable card made during his career. It is important to note that no "Washington" variation of the Winfield rookie was created. Winfield was, however, one of the players during the era that was fortunate enough to secure a rookie card of his own, unlike many of the debut cards produced in the 1970s like those of George Brett, Carlton Fisk, and Mike Schmidt. The card, while not considered a condition rarity, is often found with undesirable centering or light print defects on the face of the card.

ONE CARD TO WATCH

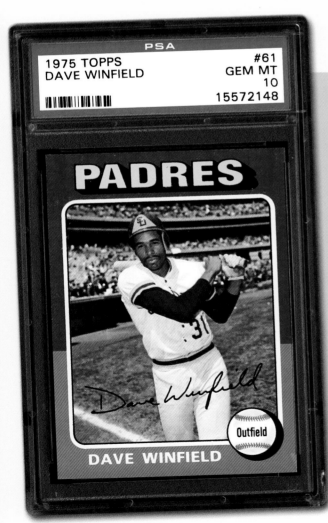

In 1975, Topps issued one of its best sets of the decade. Because of the multi-colored design and outstanding star selection, this 660-card set remains popular with active collectors today. Perhaps no other set captured the period as well as the 1975 issue did—except for the 1972 Topps offering—through the look of the cards alone. With two cards of the legendary Hank Aaron operating as bookends, the set contains several key rookie cards. The Hall of Famers who made their debut here include Brett, Gary Carter, Jim Rice, Robin Yount, and the rookie card of fan-favorite Keith Hernandez. Keep in mind that a mini version of the same card was released by Topps. While the Minis are not rare, they are tougher to find than their regular-sized counterparts. Poor centering due to image tilts, chipping along the colored edges, and print defects are all condition obstacles of which to be aware. In the case of Winfield, not only is this one of his earliest and most popular issues, it is also one of the toughest to find in PSA Gem Mint 10 condition. How difficult is it? Since 1991, only two regular 1975 Topps Winfield cards have reached such lofty heights, while no mini versions have achieved the PSA 10 grade thus far.

ROBIN YOUNT

NO ONE KNEW WHO ROBIN YOUNT WAS when he came to up to Milwaukee in 1974. Suddenly there was a tall, lanky 18-year-old kid playing starting shortstop for the Brewers. He had an inside-out swing that was something like Jeter's, in my opinion. Yount could hit the ball to left field, right field, and center field. He was a tough out even then, but once he matured, he could hit for power. As a matter of fact, Yount killed us with some big hits right out of the ballpark. At the beginning, he was a good shortstop with decent range, but as time went on, he became a tremendous all-around ballplayer.

Robin was just a great kid—a real classy guy. I only played against him for a couple of years when he was just starting out, but I liked his stuff so I followed his career closely. After I retired, Yount was moved to center field, and he became a very good outfielder. He was never controversial and always went about his business professionally.

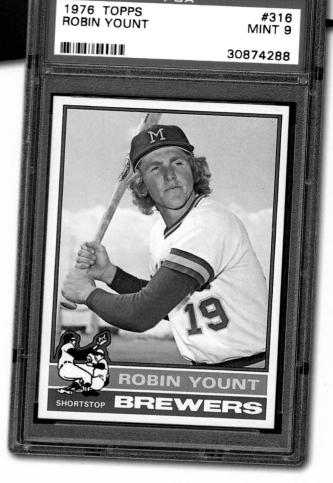

When the Brewers brought Paul Molitor in to play second base, Yount and Molitor became an awesome tandem. Besides that, they both reached the 3,000 hit pinnacle. At the plate, Robin had no weaknesses, and with that inside-out swing, he was able to put the ball over the right field fence fairly regularly. I believe Robin had over a .300 batting average against us during his career. He was a real pain in the neck! If I'm not mistaken, Yount played the last game of his career against the Red Sox.

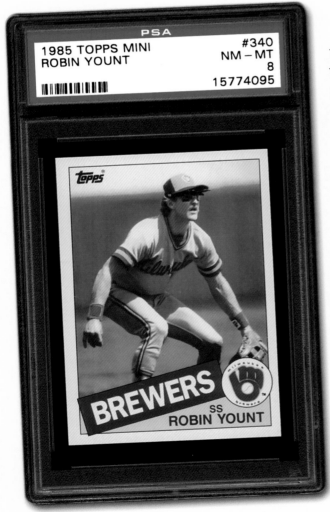

From a power perspective, Robin averaged about the same number of home runs per season as I did, but in my opinion, he was a much more polished hitter overall. I'll tell you what really baffles me. Why was Yount only a three-time All-Star? Here was a Gold Glover, League MVP, and future Hall of Famer who was certainly one of the best shortstops of all time, and he had only three appearances in the All-Star Game? Speaking of All-Stars, back in 1999 I did a signing with Robin Yount and George Brett at the All-Star FanFest in Boston. I'll tell you, I was so impressed with both of them. They are such great ambassadors for the game, very personable, and just terrific with the fans. It was great fun to talk hitting with them that day and have a few laughs. Both guys loved to hit in Fenway, but really, they could hit anywhere.

When I think about Yount's career, the thing that strikes me is how durable and consistent he was as a player. He was starting shortstop when he was only 18 years old, and he played for the Brewers until he was in his late thirties. He was so versatile, too. Yount was able to transition to the outfield without missing a beat. You know, he was MVP at both positions, and he holds a lot of Brewers team records. I've always been very impressed with Robin. I'm glad I had the chance to play against him even though he was so young at the time. It was great to see how he blossomed to become one of the top players in baseball.

THE CARDS

For 20 years, Robin Yount steadily put up the kind of numbers that are fitting for a Hall of Famer. Yount entered the 3,000 Hit Club and earned two AL MVPs before he hung up the cleats. Surprisingly, the gritty Brewer was only named to three All-Star teams during his long and productive career, but this fact helps explain why so many of his cards and collectibles remain relatively affordable. Yount played his entire career in Milwaukee, which endeared him to Brewers fans but limited Yount's exposure to a national audience at the time.

It would be difficult to choose a better set for a player's mainstream hobby debut than the 1975 Topps issue. This super-colorful Topps design was a welcomed surprise after two consecutive years of somewhat bland formats in 1973 and 1974. Keep in mind that Yount also has an O-Pee-Chee (Canadian) and mini versions of the same card. The 1975 Topps Mini issue measures slightly smaller than the standard 2½" by 3½" cards, coming in at 2¼" by 3⅛" instead. Both the

O-Pee-Chee and Topps Mini cards are tougher to find than the regular Topps issue, but neither generates the kind of interest created by the more common Yount debut. Other Yount cards were issued during his rookie era such as SSPC, but none of them carry the hobby weight of his Topps issue.

As the decade rolled on, Yount appeared in numerous collectible disc sets, which were a popular medium at the time. The disc brands included Burger Chef, Chilly Willee, Dairy Isle, Holiday Inn, MSA, Saga, and Wendy's, to name a few. While the two-time AL MVP missed the opportunity to be included in some terrific Topps test issues in the early-1970s, Yount did find his way into the elusive 1985 Topps Mini set. It is believed that only 100 cards of each player in the 132-card set were produced, creating an extreme rarity for Yount collectors. The 132 total cards represent one full sheet and each one was printed on white stock, which gives the cards a brighter appearance than the regular 1985 Topps cards. The Topps Minis are roughly 10% smaller than their standard-sized counterparts, and only a scant number of the subjects on the sheet were Hall of Famers.

During the major hobby explosion of the 1980s and 1990s, hundreds of Yount cards were issued by a host of brands. Near the end of Yount's career, the popularity of limited-edition insert or parallel cards gained in popularity. The granddaddy of these "chase" sets

is the 1993 Topps Finest Refractor issue. There was a time when no other modern-era set generated more demand or attention than this trailblazing creation. Each card in the set had a reported print run of 241, which meant that about one Refractor was inserted into every Topps box. The cards are surprisingly tough to find in PSA Gem Mint 10, but this is a result of marginal centering and a vulnerable surface. After taking his last cuts in 1993, several trading card brands paid tribute to Yount in 1994.

"The granddaddy of these 'chase' sets is the 1993 Topps Finest Refractor issue."

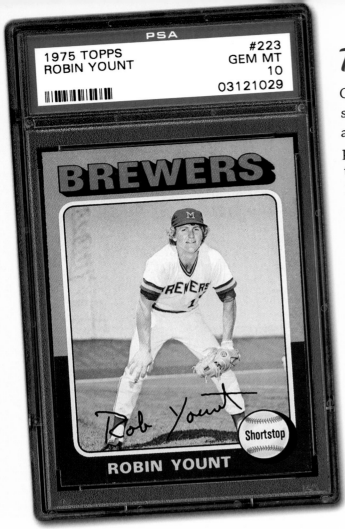

The ROBIN YOUNT CARD

One of the best Topps sets of the decade was issued in 1975. The superb star selection and colorful design makes this 660-card set a favorite of active collectors. Aside from the 1972 Topps offering, perhaps no other set captured the period as well as the 1975 issue did through the look of the cards alone. With two cards of the legendary Hank Aaron operating as bookends, the set contains several key rookie cards. The Hall of Famers who made their debut here include Yount (#223), George Brett, Gary Carter, and Jim Rice, not to mention a rookie card of fan-favorite Keith Hernandez. The Yount rookie featured the young prospect by himself, unlike the multi-player rookies of Carter and Rice. It is important to note that a mini version of the same card was released by Topps. While the Minis are not rare, they are tougher to find than their regular-sized counterparts. Poor centering due to image tilts, chipping along the colored edges, and print defects are all condition obstacles of which to be aware.

"Yount's most popular rookie card was produced in the annual Topps set."

ONE CARD TO WATCH

Over the course of his career, hundreds of Yount cards were released, which included plenty of regional issues. One of the popular brands of the era was Hostess. For years, Hostess included cards on the boxes of their snack products. These cards were designed to be removed by the collector. Dotted lines were provided for guidance to those who wanted to try their hand at cutting the cards, or the full panels if applicable, from their original homes. In 1975, Yount's most popular rookie card was produced in the annual Topps set, and two more related cards—the Topps Mini and O-Pee-Chee (Canadian) Yount rookies—were issued as well. None of them, however, are as tough as Yount's 1975 Hostess Twinkies card (#80). It's important to note that a regular Hostess card was also issued that year, but the Twinkies version is much tougher to find based on very limited distribution. While both Hostess cards look identical at first glance, the Twinkies version exhibits black bars near the top and bottom borders on the reverse if viewing the card horizontally. Each card was also issued individually along with the snack cake, versus the three-card panels used for the regular Hostess production.

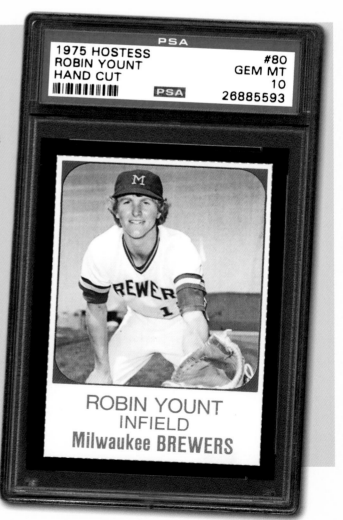

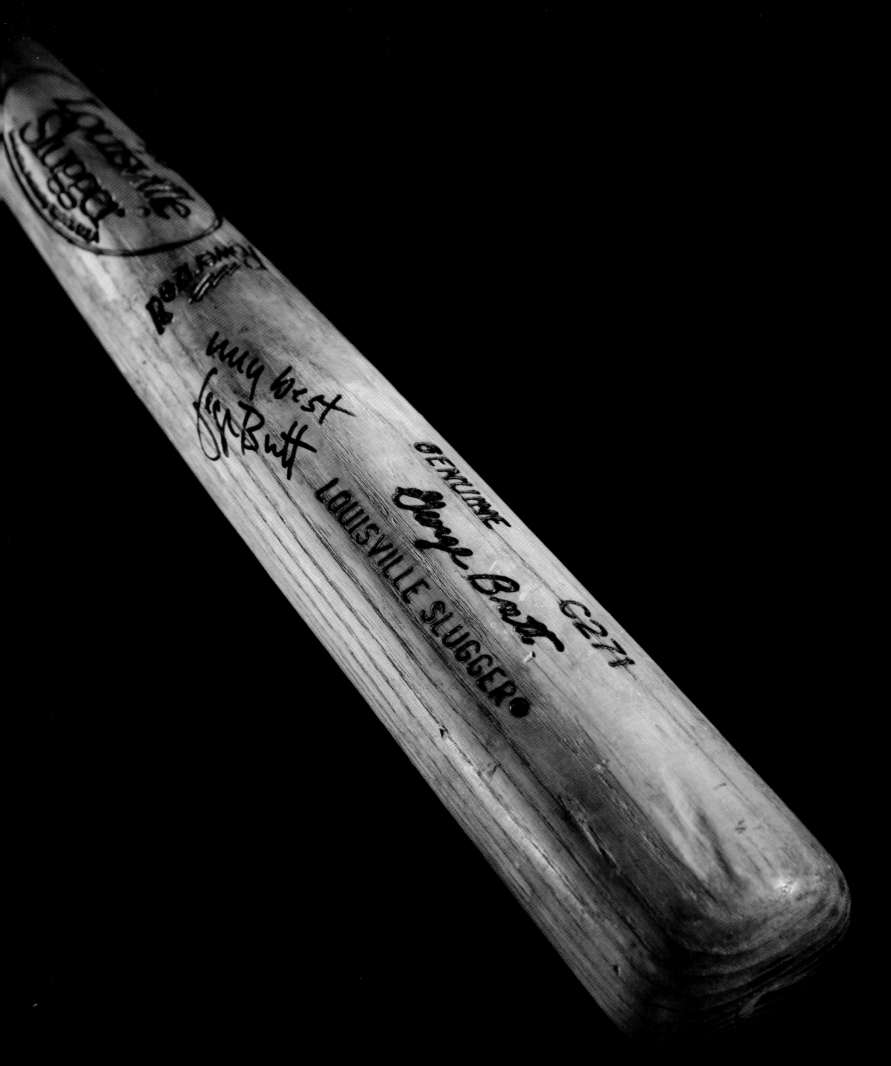

5

Mentors, Heroes, and Friends

Rico and I are sitting at a table at the Greater Boston Sports Collectibles Show. He is signing his book, and Ellen and I are signing our book. It's the last day of the show and the crowd has thinned out considerably. We start talking about some of the Hall of Famers who were working in baseball in either a managerial capacity or administrative position at the time that Rico played. In one case, although retired, one of these greats actually competed in a game against the Red Sox and surprised everyone. Every one of these men had a dramatic impact on the game, some more than others. In any event, they were all legendary players.

There is one more player that we are including in the book. No, he is not a Hall of Famer, but had his career not taken a tragic turn, he very well may have been. Tony Conigliaro was one of Rico's best friends. In 1967 Tony was struck in the face with an errant pitch, a pitch that still resonates in Boston baseball history to this day.

As a special tribute to a player that just may have made it to The Hall of Fame, we have included Rico's thoughts on Tony C.

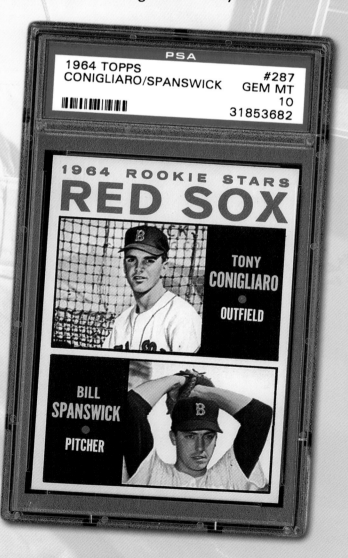

SPARKY ANDERSON

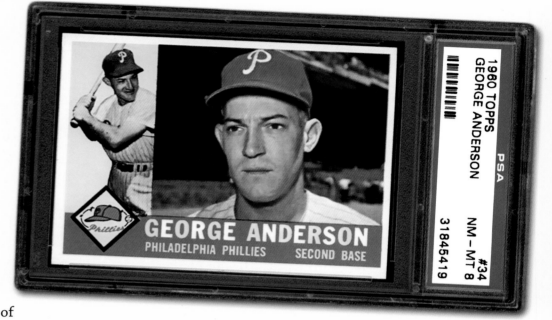

THE BIG RED MACHINE WAS

loaded with superstars. When you
have so many great players on your
team—guys like Rose, Bench, Perez,
Foster, Griffey, Morgan, and the
rest—there can be friction. Sparky
Anderson was the right manager
at the right time for the Reds. He
got that team to play together. In
public, Sparky would never knock
his players, although I know from
my conversations with some of
them, he was not afraid to tear into
them behind closed doors. With
his temper, Sparky reminded me a bit of
Dick Williams, my old manager, but he always stood up for his
players. Sparky was known for yanking pitchers pretty quickly
and most pitchers would get upset with that. That's how he got
the nickname, "Captain Hook."

Sparky always complimented me on my style of play. I think he
looked at me as a scrapper. In 1975, I was on the back nine of
my career and had slipped a bit offensively. It wasn't one of my
best years, but things came together for me when we played the
Reds in the World Series, and I had a pretty good Series. It was a
real thrill and great fun playing in Game Six, one of the greatest
World Series games ever. Some say it is the greatest World Series
game of all time. I was on base when Carbo hit the home run to
tie it up, and then of course Fisk won it in the twelfth with that
famous home run. If my memory serves me correctly, Bernie
Carbo was the number one pick ahead of Johnny Bench, but
the Reds ended up trading him after a couple of years. Bernie
had some personal problems, but Sparky was always there for
him. We played them a lot in spring training because they were
in Tampa at the time, and as I recall, Sparky would always
encourage Carbo.

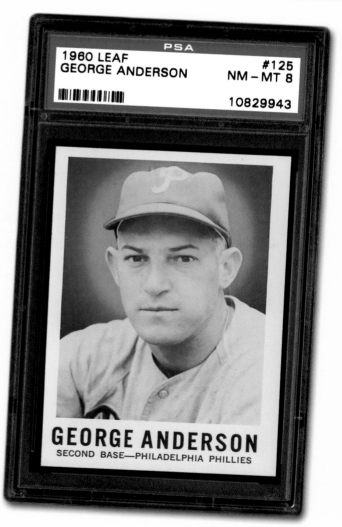

I remember talking to Sparky years later and reminiscing
about Game Six. Although they lost, Sparky said that it always
stuck out as his favorite game as a manager. Believe me, it
was a thrill for me to participate in one of the greatest games
ever against him. I only bumped into him a few times after he
retired, and I know Sparky was not well towards the end, but

that 1975 Reds team will always stick out in my mind. He did a hell of a job managing them.

When he went over to Detroit, Sparky had some very good teams and some mediocre teams. I believe Sparky was the first manager to win a World Series in both the National League and the American League. Although he managed in Detroit so many more seasons than in Cincinnati, I think managing those Big Red Machine teams was really the highlight of his career. Some of those later Detroit teams aged him. I still don't understand why he was fired by Cincinnati, but that's baseball. All I can tell you is that Sparky Anderson was a great manager. He always promoted the game and respected it, and Sparky loved his players.

The SPARKY ANDERSON CARD

Topps issued a colorful set that was full of stars in 1959. It included multi-player cards and an All-Star run in the high-number series. While the set has a lot to offer overall, the only Hall of Fame player rookie card is that of Bob Gibson, making it a clear key for collectors. There is, however, another Hall of Fame rookie card in the set. This one belongs to Hall of Fame manager Sparky Anderson. At one point in time, Anderson was a prospect for the Philadelphia Phillies. The young second baseman only played at the MLB level for one season (1959), but he did appear in 152 games that year.

The Anderson rookie (#338) is not terribly difficult in the PSA NM-MT 8 grade, but finding a well-centered copy that is absent distracting print defects may be challenging. The print defects can come in the form of traditional, dark specks in the light portion of the background or what some collectors refer to as "fish eyes" in the black frame around his portrait. Despite his brief career, Anderson appeared on a few different cards, which include Leaf and Topps issues in 1960. While the Leaf card is somewhat tough, since it is part of the high-number series (#s 73–144) which was short printed, Anderson's 1959 Topps rookie is clearly the card that garners the most interest.

"While the Leaf card is somewhat tough, since it is part of the high number series (#s 77–144) which was short printed, Anderson's 1959 Topps rookie is clearly the card that garners the most interest."

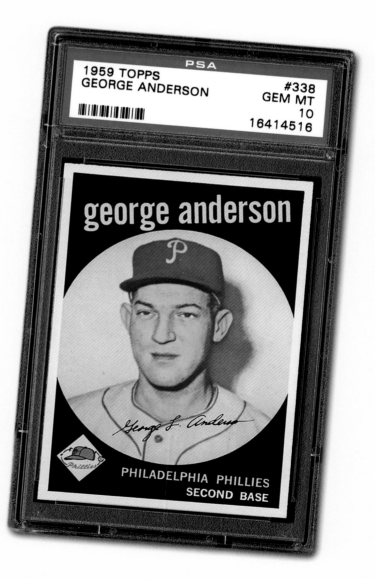

TOMMY LASORDA

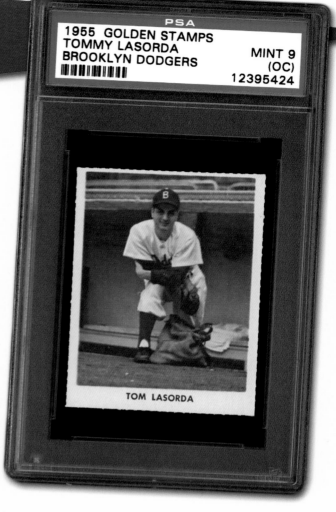

I NEVER GOT THE OPPORTUNITY TO PLAY against a Tommy Lasorda team, but he and I became friendly doing personal appearances together at various baseball events, and being members of the National Italian American Sports Hall of Fame. Tommy is one of the funniest people that I have ever met. He could have been a stand-up comedian.

The National Italian American Sports Hall of Fame is in Chicago, and we have attended quite a few events there together. As a matter of fact, they hold a golf tournament every year named the Tommy Lasorda Open.

Tommy was a hell of a pitcher in the minors. He played for Montreal in the 1950s, and he told me that one year he was named the pitcher of the year. For whatever reason, he did not have a long career as a player in the majors, but later on he became one of the great managers in the game. Tommy and I used to talk about his career. He managed Los Angeles for 21 years and they were contenders off and on throughout that time. Just think about that. There was a whole generation of fans that only knew Lasorda's Dodgers. Over the years, he had some darn good teams with guys like Mike Piazza, Steve Sax, and Rick Sutcliffe.

Whenever we got together, Tommy and I would find a great Italian restaurant and shoot the breeze for a couple of hours. One of our favorite restaurants was

Joe Tecce's in Boston's North End, the Italian section of the city. We would order some pasta and have a few laughs.

You never got a word in edgewise with Tommy though, because he would hold court and have us howling with stories about other players or managers.

One bond that Tommy and I have is that family is very important to both of us. We were brought up in Italian families, so we had a lot in common. Both of his parents were immigrants, as were mine, and we both shared the same values when it came to family. I hear that he has an Italian restaurant at Dodger Stadium. I haven't been

out there yet, but the food is supposed to be really good. One thing about Tommy is that he loves to eat.

Once Tommy got on the field, he was all business and as competitive as they come. Tommy had no problem butting heads with some of his players and he took no bull from them. As a manager, I think he is right up there with the greatest of all time. Tommy always said he liked how I played the game. I'm not sure what that meant, but I'm sure being Italian had something to do with it. Hey, the bottom line is that he won a couple of world championships and was Manager of the Year a couple of times, so Tommy was doing something right.

The TOMMY LASORDA CARD

The 1954 Topps set has always been one of the most revered baseball card issues of all time. With its booming colors and immense star selection, it's easy to see why. Between the Ted Williams bookends (#1 and #250) are three key Hall of Famer rookie cards. Hank Aaron, Ernie Banks, and Al Kaline made their debuts here and were exclusive to Topps that year. Technically, however, there is one more Hall of Famer rookie in the set. This one belongs to Tommy Lasorda (#132). Lasorda was once a promising young lefty for the Brooklyn Dodgers long before becoming the outspoken manager of the Los Angeles Dodgers years later.

After a brief stint with Brooklyn, Lasorda joined the Kansas City Athletics after being purchased in 1956. Even though Lasorda didn't pan out with Brooklyn, the team had another young lefty waiting in the wings named Sandy Koufax. Lasorda pitched in parts of three MLB seasons (1954–1956), logging a little over 58 innings altogether. His eye-catching 1954 Topps card features a bright yellow background, which can be a haven for print defects. In addition, the card can be somewhat tough to find well centered, and keep in mind that the green portion on the reverse is easily chipped.

Lasorda did appear in another period MLB issue called 1955 Golden Stamps, but there is no doubt that his classic 1954 Topps debut is the card collectors desire most.

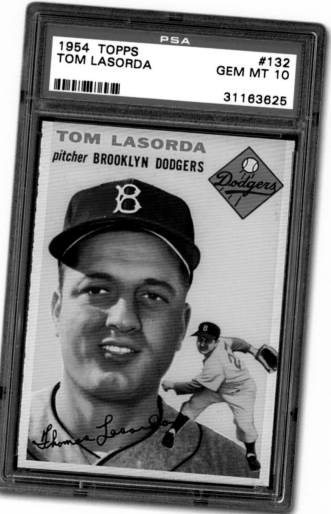

"Lasorda was once a promising young lefty for the Brooklyn Dodgers."

SATCHEL PAIGE

ON SEPTEMBER 25, 1965, we were playing the Kansas City Athletics in a game that really meant nothing for either team. As a matter of fact, we were the two worst teams in the American League! Charlie Finley, the owner of the A's, decided to try to boost attendance by honoring legendary pitcher Satchel Paige. You probably know that Satchel was practically a god in Kansas City because, back in the day, he was the star pitcher for the Kansas City Monarchs in the Negro Leagues. As a matter of fact, the A's signed Paige to a one-day contract so he would be able to pitch against us. I believe he was about sixty years old at the time.

Eddie Bressoud got the start that day for us at shortstop. I had played in the game the night before,

in front of only about 2,000 people, so Eddie got the start. That meant I got to enjoy watching one of the greatest pitchers of all time. Before the game, they had Satchel sitting in a rocking chair in the bullpen while they made a big show of massaging his pitching arm. He was having a great time, waving to fans, and he seemed to be totally enjoying the moment. We watched as Paige warmed up and it looked like he was throwing pretty well for his age, or for that matter, any age. We were there to win a ball game though, and our manager told us to go out there and do our job.

We didn't know what to expect, but I'll tell you, Satchel was the real deal, even at that age.

In the first inning, Jimmy Gosger led off and popped out. When he got into the dugout, he told me that this guy, although not overpowering, had great command.

In that first inning, I think Yaz was the only one to get a hit off him. I can remember we were all talking about how great Paige must have been in his younger days. He was tall and lanky and had a nice flawless motion. Satchel pitched for three innings. He did not exactly overpower us but he did manage to shut us out for the last two of those innings. The guys kept coming into the dugout just shaking their heads. In those three innings, I think Satchel gave up only that one hit to Yaz.

I remember Satchel came out for the fourth inning, but the Kansas City manager, Hayward Sullivan, walked out and replaced him so he would get a nice reception from the crowd. Paige got a standing ovation that day. We also acknowledged him. He tipped his hat and bowed to the fans. Although I did not get into that game, I have always felt lucky to even witness it. As a matter of fact, now that I think back, I was very fortunate to play when I played. I had a good career and made a lot of friends and I always appreciated the fans. I was very lucky to play against some of my childhood idols and many future Hall of Famers, but honestly, I never expected to witness the great Satchel Paige in action.

The SATCHEL PAIGE CARD

Baseball fans were deprived of seeing some of the most talented players on earth before Jackie Robinson broke the color barrier in 1947. Negro League legends like Oscar Charleston and Josh Gibson never had the chance to showcase their skills at the MLB level. There were some, however, who did get that opportunity, even though they were past their prime. Satchel Paige, at the age of 42, was one of those players. Not only did Paige pitch for five consecutive years (1948–1953), he came back for a three-inning stint in 1965 at the age of 59, when he didn't surrender a run. During his playing career, only a handful of cards were issued, but all of them carry meaningful weight.

Only one Topps card (1953) and one Bowman card (1949) were produced. The Bowman card has gained more attention in recent years and is worth considerably more than his lone Topps issue. While true, the card that is the unquestioned king of all Paige cards is his 1948/1949 Leaf. The card (#8) resides in one of the more popular but tough sets in the post-WWII era. There are other Hall of Famer rookie cards in the set, such as those of Stan Musial and Robinson. There are also some terribly difficult cards to find in high grade like the #1 card of Joe DiMaggio and the Bob Feller condition rarity. That all being said, none hold a candle to the Paige card in terms of desirability or market value. One of several scarce short prints, the Paige card suffers from poor print quality and registration to complicate matters. At the time of this writing, less than half a dozen Paige cards have reached the PSA NM-MT 8 grade, with none grading higher.

"...the card that is the unquestioned king of all Paige cards is his 1948/1949 Leaf."

TED WILLIAMS

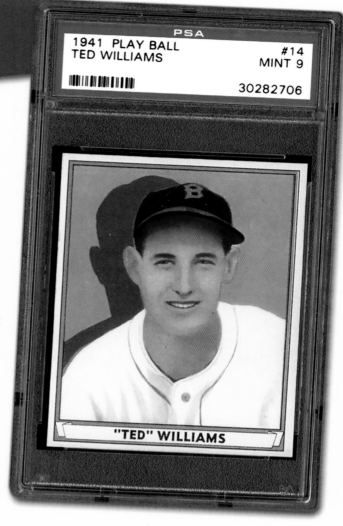

WITHOUT A DOUBT, TED WILLIAMS was one of the greatest hitters of all time. When he worked with us in spring training, he never hesitated to yell at us if we needed it. Ted was as salty as they came. He was loud and definitely had a presence, but man could he hit! He was great with us in spring training and he took no bull. One of the things he taught me was to anticipate the pitch. He advised me not to make any movement until the ball left the pitcher's hand and then to make my adjustment based on what I thought was coming. Because he was probably the greatest hitter that ever lived, he had a hard time understanding that he could adjust a hell of a lot more quickly than us kids. Sometimes he got frustrated because we could not hit like him. Ted would hit fungoes to us and deliberately hit the ball just

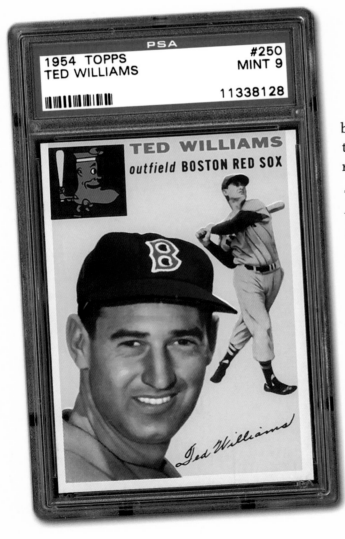

beyond our reach. He always laughed when we could not get to it because, of course, he was doing it to help improve our range.

Ted had unbelievable eyesight and very quick hands, even when he was in his fifties, and we used to joke that he had three lungs because he was so loud. I remember Ted watching a young player in the batting box who was having a hard time grasping what he was trying to teach him. Finally, he told the kid to give him the bat. Ted stepped into the batter's box and started lacing pitches all over the park. He handed the bat back to the kid and told him to get back in there and do it like he did. Honest to God, I thought the kid was gonna faint, but after a little LOUD encouragement from Ted, the kid began hitting the ball with authority. The whole time, Ted was giving the kid encouragement yelling, "Ya see? Ya see? That's how you do it 'Bush.' That's how ya do it!" Ted's nickname for all the younger players was "Bush" as in bush leaguer. Ted helped Yaz a lot with his hitting in the early days. He also used to tell me that my stroke was tailor-made for Fenway. When you got praise from Ted, you were on top of the world.

We did a lot of work together because Ted was very involved with the Jimmy Fund Children's cancer clinic at the Dana Farber Hospital in Boston and so was I. Ted always tried to stay under the radar and would just show up and visit with those sick kids. He also helped other ballplayers who were down on their luck. He was a good guy but very complex. He played angry, which I think made him great. He also had a running feud with the press that did not help things.

I did a few events with Ted towards the end of his life, and he always remained feisty yet engaging. He loved talking about hitting with anyone. We appeared at a fundraiser in Manchester, New Hampshire, for then President Bush Sr. and what did the three of us talk about? Hitting. That's what Ted loved. I'll never forget the 1999 All-Star Game towards the end of his life when all of the players circled Ted like he was a god. It's a shame how his life ended with the family stuff and all that. For me personally, it was an honor to be his friend and to learn from him.

THE CARDS

During his unforgettable career, dozens of memorable Ted Williams cards and collectibles were issued, which seems fitting for the man who wanted to be known as the greatest hitter who ever lived. When you consider that Williams lost around five years of his prime as a result of serving in the military and the fact that no major trading card sets were issued between 1941 and 1948, collectors can only dream of what might have been for the legendary

lefty and for the hobby. Even though Williams did lose time and the hobby went through a period of limited production in the 1940s, there are still dozens of great Williams cards to collect.

The same year Williams entered the league, he also made his hobby debut. The card that most collectors are familiar with is his popular 1939 Play Ball rookie; however, there is another card worthy of mention, and it's one that appears to be currently underrated based on its comparative rarity. Williams was also included in the 1939 Goudey Premiums issue. This oversized card, which was printed on thin paper, measures approximately 4" by 6³⁄₁₆" and is part of a 48-subject set. The front of each card features a facsimile signature of the subject, while the reverse contains an illustrated baseball tip. The sepia-toned Williams card is seldom discussed as an alternative to the mainstream 1939 Play Ball rookie, and quite frankly, it is a bit

perplexing, since Goudey is such a revered name in the hobby.

Over the years, Williams was a staple in many intriguing sets. In 1941, Play Ball injected color for the first time after producing a black-and-white set in 1939 and then

"In 1941, Play Ball injected color for the first time after producing a black-and-white set in 1939 and the sepia-toned cards in 1940. This was also the year that Williams hit .406 for the season, making him the last person to hit .400."

sepia-toned cards in 1940. This was also the year that Williams hit .406 for the season, making him the last person to hit .400. Bowman entered the fold in 1948, issuing trading card sets through 1955. Williams started to appear in Bowman's annual release in 1950, but it would be his 1954 Bowman card that captivates collectors more than any other. The Williams card (#66) was withdrawn due to a contractual dispute and replaced by Jimmy Piersall. The card is not quite as rare as once thought, but it remains one of Williams' most desirable issues.

Speaking of 1954, Williams started to appear in Topps sets that year, and he began with a bang: acting as the bookend for the set in its first and last slots. Williams would also serve as the #1 card in the 1957 and 1958 Topps sets before signing with Fleer in 1959. That year, the manufacturer dedicated an entire 80-card set to the Red Sox icon, one that covered his personal and professional life. Card #68 (Ted Signs for 1959) was pulled from production early since Fleer did not have permission to use the image of manager Bucky Harris. Like the 1954 Bowman Williams, the rarity of this card may have been exaggerated in the past, but it is still the most valuable card in the set by far. Even though Williams remained active through 1960, his 1960 and 1961 Fleer cards have been treated more like commemorative issues by collectors, since both issues are primarily made up of retired stars.

"His 1954 Bowman card captivates collectors more than any other. The Williams card (#66) was withdrawn due to a contractual dispute and replaced by Jimmy Piersall. The card is not as rare as once thought, but it remains one of Williams' most desirable issues."

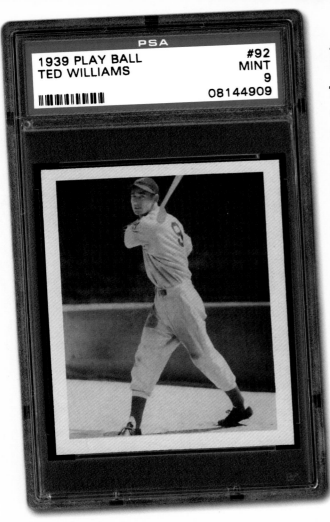

The TED WILLIAMS CARD

There are so many iconic, rare, and valuable Williams cards available to the collector. The Hall of Famer is like Mickey Mantle or Babe Ruth in that respect. If Williams is involved, the card or collectible is usually taken to a new level of importance. While there are many great Williams items to choose from, the overwhelming popularity of mainstream rookie cards cannot be overstated. So, when it comes to Williams, the card that fits that definition better than any other is his 1939 Play Ball rookie. The simple, black-and-white design certainly isn't quite as visually attractive as many of Williams' later issues, but that basic look is also part of its charm. The young, slender slugger is pictured doing what he does best, swinging the lumber that made him famous and turning just enough to reveal the "9" on his back. Considering the era, the card isn't too challenging to find, but finding PSA Mint 9 or better copies is another story. Beyond general wear from handling, unattractive centering and print defects are somewhat common to the issue.

ONE CARD TO WATCH

As we just discussed, trying to single out a Williams card from the seemingly endless list of important hobby issues is almost impossible. Once you get past his classic 1939 Play Ball rookie card, it gets even harder. That said, the Williams card that is arguably his most valuable overall, and is perhaps the most important regional issue ever released, is one that resides in the 1954 Wilson Franks set. These cards were inserted into packages of hot dogs, creating obvious condition obstacles for those that accompanied the consumer products. As is the case with many vintage issues, some copies never made it into product circulation, which means some high-grade copies have been discovered over the years. The set only contains 20 unnumbered cards, but several of them feature the top stars of the day like Roy Campanella, Bob Feller, and Williams. The bad news is that a good portion of the cards are found with poor centering, which is partially a result of the borders being so narrow, leaving little room for error. The good news is that the Williams card has a solid white background, so marginal centering does not impact eye appeal in a negative way like it would on a card with a more traditional frame.

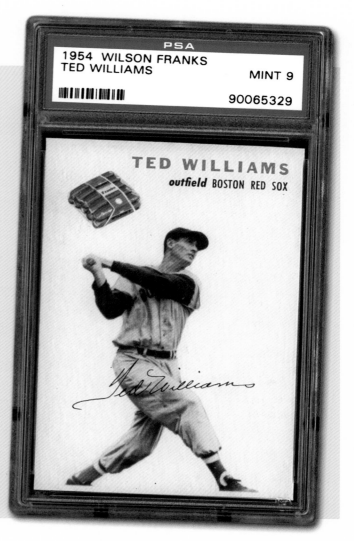

TONY CONIGLIARO

TONY CONIGLIARO WAS ONE OF MY closest friends. The two of us along with Tony's roommate, Mike Ryan, were like the Three Amigos. Even though Tony made it to the big leagues before I did, we developed a very close friendship. We liked to hang out at Regina's Pizza in Boston's Little Italy, the North End. It was a blast. When we walked down the street, the old Italians would shout out of their windows, "Hey Tony, Hey Rico!" On the road, we always went out to dinner together. Tony was single and movie-star handsome. I married Elsie in 1965, so after dinner, I would go back to the hotel and Tony would go out. He was a ladies man, but not a big drinker. Tony actually took good care of himself and was in good condition for every game.

Tony had a legitimate home run swing. As a matter of fact, he was the youngest player in American League history to reach 100 home runs.

He had that little uppercut and tremendous power to all fields. Tony was 6'3", about 205 lbs., and he was as strong as a bull. He was also fearless at the plate and very aggressive. Tony could hit the curve, the inside fastball, and the outside fastball. If you were gonna throw a fastball to Tony, it had better be 100 miles per hour. Had Tony not gotten hit, and with the DH position coming along, I am certain he would have hit 500 home runs.

Growing up just outside of Boston, it was a dream for Tony to play for his hometown team. He was very competitive and told me he wanted to be the best, like Ted Williams. Tony's parents, Sal and Theresa, invited my family to spend Thanksgiving and Christmas with the family every year. We would have great Italian food which reminded me of my mother's cooking. Tony's brothers, Richie and Billy (who later played for the Red Sox) would also hang out. I am still very close with both of them. The three of us ganged up on Tony and teased him a lot.

Everything changed when Tony got hit. It was in August of our 1967 Impossible Dream season. I was on deck and saw the pitch coming in high from Angels pitcher, Jack Hamilton. Tony didn't get out of the way quick enough and the ball hit him right underneath the eye. I ran to him as soon as he got hit. At first I thought that he was dead. Then he started moaning, and I could not believe how much his eye swelled up. I thought he would lose his eye. He was rushed to the hospital where they determined Tony had a detached retina, a broken bone under his eye, and a broken jaw. I was certain that at 22 years old, his career was over. Tony sat out the entire 1968 season, but he worked hard to rehab so he could make a comeback.

In 1969, Tony came back. He hit a home run in our first game of the season against Baltimore. Even though he had vision and depth-perception problems, Tony went on to hit 20 home runs that year,

and he hit 36 home runs in 1970. At that point, his eyesight started to deteriorate from scar tissue in his sight line. He was finally traded to Los Angeles where he played one year and hit four home runs. He came back to us in 1975 to end his career. We all felt bad that Tony's career was cut short and that his potential to be one of baseball's greats could not be realized. Although his body of work is incomplete, he did have one All-Star appearance and he led the league in home runs one year. In my opinion, my friend would have had a very special career.

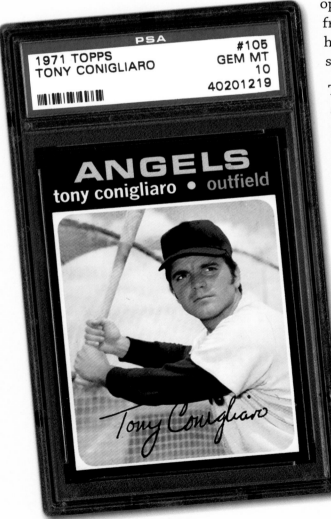

Tony became a color analyst, and he even recorded a few records because he had a good voice. He worked in Rhode Island and then California. In 1982, on his way to the airport, Tony suffered a massive heart attack and stroke. Was it the result of the beaning? We will never know.

For the next eight years he was confined to a hospital bed and lost the ability to speak. I visited him often and would just sit with him. Sadly, Tony passed away at the age of 45 after developing pneumonia. I was a pallbearer

at his funeral. It was a very sad time. I remember talking to Yaz and how sad he was, too. Yaz and Tony were very competitive in the old days because they were both stars, but after they worked out their differences they were great teammates.

There is a special section in Fenway called Conigliaro's Corner. I hope that at some point, Tony's number will be retired. I keep in touch with Billy and Richie to this day. We recently honored Tony during the fiftieth anniversary celebration of the Impossible Dream Team. Tony Conigliaro was one of the catalysts who got us to that World Series. He was one of my closest friends and I still miss him today.

The TONY CONIGLIARO CARD

Tony Conigliaro seemed to be well on his way to superstardom prior to being struck in the face by a pitch in 1967, and even though he made a successful comeback from the horrific injury, it was short-lived. Although his career was limited, a few dozen different cards and collectibles were issued during his playing days. It was quite clear that the hobby had high hopes for Conigliaro, as he was included in a variety of Topps sets early on in his career. One of Conigliaro's toughest, and perhaps his most valuable card pound-for-pound, is his 1964 Topps Rookie All-Star Banquet issue. The black-and white, oversized card measures approximately 3" by 5¼" and is seldom offered today. As elusive as the aforementioned issue is, the Conigliaro card that gets the most attention from collectors is his 1964 Topps rookie card from their standard, annual set.

Like many prospects of the period, Conigliaro had to share the spotlight with another newcomer. In this case, teammate and pitcher Bill Spanswick took the lower half of the card while Conigliaro is featured in the upper portion. While the card is not considered a condition rarity, well-centered copies can be somewhat hard to find, and keep in mind that the reverse of the card is surrounded by colored edges that sort of reminds us of orange sherbet (well, at least for those of us old enough to know what that is). It is important to note that a Venezuelan Topps rookie was also issued in 1964, and despite being less popular, it exists in far fewer numbers than the regular Topps card. Conigliaro's final hobby appearance as an active player came in 1971 when several collectibles were released, including a collectible coin and tattoo from Topps. Interestingly, even though Conigliaro made a brief comeback in 1975, no card was issued to help document his attempt.

"The Conigliaro card that gets the most attention from collectors is his 1964 Topps rookie card from their standard, annual set."

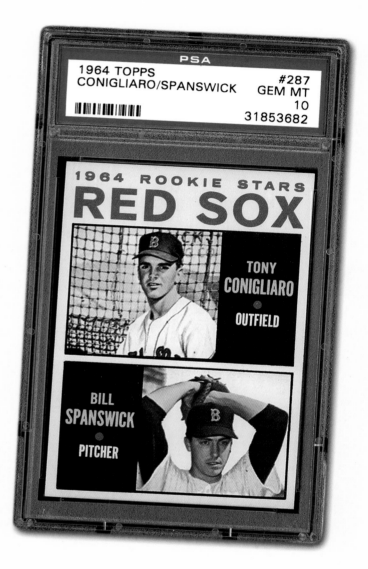

"It was quite clear that the hobby had high hopes for Conigliaro, as he was included in a variety of Topps sets early on in his career."

Index

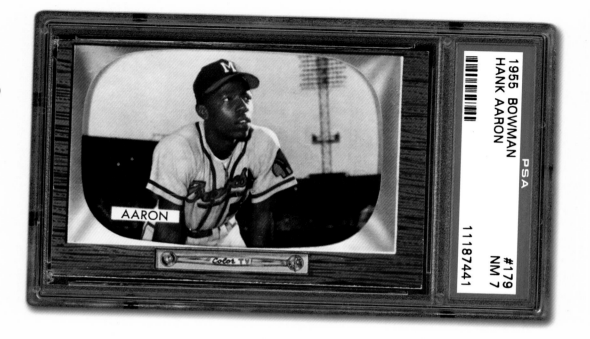

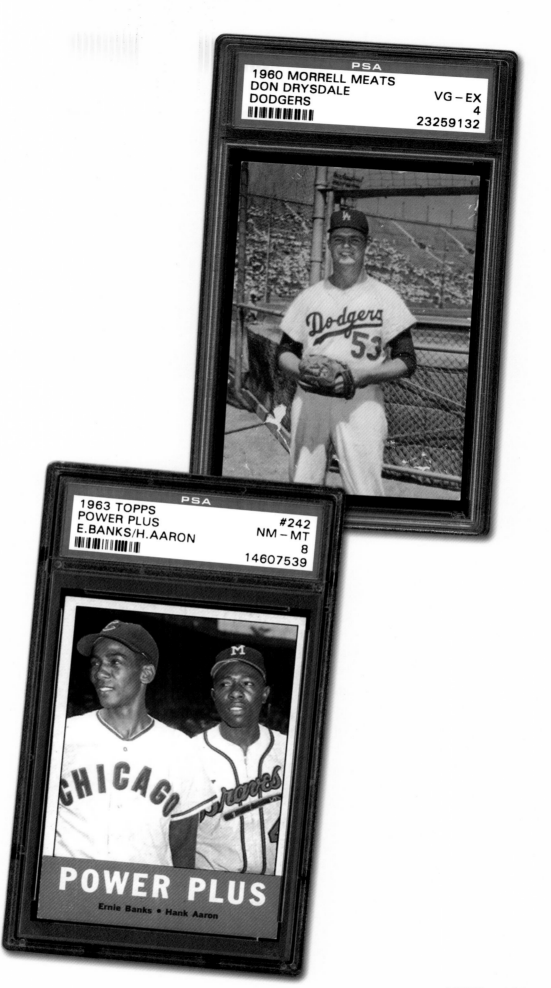

About the Authors and Contributors

Tom Zappala is a businessman in the greater Boston area who is passionate about maintaining the traditions and historical significance of our National Pastime. He is co-author of the award-winning books *The T206 Collection: The Players & Their Stories*, *The Cracker Jack Collection: Baseball's Prized Players*, *The 100 Greatest Baseball Autographs*, and *Legendary Lumber: The Top 100 Player Bats in Baseball History*. In addition to co-hosting a popular Boston area radio talk show, Zappala co-hosts *The Great American Collectibles Show*, which airs nationally every week. As co-owner of ATS Communications, a multimedia and consulting company, he handles publicity and personal appearances for several authors and a variety of artists in the entertainment field. He enjoys collecting vintage baseball and boxing memorabilia, using the simple philosophy of collecting for the love of the sport. Proud of his Italian heritage, Zappala recently authored *Bless Me Sister*, a humorous book about his experience attending an Italian parochial school.

Ellen Zappala is president of ATS Communications, a multimedia marketing and consulting company. Co-author of the award-winning books *The T206 Collection: The Players & Their Stories*, *The Cracker Jack Collection: Baseball's Prized Players*, *The 100 Greatest Baseball Autographs*, and *Legendary Lumber: The Top 100 Player Bats in Baseball History*, Zappala also worked with former welterweight boxing champ Tony DeMarco on his autobiography *Nardo: Memoirs of a Boxing Champion*. Zappala was publisher of a group of weekly newspapers in Massachusetts and New Hampshire for many years and served as president of the New England Press Association. She works closely with various publishing companies on behalf other authors, and handles publicity in both print and electronic media. She especially enjoys bringing the stories of the Deadball Era and Golden Age players to life.

Joe Orlando is CEO of Collectors Universe, Inc. and president of Professional Sports Authenticator (PSA), the largest trading card and sports memorabilia authentication service in the hobby. Editor of the nationally distributed *Sports Market Report* (SMR), a Juris Doctor, and an advanced collector, Orlando has authored several collecting guides and dozens of articles for Collectors Universe, Inc. He authored *The Top 200 Sportscards in the Hobby* (2002) and *Collecting Sports Legends* (2008), and was the lead author of *Legendary Lumber: The Top 100 Player Bats in Baseball History* (2017). Orlando contributed to the award-winning *The T206 Collection: The Players & Their Stories* (2010), *The Cracker Jack Collection: Baseball's Prized Players* (2013) and *The 100 Greatest Baseball Autographs* (2016). As a hobby expert, Orlando has appeared as a featured guest on numerous radio and television programs, including ESPN's *Outside the Lines*, HBO's *Real Sports*, and the Fox Business Network.

Rico Petrocelli defined the position of "power-hitting" shortstop in his 13 years with Boston. In 1969, he was the first AL shortstop to hit 40 home runs in a season, a record that stood until Alex Rodriguez broke it in 1998. The Red Sox Hall of Famer and two-time All-Star was a versatile infielder, leading the league in fielding at both shortstop and third base. He helped the team advance to two World Series appearances, including the 1967 "Impossible Dream" season. That season is detailed in his book, *Tales from the 1967 Red Sox Dugout*. Petrocelli has worked as manager, coach, and TV analyst for the Pawtucket Red Sox, as radio/television analyst for the Boston Red Sox and the Seattle Mariners, and as host of a weekly sports talk show on Boston's 1510AM "The Zone." He currently co-hosts *The Great American Collectibles Show*, which airs nationally every week, and the Sirius MLB Radio Show *Remember When* with Ed Randall of New York's WFAN. He is president of Petrocelli Marketing Group, and continues his close association with the Jimmy Fund Clinic for pediatric cancer.

Dr. Jim Lonborg was the first pitcher in Red Sox history to win the Cy Young Award. The Red Sox Hall of Famer and All-Star starting pitcher was known for fearlessly pitching inside the plate over his 15-year major league career. The AL wins and strikeout leader in 1967, his 22 wins that year helped the Red Sox advance to the World Series in their famous "Impossible Dream" season. After his stint with the Red Sox, Lonborg pitched for the Milwaukee Brewers and the Philadelphia Phillies, but his best career season by far was with Boston in 1967. After retiring from baseball, Dr. Lonborg graduated from the Tufts University School of Dental Medicine and started his second career with a dental practice in Hanover, Massachusetts, in 1983. He retired from his dental practice in 2017 but he continues to be active in several non-profit organizations including The Jimmy Fund Clinic for pediatric cancer, the Cystic Fibrosis Foundation, and Learn Live Love Cancer Outreach Organization.

Christina Good is a senior photographer for Collectors Universe, Inc. A Seattle native and 2005 graduate of Brooks Institute of Photography in Santa Barbara, Good initially honed her skills on portraiture and wedding photography. Since joining the company in 2013, she has become a key part of the photography team and especially enjoys the opportunity to use her photography skills to artistically document rare coins and collectibles.